PETERSON'S

LOGIC & READING REVIEW

for the

GRE*, GMAT*, LSAT*, MCAT*

*GRE is a registered trademark of the Educational Testing Service, which does not endorse this book.

*GMAT is a registered trademark of the Graduate Management Admission Council, which does not endorse this book.

*LSAT is a registered trademark of the Law School Admission Council, Inc., which does not endorse this book.

*MCAT is a registered trademark of the Association of American Medical Colleges, which does not endorse this book.

Peterson's
Princeton, New Jersey

Logic Review: Edward J. Rozmiarek

Reading Review: Jo Norris Palmore

Editorial Development: American BookWords Corporation

Visit Peterson's Education Center on the Internet (World Wide Web) at
www.petersons.com

Library of Congress Cataloging-in-Publication Data

Rozmiarek, Edward J.

    Logic and reading review for the GRE, GMAT, LSAT, MCAT/Edward J. Rozmiarek, Jo Norris Palmore.
      p. cm.
    At head of title: Peterson's.
    ISBN 0-7689-0229-0
    1. Universities and colleges—United States—Graduate work—Examinations Study guides. 2. Universities and colleges—United States—Entrance examinations Study guides. I. Palmore, Jo Norris. II. Peterson's (Firm) III. Title. IV. Title: Peterson's logic & reading review for the GRE, GMAT, LSAT, MCAT. V. Title: Logic and reading review for the GRE, GMAT, LSAT, MCAT.
LB2366.2.R69 1999
378.1'662—dc21
                                                99-28088
                                                 CIP

Printed in the United States of America

10 9 8 7 6 5 4 3 2 1

Contents

Introduction

The purpose of this book is to help you to focus on and improve specific skills that are tested on the four major graduate-level examinations—the Graduate Record Examinations (GRE), the Graduate Management Admission Test (GMAT), the Law School Admission Test (LSAT), and the Medical College Admission Test (MCAT). Although these tests are dramatically different, they all require that test-takers have strong reading comprehension skills, and the GRE, GMAT, and LSAT also have sections that test students' analytical and logical ability. Therefore, we decided to focus on these four exams and two of the most important skills you must have to score well on these exams: logic and reading. Through our in-depth analysis of both Logic questions and Reading Comprehension passages, you will quickly learn how to identify and answer the various types of questions you will encounter on the exams.

THE FORMAT

The book is divided into logical sections. The first part of the book covers Logic questions, which appear on the GRE, GMAT, and LSAT. The second part of the book covers Reading Comprehension, which appears on the GRE, GMAT, LSAT, and MCAT. Within those two major sections you will find in-depth explanations of each type of question you will encounter on any of these exams. What you will notice is that there are really only a few types of questions, and once you are able to recognize them and identify the skills they are testing, you'll learn to answer them correctly.

Both sections of the book offer you comprehensive analysis of the different types of questions and samples to illustrate the concepts. Following each of the instructional chapters, there are several generic tests that allow you to analyze your progress and gauge how much you have learned and how well you can apply what you've read. There are enough tests in both sections to give you a good indication of what you know and what needs further study.

THE CONTENTS

LOGIC QUESTIONS

Questions that test your logic skills may be called different names on each test, but they all have similar requirements. You must be able to read a situation or question presented to you and then logically deduce the answers, using a technique such as the process of elimination or diagramming the solutions. There are two major question types covered here.

- Analytical Reasoning problems (sometimes called "Logic Games") appear on both the GRE and the LSAT.
- Logical Reasoning questions also appear on both the GRE and LSAT. On the GMAT, these questions are called Critical Reasoning.

READING COMPREHENSION QUESTIONS

Reading Comprehension questions are probably more familiar to you than the Logic questions are, since your reading skills have probably been tested on most of the tests you've taken throughout your school career, including the SAT and the ACT. Reading comprehension may be the most important skill you need in order to do well on any test, whether you're taking an undergraduate exam or one of these graduate tests. After all, there's always a strong element of reading comprehension that comprises a logic question. If you can't read and understand the situations presented in a logic question, how can you answer the question?

Regardless of what the questions are called, there is the basic premise that you are able to read a passage—whether it's related to the law, science, social science, humanities, or literature—and then answer the questions pertaining to that passage. This book is designed to give you those skills to help you understand and comprehend any type of reading passage.

Take your time reading through the analysis and review material. This is important information, and we have tried to cover all of the possible question types that you will encounter on any of these four exams. The step-by-step approaches that are prescribed in this book are for your benefit. They should significantly increase your understanding of what you will encounter on any of these exams.

Part I

LOGIC: REVIEW OF QUESTIONS GRE, GMAT, LSAT

INTRODUCTION

A significant portion of most of the standardized tests that are required for graduate school applications—the GRE, the GMAT, and the LSAT—consists of questions and problems related to your ability to think logically. Recognizing that fact, this portion of the book is designed to help you in preparing for all forms of logic questions that appear on each of the graduate school tests.

This section is based on the belief that no knowledge or studying of formal logic is necessary for you to succeed on the logic sections of the standardized tests. Instead, you need to recognize the kinds of questions that appear frequently on the tests and the different skills they are testing. Once you recognize the questions and the various ways that they test your ability to think logically, you can begin to work on analyzing the material so that you can succeed on the tests. This book can show you how to identify the questions you will encounter and help you prepare for the tests.

In the beginning of this section, you will be introduced briefly to both of the two primary question types, together with an outline of the style of presentation of each question type, and you will also see sample questions of each type, so you can begin to recognize them.

The second section presents you with an in-depth analysis of each question type. You will learn more completely how to recognize each question type and how to differentiate among them. You will learn how to analyze each question and the various approaches that will maximize your success rate and help you in answering each question type as quickly and correctly as possible. You will learn the styles of the various questions, the best methods for selecting correct answers, and the hints that will assist you in eliminating incorrect answer choices.

Finally, the third section of this book provides you with sample test sections. These sections are designed to mimic actual logic-related test sections that you might see on the GRE, GMAT, or LSAT.

TYPES OF QUESTIONS

Logic questions appear in the standardized tests—the GRE, GMAT, and LSAT—in two different forms. This chapter provides you with an outline and brief discussion of the two primary question types.

The question types that you will encounter are:

1. Analytical Reasoning
2. Logical Reasoning

Each type of question has its own style and, as a result, its own style of setting up and answering the problem. This chapter will introduce you to the styles so that you can recognize both question types and quickly and efficiently decide on the method that will lead you to an effective solution.

1. ANALYTICAL REASONING

What is an Analytical Reasoning question?

Analytical Reasoning problems require exactly what the name implies—an ability to reason and think in an analytical manner, weeding through various bits of information, selecting relevant material and discarding any irrelevant material. These problems are the kind that sometimes appear in crossword puzzle books, asking you to determine, for example, the order of people standing in a line or to arrange people by height or to identify the chosen professions of several individuals.

An Analytical Reasoning problem provides you with an initial set of statements describing the circumstances of the problem. This set of statements is followed by a set of "rules" that will assist you in making decisions about the problem. Finally, you are asked to answer from five to seven specific questions, based on the initial information.

A sample Analytical Reasoning problem looks like this:

A hallway in an elementary school has six classrooms in a row, all on the same side of the hallway. The rooms are numbered 1 through 6, in order from left to right. Six new students—Kevin, Laura, Michael, Nellie, Oscar, and Pat—all begin attending the school on the same day, and they must be assigned to the six classrooms as follows:

> *One student must be assigned to each classroom.*
> *Pat must be assigned to one of the classrooms at one of the ends of the hallway.*
> *Kevin may not be assigned to a classroom next to Pat.*
> *Laura's classroom and Oscar's classroom may not be separated by more than one other classroom.*

Which of the following is a possible list of the classroom assignments, in order from classroom 1 to classroom 6?

(A) Pat, Oscar, Kevin, Michael, Laura, Nellie
(B) Kevin, Laura, Oscar, Pat, Nellie, Michael
(C) Laura, Oscar, Nellie, Michael, Kevin, Pat
(D) Nellie, Oscar, Kevin, Laura, Michael, Pat
(E) Pat, Michael, Oscar, Nellie, Kevin, Laura

The correct answer is: (D)

A more in-depth analysis of solution methods for Analytical Reasoning problems follows in the Analytical Reasoning section of Part 2.

2. LOGICAL REASONING

What is a Logical Reasoning question?

Logical Reasoning questions require you to think and reason just as logically as you must for Analytical Reasoning problems, but the questions are presented in a very different format. While Analytical Reasoning problems are presented in sets of five to seven questions based on a single set of initial facts, the Logical Reasoning questions present only one question (or occasionally two) based on a single statement, or "argument." The question requires more reading comprehension skill and less of a sheer analytical organization structure.

Logical Reasoning questions begin with an "argument." This "argument" is one or more sentences about some topic, ranging from social sciences to current events to politics. The subject matter of the argument varies widely, but no knowledge of any specific subject is necessary or even, in most cases, helpful. You are being tested on your ability to reason logically and make decisions based on the brief information provided to you in the argument alone—not on any additional outside information. Following the argument is a very brief question, asking you to interpret the argument and select certain relevant information from it. Finally, you have five answer choices, from which you will be instructed to select the "best" answer for the question asked.

A sample Logical Reasoning question looks like this:

Some psychologists believe that humans, like porpoises, are benevolent creatures by nature. These psychologists assume that human nature is essentially disposed to benevolent conduct. To account for social evils, psychologists have to blame institutions that corrupt the native disposition of humans.

The psychologists' argument described above would be most strengthened if it were to explain how . . .

(A) a way of life consistent with benevolent ideals is possible in the modern world.

(B) people can be persuaded to abandon technology, urbanization, and mass production.

(C) benevolent conduct can result from humans living in accordance with their own natural dispositions.

(D) benevolent dispositions give rise to evil institutions.

(E) corrupt institutions can be eliminated or reformed.

The correct answer is: (B)

More in-depth analysis of different styles of Logical Reasoning questions and solution methods follows in the Logical Reasoning section of Part 2.

Summary of Logic Question Distributions

	Number of Logic Sections	Minutes per Section	Questions per Section	Arrangement of Questions
GRE Computer Adaptive Test	1	60	35	21–25 Analytical Reasoning; 10–14 Logical Reasoning
LSAT	3	35	24	One section Analytical Reasoning; two sections Logical Reasoning
GMAT Computer Adaptive Test	1 (part of combined verbal score)	75	41	Approximately 14 Critical Reasoning questions (same as Logical Reasoning) interspersed with other verbal questions

Part II

LOGIC SKILLS REVIEW

ANALYTICAL REASONING

The Analytical Reasoning questions of the GRE and LSAT begin with the following instructions:

> **Directions:** Each question or group of questions is based on a passage or set of conditions. In answering some of the questions, it may be useful to draw a rough diagram. For each question, select the best answer given.

To succeed on the Analytical Reasoning questions, the most important part of these directions is the recommendation "to draw a rough diagram." An accurate diagram can help you simplify an Analytical Reasoning problem so much that you merely have to glance at the diagram to answer some of the questions.

But first, let's review the basic structure of the Analytical Reasoning problems.

THE BASIC STRUCTURE

Analytical Reasoning questions appear in groups of four to seven questions, all based on an initial set of conditions, or "rules." The entire set of questions, including its rules, is what we call a single Analytical Reasoning "problem." Each problem begins with a few introductory sentences describing a particular situation. The introduction suggests what you are being asked to do with a particular problem. The problem types that you will encounter are: (1) ranking (to place people or objects in some specific order), (2) distributing (to organize items in arranged locations), (3) scheduling (to schedule the timing of certain events), (4) connections, (5) maps, and (6) hybrid problems. The introduction tells you how many people or things you are going to be working with in the problem. Typically you will be asked to manipulate between five and eight people or things— sometimes more, sometimes less.

The introduction is followed by several short statements, called "rules," which set certain conditions that must be followed. These rules tell you what you can and cannot do with the people or things that you are moving around for the problem. The rules that you are given at the beginning of an Analytical Reasoning problem must be followed for all of the questions that are part of that problem. Very often, the individual questions may add additional conditions of their own. If a question adds a new condition, that new condition applies to that question only; but the initial rules apply to the entire set of questions.

A sample Analytical Reasoning problem begins with an introduction and rules that look like this:

> *Six people—Jim, Kathy, Lewis, Mary, Ned, and Olivia—were born during the years 1960 through 1965, inclusive. No two people were born in any one year.*
>
> *Jim was born before Kathy but after Lewis.*
> *Kathy was born in 1963.*
> *Ned and Mary are both younger than Olivia.*

In this sample, the introduction tells you that you will be working with six people and that you will be arranging them in order according to their ages. The people's names are supplied for you, but their names are unimportant except as a way of identifying them.

> **LOGIC TIP:** People in an Analytical Reasoning problem are usually named in alphabetical order. Take advantage of this and work with their initials—this saves you time in making your notes, and it is just as effective in answering the questions. And you do not need to worry about remembering anyone's actual name.

Usually, the best procedure for beginning an Analytical Reasoning problem is to read the introduction so you understand generally what you are being asked to do, and then use the rules to create a "diagram" of the situation. A good diagram can simplify an Analytical Reasoning problem so that you may have very little work left to do.

SUCCESSFUL DIAGRAMMING

Depending on the type of problem that you are faced with, your diagram will differ.

Specific problem types are addressed below. However, successful diagramming for any problem type depends upon certain basic principles. You must pay careful attention to the details that are given to you in the introduction and in the rules for the problem you are working on. Using these details in the introduction and rules, you will sketch out a table, chart, graph, or whatever kind of diagram seems most appropriate for the problem type. Working with one rule at a time, fill in whatever information you can into your diagram. When you have finished diagramming as much information as you can with the first rule, then move to the second and do the same. Keep adding information to your diagram bit by bit until you use up all the rules.

While you are working on your diagram, be very careful to pay attention to details. Some rules will give you more than one piece of information, and you must be sure to include all possible information. Some rules will not give you the kind of information that is easily incorporated into a diagram. When that happens, you will have to read the rule, make a "mental note" of the information, and then remember to come back to it when a particular problem calls for it.

As noted above, you will encounter six general types or categories of Analytical Reasoning problems. Again, the six most common problem types are:

1. Ranking

2. Distributing

3. Scheduling

4. Connections

5. Maps

6. Hybrid (or "Other")

Quickly recognizing the type of problem you are facing will assist you in identifying the best way to solve it. The next section of this book addresses each of the six primary problem types in turn, highlighting the keys to look for in identifying the problem types and outlining the best methods for solving each one. You will be shown an example of each problem type, with a thorough analysis of the method used for diagramming and solving the problem. You will then be given a section of practice problems to perfect your own skills. Using this section of the book, you can work on all six problem types, identify your own strengths and weaknesses, and then focus on your problem areas to improve your scores. Complete answers and explanations to these problems are provided in the following section.

1. RANKING PROBLEMS

The sample problem shown above is an example of a ranking problem. Ranking problems are the kinds of problems in which you are asked to place people or objects in order according to some kind of ranking. You may be working with age (as in the preceding sample problem), height, weight, seating arrangements, finishing order in a race, or any other kind of situation in which you can organize people or objects you are given. In a typical ranking problem, you will have one space, or "slot," for each person or object you are ranking. In the preceding example regarding the ages of the six individuals, you had exactly one year for each of the six individuals.

Review the sample ranking problem, as given to you:

Six people, Jim, Kathy, Lewis, Mary, Ned, and Olivia, were born during the years 1960 through 1965, inclusive. No two people were born in any one year.

Jim was born before Kathy but after Lewis.
Kathy was born in 1963.
Ned and Mary are both younger than Olivia.

This problem is easily identified as a ranking problem because the number of people, or "players," involved in the problem matches exactly with the number of "spaces" (in this case, years) to place them. You have six people, Jim, Kathy, Lewis, Mary, Ned, and Olivia, and you are instructed to arrange or place them each in one year for the six-year period from 1960 through 1965. Because of the requirement that "No two people were born in any one year," you can tell that the match must be "one-to-one" between players and spaces. This "one-to-one" match is the key element of ranking problems.

The introduction tells you that you will be taking the six people and ranking them according to their ages. The introduction for the sample problem also tells you that you have six years to work with: 1960, 1961, 1962, 1963, 1964, and 1965.

Because no two people were born in the same year, your task will be to assign one person to each of the six years. With this much information to begin with, your basic diagram will be a chart of the six years, and your task will be to fill in each of the years with one person's name. The chart may look something like this:

1960	1961	1962	1963	1964	1965

So far, the spaces underneath the years are blank because you have not yet begun using the rules to complete the diagram. That will be the next step.

Following the introduction, you are given three separate rules for this problem:

1. Jim was born before Kathy but after Lewis.

2. Kathy was born in 1963.

3. Ned and Mary are both younger than Olivia.

The rules will give you some information about the ranking of the people, but they do not tell you everything. For example, the only person you can specifically assign to any year is Kathy, who you are told was born in 1963.

As soon as you see a rule that lets you place a specific person in a specific slot of your diagram, go ahead and fill in that much:

1960	1961	1962	1963	1964	1965
			Kathy		

Now, for all of the questions in this problem, you will always know that Kathy was born in 1963.

You also know, from rule #1, that Jim was born before Kathy but after Lewis. This is an example of a single rule that gives you two pieces of information. You know that Jim was born in either 1962, 1961, or 1960, since these are the only available years before Kathy. So far, the diagram looks like this:

	1960	1961	1962	1963	1964	1965
A	Jim			Kathy		
B		Jim		Kathy		
C			Jim	Kathy		

Each line in this diagram, labeled here as A, B, and C, represents a possible arrangement of Jim and Kathy, based on the information you have gathered from the rules so far.

Since rule #1 also tells you that Jim was born after Lewis, you know that line A in the preceding diagram is impossible, since Jim could not have been born in 1960 if Lewis was born before Jim. If Jim was born in 1961, as in line B, then Lewis would have been born in 1960.

Finally, if Jim was born in 1962, then Lewis could have been born in either 1961 or 1960. Therefore, analyzing rules 1 and 2 of this sample problem, you will have the three following possibilities:

	1960	1961	1962	1963	1964	1965
A	Lewis	Jim		Kathy		
B	Lewis		Jim	Kathy		
C		Lewis	Jim	Kathy		

Based on rules 1 and 2, you have three possible arrangements for placing Kathy, Jim, and Lewis. You do not yet have enough information to assign Jim and Lewis to either specific year, but you have enough information to limit their placement significantly.

Rule #3 for this sample problem tells you: "Ned and Mary are both younger than Olivia." This is an example of a kind of rule that appears not to allow you to diagram it immediately. You do not know in which year any of them—Ned, Mary, or Olivia—was born. All you know is that Olivia has to be older than both Ned and Mary. It is also important for you to recognize that you do not know whether Ned is older than Mary or whether Mary is older than Ned.

LOGIC TIP: Sometimes it is as important to focus your attention on the information that you DON'T know as it is to focus on the information you DO know. When you are told, for example, that one person is older than two others (or is taller or faster or has higher grades—depending on the problem), you often will not be told anything about the relationship of those other two people to each other. You must not assume anything, such as expecting that the first one named is older simply because he or she comes first in the list. You must constantly be on the lookout for information that is missing, as well as information that you have.

Although you do not know if Ned is older than Mary or if Mary is older than Ned and you have not been told in which year either of them was born, you still can add some of this information to the diagram you have started. Review the diagram as it stands up to this point:

	1960	1961	1962	1963	1964	1965
A	Lewis	Jim		Kathy		
B	Lewis		Jim	Kathy		
C		Lewis	Jim	Kathy		

You will note that in each of the three possibilities—A, B, and C—there remain three empty spaces. These three spaces will have to be occupied by Olivia, Ned, and Mary. In each possibility, there is one empty space in a year before Kathy's birth in 1963 and two empty spaces after it. Since Olivia will have to be older than both Ned and Mary, no matter what the final diagram, then it is obvious that Olivia will have to take that one empty slot before 1963.

Therefore, the three possibilities in the diagram can have one more piece of information added:

	1960	1961	1962	1963	1964	1965
A	Lewis	Jim	Olivia	Kathy		
B	Lewis	Olivia	Jim	Kathy		
C	Olivia	Lewis	Jim	Kathy		

You still do not know for certain where Ned and Mary go, but you do know that for any of the three possibilities, Ned and Mary will be in 1964 and 1965, in either order. If any question asks you to limit them to any specific year, you will be given additional information when necessary.

LOGIC TIP: A key to success with Analytical Reasoning problems is to stay relaxed and focus on whatever information you know. The problems purposely give you only limited information, but the information they give you will always be enough to answer the questions you are asked. If you ever find yourself asking questions like, "How do they expect me to know that?" or "Why don't they just tell me what year Lewis was born?" then you need to take a deep breath and begin again. You may never know the complete order of the people in the problem (sometimes you might!), but you will always have enough information to answer the questions.

The diagram as it has been developed so far uses all the information that you know from the introduction and the rules. You cannot fill in all the spaces exactly, but the diagram significantly narrows down the possibilities. When you have practiced working on the Analytical Reasoning questions, the skill of creating a useful diagram will come to you quickly, so that you can move through these introductory steps fairly smoothly. Then you can use the diagram to answer the specific questions.

Let's look at the questions that accompany this sample problem, and you can see how the diagram can help.

1. Which of the following could be a list of the six people, from oldest to youngest?

    (A) Jim, Kathy, Olivia, Lewis, Ned, Mary
    (B) Lewis, Jim, Kathy, Olivia, Mary, Ned
    (C) Olivia, Lewis, Jim, Kathy, Ned, Mary
    (D) Ned, Lewis, Jim, Kathy, Olivia, Mary
    (E) Lewis, Olivia, Ned, Kathy, Mary, Jim

    By comparing the answer choices to your diagram, you should be able to notice quickly that answers (A) and (B) must be wrong because Kathy must always be the fourth person in the list. You can also tell immediately that answer (D) is wrong because Olivia must come before Kathy in the list. Finally, you can see that answer (E) is wrong because Ned will always be one of the last two people in the list. Therefore, the answer must be (C). Using the diagram makes this type of question very simple to answer.

2. Which of the following statements must be true?

    (A) Olivia is older than Kathy.
    (B) Ned is younger than Mary.
    (C) Jim is older than Olivia.
    (D) Kathy is younger than Ned.
    (E) Mary was born in 1965.

    Because of the preparation in making the diagram, this question also becomes very easy. Answer (A) must be the true statement, since your diagram shows that in any possibility, Olivia will always be listed before (i.e., "older than") Kathy. Because only one answer choice can be the correct answer, your job is finished and you can move on to the next problem.

> **LOGIC TIP:** With the Analytical Reasoning questions, there can be only one correct answer. Therefore, when you have found an answer choice that you are sure is correct, you do not need to spend valuable time reviewing all the other answer choices. On other types of questions, such as Reading Comprehension or even the Logical Reasoning logic questions, you are asked to choose the "best" answer choice out of several that could possibly be answers to the question. However, with Analytical Reasoning, only one answer choice will correctly answer the question, and the other four choices will not even be possible. (CAUTION: If your diagram is incorrect, then you may think an answer choice is correct when it really is not. Therefore, this time-saving technique could backfire if you are not careful.)

If you take the time to review the other answer choices, however, you will see that all of them are incorrect. (B) is incorrect because, as we discussed above, you do not know anything about the relationship between Ned and Mary; Ned might be older, but he might be younger. Since the question asks you for a statement that "must be true," you cannot select answer (B). Answer (C) is incorrect for the same reason, since Jim may or may not be older than Olivia. Answer (D) is incorrect because it will always be a false statement; in any possible arrangement of your diagram, Kathy will always be older than Ned. Finally, answer (E) is incorrect because you do not know if Mary was born in 1964 or 1965.

LOGIC TIP: It is essential that you pay attention to what the question asks you. Questions will ask you to decide what information "must be true," "could/might be true," "must be false," or "could/might be false." Each of these four possible questions will require you to focus your attention slightly differently on the information you have before you. If you mistake a "must be true" for a "could be true," you will not be able to select the correct answer.

---

3. If Lewis was born in 1960, then which people could have been born in 1961?

   (A) Jim or Mary
   (B) Olivia or Jim
   (C) Jim, Mary, or Ned
   (D) Olivia, Jim, or Mary
   (E) Olivia, Jim, Mary, or Ned

This is an example of a question that adds some extra information to what you already know from the rules and introduction. You are now being told to assume that Lewis was born in 1960.

When you are given extra information like this, you must remember that the extra information applies ONLY to this one question. When you move on to the next question, you must rely ONLY on the initial rules.

With this added information in mind, review your diagram:

	1960	1961	1962	1963	1964	1965
A	Lewis	Jim	Olivia	Kathy		
B	Lewis	Olivia	Jim	Kathy		
C	Olivia	Lewis	Jim	Kathy		

If you are now to assume that Lewis was born in 1960, then you can tell that line C here is no longer possible. Therefore, the only possibilities are:

	1960	1961	1962	1963	1964	1965
A	Lewis	Jim	Olivia	Kathy		
B	Lewis	Olivia	Jim	Kathy		

Using this diagram now to answer the question, you can see that the only possibilities for people born in 1961 are Jim or Olivia. Therefore, the answer must be (B).

You should recognize already that a clear diagram can take only a few seconds to prepare, but it can make your task of answering questions much easier. There is no single way to prepare a diagram. You may find that a combination of a chart, arrows, abbreviations, or whatever seems useful to you at the moment will work best for your own needs. Whatever you choose, you must make sure that your notes and diagrams are clear and consistent, so that you do not needlessly confuse yourself with extraneous information that can only result in incorrect answers.

Ranking Practice Questions

> **Directions:** Each question or group of questions is based on a passage or set of conditions. In answering some of the questions, it may be useful to draw a rough diagram. For each question, select the best answer given:

The following information applies to questions 1–5

A section of a kindergarten class has eight children, Barry, Carol, Donna, Eddie, Frank, Gary, Hanna, and Iris. When they leave the class to go to the library, they line up according to the following instructions:

Frank may not be first.
Donna must be either second or last.
At least two students must stand between Frank and Gary.
Iris must stand either immediately in front of or immediately behind Hanna.
Eddie must be fifth.

1. Which of the following is a possible lineup for the eight children, from first to last?

    (A) Iris, Donna, Frank, Hanna, Eddie, Barry, Carol, Gary
    (B) Frank, Donna, Iris, Hanna, Eddie, Gary, Carol, Barry
    (C) Gary, Iris, Hanna, Donna, Eddie, Frank, Barry, Carol
    (D) Hanna, Iris, Frank, Carol, Eddie, Barry, Gary, Donna
    (E) Carol, Gary, Barry, Frank, Eddie, Hanna, Iris, Donna

2. If Gary is last in line, which of the following must be true?

    (A) Barry is either first or third.
    (B) Carol is either fourth or sixth.
    (C) Iris is either sixth or seventh.
    (D) Hanna is either third or fourth.
    (E) Frank is third.

3. If exactly two students stand between Gary and Frank, which of the following must be false?

    (A) Carol is third and Barry is sixth.
    (B) Gary is fourth and Donna is eighth.
    (C) Donna is in front of Frank.
    (D) Barry is seventh and Donna is eighth.
    (E) Donna is second and Hanna is third.

4. If Gary is fourth and Iris is somewhere ahead of Donna, then which of the following is a complete list of the students who could be in sixth place?

   (A) Barry, Carol
   (B) Carol, Iris
   (C) Iris, Hanna
   (D) Carol, Iris, Hanna
   (E) Barry, Carol, Iris, Hanna

5. If Iris and Hanna are the only people standing between Frank and Gary, then how many different lineup combinations of all eight students are possible?

   (A) 2
   (B) 4
   (C) 6
   (D) 8
   (E) 10

The following information applies to questions 6–10

A person visiting the United States wants to visit eight different cities, Alexandria, Boulder, Cleveland, Dallas, East Lansing, Ft. Lauderdale, Gary, and Honolulu. The visitor's itinerary must adhere to the following restrictions:

Boulder and Cleveland must be visited consecutively.
Alexandria must be visited before Gary.
Ft. Lauderdale must be one of the first four cities on the trip.
Honolulu must be third.

6. Which of the following is a possible arrangement of the cities, in order from first to last?

   (A) Boulder, Cleveland, Honolulu, Ft. Lauderdale, Gary, Dallas, East Lansing, Alexandria
   (B) Alexandria, Dallas, Honolulu, Ft. Lauderdale, Cleveland, Boulder, Gary, East Lansing
   (C) Ft. Lauderdale, Cleveland, Boulder, Honolulu, Alexandria, East Lansing, Gary, Dallas
   (D) Dallas, Alexandria, Honolulu, Ft. Lauderdale, Gary, Boulder, East Lansing, Cleveland
   (E) East Lansing, Ft. Lauderdale, Honolulu, Cleveland, Boulder, Dallas, Gary, Alexandria

7. How many different cities could be the last city on the list?

    (A) 2
    (B) 3
    (C) 4
    (D) 5
    (E) 6

8. If Alexandria is visited first, which of the following must be true?

    (A) Dallas is visited before Honolulu.
    (B) Gary is visited after Honolulu.
    (C) Boulder is visited sixth.
    (D) Ft. Lauderdale is visited before Cleveland.
    (E) Dallas is visited immediately after Gary.

9. If Boulder is visited before Ft. Lauderdale, then which of the following is a complete list of the cities that could be visited fifth?

    (A) Alexandria, Dallas
    (B) Dallas, East Lansing
    (C) Alexandria, Dallas, Gary
    (D) Alexandria, Dallas, East Lansing
    (E) Alexandria, Dallas, East Lansing, Gary

10. Which of the following must be false?

    (A) Cleveland is visited immediately after Honolulu.
    (B) Dallas is visited after Alexandria.
    (C) Boulder is visited immediately before Ft. Lauderdale.
    (D) Ft. Lauderdale is visited before Honolulu.
    (E) Honolulu is visited before both Cleveland and Gary.

2. DISTRIBUTION PROBLEMS

Distribution problems are similar to ranking problems, but you will not always have a simple linear arrangement for ordering the people or objects in the problem. Distribution problems may involve placing cars in a multilevel parking garage, where there can be one, two, three, or more cars on any particular floor of the garage; arranging businesses into office spaces in a building, where more than one business can occupy any particular floor; or placing people in seats in a theater, where people do not necessarily appear in the same row. A successful diagram for a distribution problem, instead of containing a single line across, as in the ranking problem, will often have several rows and several columns available for distribution. The method of answering the questions will be very similar to the method used for the ranking problems, but you simply have to realize that there may be more than one person or object on any given level of the diagram.

The key to recognizing that a problem is a distribution problem and not a ranking problem is that a distribution problem will not have a direct "one-to-one" match of players with spaces. Some keys to recognizing a distribution problem are:

1. The items do not fit neatly into a single row, column, or similar arrangement;

2. The number of items does not exactly match the number of spaces; and

3. The problem may directly tell you that you will have two or more rows, columns, etc.

As with all Analytical Reasoning problems, the key to success with a distribution problem is a complete and accurate diagram. The diagram will appear somewhat different from the diagram for the ranking problems, but most of the principles are the same.

Consider the following sample problem:

An apartment building has six floors, with two apartments on each floor. Eight families—named Harrison, Inker, Jones, Kelly, Lewis, Michaels, Nesmith, and Otterman—live in the apartment building, according to the following specifications:

> *At least one family lives on each floor.*
> *The Otterman family lives on the same floor as the Jones family.*
> *The Harrisons are on the third floor.*
> *The Kellys are on one of the top two floors.*
> *The Michaels family lives one floor below the Kelly family.*

The first step in creating a useful diagram for a distribution problem is recognizing the "shape" or "layout" of the situation. In this case, the problem describes an apartment building that has six floors, with two apartments on each floor. This suggests the following structure for your diagram:

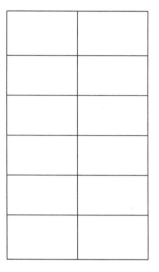

To assist you in quickly, easily, and accurately spotting the correct "floors" for placing families in this problem, it would be helpful to number the floors.

LOGIC TIP: Be careful, whenever you are assigning numbers to spaces in an Analytical Reasoning problem, that you read the problem VERY CAREFULLY so that you are sure whether the spaces are numbered from the bottom up, from the top down, from left to right, from right to left, or some other method. In some cases, the problem may not specify. In those cases, the numbering may not be essential to the problem, but it is important that you remain consistent.

In this case, the problem does not specify which floor is to be number 1 and which floor is to be number 6. Because the problem does not give you any definition, you can use common sense and label the bottom floor Number 1 and the top floor Number 6, as shown below:

6		
5		
4		
3		
2		
1		

Numbering the floors assists you in identifying quickly where to place the names as you work through diagramming the problem.

Once you have set up the general structure for your diagram, the next step is to begin reviewing the rules for the problem and placing information in your diagram according to the rules. As with ranking problems, most of the rules for a distribution problem lend themselves fairly easily to notations in your diagram. Occasionally, rules are not simple enough to make direct notes in the diagram. In these cases, just make a brief summary of the rule off to the side of the diagram so that you do not risk forgetting about that particular rule later. It is important to note that the creators of the Analytical Reasoning problems very rarely include "red herrings"—if a rule is provided, it probably will be used at some point in the problem.

When reviewing the rules, you first want to start with the rules that most directly provide you with clear information about the placement of a particular player. In this problem, the third rule, "The Harrisons are on the third floor," allows you to place a family directly in its place. This is the best place to begin, by placing that family in place:

6		
5		
4		
3	Harrison	
2		
1		

This is the only rule that makes a direct placement. Next, move on to rules that perhaps provide less concrete information but still allow you to make a placement into your diagram. The second rule, "The Otterman family lives on the same floor as the Jones family," does not tell you exactly where to place the Ottermans and Joneses, but you do know that they will be together. So make this note below your table:

6		
5		
4		
3	Harrison	
2		
1		

Otterman—Jones together

The two last rules, "The Kellys are on one of the top two floors," and "The Michaels family lives one floor below the Kelly family," allow for a partial placement of information. You know that the Kellys are on either 5 or 6 and the Michaels are one floor below, on either 4 or 5. This creates two possibilities for the diagram:

6	Kelly	
5	Michaels	
4		
3	Harrison	
2		
1		

6		
5	Kelly	
4	Michaels	
3	Harrison	
2		
1		

Otterman—Jones together

The final rule, just to make sure that you do not forget it, is the very first one on the list which requires that at least one family live on each floor. This is a common rule but not one that you can diagram very well. You simply need to remember, for the purpose of this problem, that there must be at least one family on each floor—that no floor is left completely blank.

Now that you have accounted for all the rules, reconsider the diagram that you have created and try to identify any additional relationships that may not have been stated as rules for the problem but that must be true because of the way the other information has fallen into place. Recognizing that the Otterman—Jones combination will take up a complete floor, you can tell that the Otterman—Jones combination may be only on Level 1, 2, 4, or 6—i.e., they cannot ever be on Levels 3 or 5. By noting this information at this stage, you may be able to anticipate a later question.

6	Kelly	
5	Michaels	
4		
3	Harrison	
2		
1		

OR

6		
5	Kelly	
4	Michaels	
3	Harrison	
2		
1		

Otterman—Jones together
(NOT on 3 or 5)

The final step before beginning with the actual questions is to note which of the names, if any, are not already accounted for. These names are people who are free to be placed anywhere in the diagram. Recognizing this information early can help you quickly eliminate incorrect answers later. For example, in this problem, the three names Inker, Lewis, and Nesmith are not accounted for. As a result, they may freely be placed anywhere (subject, of course, to any additional rules that are provided later). If you are faced with a question that asks, "Which of the following MUST be TRUE . . .," you can eliminate any answers that involve Inker, Lewis, or Nesmith, since there are no requirements that any of these names "MUST" be placed anywhere.

Now review the completed diagrams, with the additional information gleaned from the introductory rules:

6	Kelly	
5	Michaels	
4		
3	Harrison	
2		
1		

OR

6		
5	Kelly	
4	Michaels	
3	Harrison	
2		
1		

Otterman—Jones together
(NOT on 3 or 5)
Inker, Lewis, Nesmith—Anywhere

Now that your diagram is complete, you are ready to begin working on the questions.

1. If the Kelly family lives alone on the fifth floor, then which of the following statements must be false?

    (A) The Nesmith family lives on Floor 6.
    (B) The Inker family and Lewis family are on the same floor.
    (C) The Michaels family lives above exactly six other families.
    (D) The Jones family lives on Floor 6.
    (E) The Kelly family lives below only one family.

To begin solving this question, first recognize that the question adds a new fact to the initial rules. For this question, and ONLY this question, you are to assume that the Kelly family lives on the fifth floor and that no other family lives on that floor. Therefore, of the two possible diagrams that were created above, one with the Kelly family on the sixth floor and one with the Kelly family on the fifth floor, the first diagram can be discarded. Therefore, the diagram for this particular question is as follows:

6		
5	Kelly	EMPTY
4	Michaels	
3	Harrison	
2		
1		

Otterman—Jones together
(NOT on 3 or 5)
Inker, Lewis, Nesmith—Anywhere

Now work on answering the question by checking each answer, one at a time, to see if your diagram points out a configuration that "must be false." You can quickly tell from your notes below the table that answer (A) is incorrect because there is no rule that limits where the Nesmith family may be. Likewise, the diagram does not suggest any reason that answer (B) "must be false." Without spending too much time at this point searching for an answer, it would make more sense to continue checking the remaining answers for an answer that is more blatantly incorrect. Answer (C) has the Michaels family above exactly six other families. Recognizing that the Michaels family is on the fourth floor, with three floors below, this would require that two families live on each of the first three floors, making up the six families. The Michaels family is on the fourth floor, and the Kelly family is on the fifth. This accounts for all eight families in this problem. However, this arrangement would leave the sixth floor empty. Because at least one family must live on each floor, answer (C) presents the impossible statement and therefore the correct answer.

Because answer (C) is the correct answer, you need not waste time reviewing answers (D) and (E), which must be false.

2. If the Otterman family lives above the Kelly family, then which of the following statements must be true?

   (A) The Inker and Lewis families live on the same floor.
   (B) The Michaels family lives directly below the Harrison family.
   (C) At least three families live on floors 1 and 2 combined.
   (D) At least three families live on floors 5 and 6 combined.
   (E) Exactly two floors have only one family.

The first step to answering this question is to recall your diagram using the original rules and add to it the new information for this question. Also add to it any new conclusions you can draw.

Recall that the original diagram alternatives for this problem are as follows:

6	Kelly	
5	Michaels	
4		
3	Harrison	
2		
1		

OR

6		
5	Kelly	
4	Michaels	
3	Harrison	
2		
1		

Otterman—Jones together
(NOT on 3 or 5)
Inker, Lewis, Nesmith—Anywhere

For this particular question, you are now required to add to the diagram the fact that the Otterman family lives directly above the Kelly family. Note that the first alternative diagram, with Kelly on the sixth floor, would make this impossible, since there is no higher floor for the Otterman family. Therefore, you know immediately that Kelly must be on 5 and Otterman on 6. Since Otterman and Jones must be on the same floor, the diagram becomes the following:

6	Otterman	Jones
5	Kelly	
4	Michaels	
3	Harrison	
2		
1		

Now, still before considering the answers, also note which names have not yet been placed. These are Inker, Lewis, and Nesmith. There are three remaining names, and there are two floors with no occupants left. Therefore, of these three names, two of them will be used on floors 1 and 2. You have no rules directing which of the remaining names must go in which spaces, so you must assume that any of them could go in any space. But since two of them must take the spaces on floors 1 and 2, then only the single remaining name is left to share a floor with anyone. After this initial analysis, you are ready to begin checking the answers.

Note that the question asks for the one statement that "must be true." Therefore, any statement that "could be false" is an automatically incorrect answer. This is your method for testing the answers.

Answer (A) places Inker and Lewis on the same floor. Because there are no rules dictating where either Inker or Lewis must go, this statement could probably be true, but it could also probably be false. If you can arrange even one organization of the names that would make this statement false, then (A) must be an incorrect answer. Such a possible arrangement is:

6	Otterman	Jones
5	Kelly	
4	Michaels	
3	Harrison	Nesmith
2	Inker	
1	Lewis	

The above diagram satisfies all the conditions of the rules but has Inker and Lewis on separate floors. Therefore, it would be incorrect to say that Inker and Lewis "must" be on the same floor. Therefore, answer (A) is incorrect. Answer (B) is immediately counted as an incorrect statement, since the diagram clearly shows that the Michaels family lives ABOVE the Harrison family, not below. Answer (C) is incorrect because the diagram above, used to analyze answer (A), shows a possible arrangement of the eight families in which only two families are on floors 1 and 2 combined. This arrangement satisfies all the rules but shows that answer (C) is not a statement that "must be true." Answer (D), just as clearly, must be true, and therefore must be the correct answer, since a quick look at the diagram shows that there are at least three families on the top two floors. There could be a fourth, but that is not necessary for answer (D) to be correct. Answer (E) is incorrect for two reasons. The first reason is that (D) is already shown to be the answer, so all other answers must be incorrect. Answer (E) can also be shown to be incorrect by reviewing the diagram and counting the number of available names. The initial analysis of the diagram for this question resulted in recognizing that there are two available floors, 1 and 2, with three available names, Inker, Lewis, and Nesmith. Since one of those must go on level 1 and one on level

2, the final name will be a second occupant on any of the floors of the building except the sixth floor, which is already occupied by Otterman and Jones. Therefore, there will be exactly two floors with two families and exactly four floors with one family. So answer (E) is incorrect.

3. If the Inker family shares a floor with the Harrison family, then which of the following could be true?

(A) The Kelly and Nesmith families live on the same floor.
(B) The Lewis family lives directly below the Kelly family.
(C) The Otterman family lives directly above the Michaels family.
(D) The Jones family lives directly below the Inker family.
(E) Exactly four families live on floors 5 and 6 combined.

As always, begin by revising the initial diagram to add the new material for this question. Because Harrison is on 3, then this question requires that Inker is also on 3. Recall that the original diagram alternatives for this problem are as follows:

6	Kelly	
5	Michaels	
4		
3	Harrison	
2		
1		

OR

6		
5	Kelly	
4	Michaels	
3	Harrison	
2		
1		

Otterman—Jones together
(NOT on 3 or 5)
Inker, Lewis, Nesmith—Anywhere

By adding the new information, the diagram alternatives become the following:

6	Kelly	
5	Michaels	
4		
3	Harrison	Inker
2		
1		

OR

6		
5	Kelly	
4	Michaels	
3	Harrison	Inker
2		
1		

Otterman—Jones together
(NOT on 3 or 5)
Lewis, Nesmith—Anywhere

At this point, it is also useful to note that four names have been used (Kelly, Michaels, Harrison, and Inker), even though you cannot be certain yet about the placement of Kelly and Michaels, and that four names remain. In either of the possible alternative diagrams, there are three floors left unoccupied. Therefore, the four names remaining must be placed so that there is at least one name on each floor. Since Otterman and Jones must be placed together, then neither Otterman nor Jones can share a floor with anyone else, and the Otterman—Jones combination must be on one of the three empty floors. That placement will leave two empty floors, with two names, Lewis and Nesmith, left to be placed. As a result, you can quickly tell that the remaining two families, Lewis and Nesmith, must be placed by themselves on those two remaining floors. Note that you do not have enough information to know the exact placement of any of these names, but the analysis of the general placement can save you a lot of time later.

Answer (A) suggests placing Nesmith on the same floor as Kelly. Because of the above analysis, you know that Nesmith must be alone on some floor, so (A) must be false and is therefore an incorrect statement for a question that asks for statements that "could be true." Answer (B), by placing Lewis directly below Kelly, would force Lewis to share a floor with Michaels in either of the diagram alternatives. However, since the analysis requires Lewis to be alone, this statement must be false and is therefore an incorrect answer. Answer (C) creates an impossible situation, since Otterman and Jones must be placed on the same floor, and the diagram shows that there is only one vacancy on the floor directly above Michaels. Answer (D) places Jones on the second floor, directly below Inker, which would also place Otterman on the second floor, since Otterman and Jones must remain together. In either of the alternative diagrams for this question, this much is possible:

6	Kelly	
5	Michaels	
4		
3	Harrison	Inker
2	Otterman	Jones
1		

OR

6		
5	Kelly	
4	Michaels	
3	Harrison	Inker
2	Otterman	Jones
1		

Lewis, Nesmith—Anywhere

Each possibility leaves two empty floors, with two names, Lewis and Nesmith, to be placed. Since Lewis and Nesmith can be placed anywhere and since all floors can be filled, this is a possible arrangement, so answer (D) is a statement that "could be true" and is the correct answer. Answer (E) would have two families on the fifth floor and two families on the sixth floor. Combined with the two families on the third floor, this accounts for a total of six families, with only two left, but with three empty floors:

6	occupied	occupied
5	occupied	occupied
4		
3	Harrison	Inker
2		
1		

This is an impossible arrangement, with only two names left to fill the three remaining floors, so answer (E) is incorrect.

4. If the Kelly, Lewis, and Otterman families all live on odd-numbered floors, then which of the following statements could be false?

(A) Inker lives on an even-numbered floor.
(B) Lewis lives somewhere above Jones.
(C) Harrison lives somewhere above Otterman.
(D) Inker lives somewhere above Otterman.
(E) Nesmith lives somewhere above Harrison.

As always, the first step is to place the new information into the diagram and create a new diagram for this specific question as completely as possible. Begin with the two original diagram alternatives:

6	Kelly	
5	Michaels	
4		
3	Harrison	
2		
1		

OR

6		
5	Kelly	
4	Michaels	
3	Harrison	
2		
1		

Otterman—Jones together
(NOT on 3 or 5)
Inker, Lewis, Nesmith—Anywhere

Because this question requires that Kelly must be on an odd-numbered floor, the alternative on the left, placing Kelly on the sixth floor, must be incorrect. As a result, focus on the second alternative alone:

6		
5	Kelly	
4	Michaels	
3	Harrison	
2		
1		

Because Otterman must be placed together with Jones, the only odd-numbered floor where Otterman can be placed is the first floor:

6		
5	Kelly	
4	Michaels	
3	Harrison	
2		
1	Otterman	Jones

The final bit of new information for this question is that Lewis is on an odd-numbered floor. Both floor 3 and floor 5 have openings, and it appears that Lewis could take either of those vacancies. So mark this in the diagram with a question mark, to show uncertainty:

6		
5	Kelly	Lewis (??)
4	Michaels	
3	Harrison	Lewis (??)
2		
1	Otterman	Jones

It is up to you to remember that the question marks mean that Lewis might be on the fifth floor or might be on the third floor. Even so, having these notes marked in the diagram makes the problem much easier to solve.

> **LOGIC TIP:** When you can limit the placement for a particular name to exactly one space in your diagram, write it in. When you can limit the placement for a particular name to two or three spaces it is often helpful to write the name into all the possible spaces, with a question mark (??) to remind you that the placement is not permanent. This still provides you with a quick visual aid for answering the questions, but it reminds you of the information that you do not certainly know.

This diagram shows that six names have been used, with two names, Inker and Nesmith, remaining to be placed. There are two floors, the second and sixth, that have no occupants yet, so you know that Inker will be alone on one of these floors and Nesmith with be alone on the other. This information can be shown by writing both names into both spaces, showing the alternatives available to you. Also, you can write "Empty" into the spaces that you know must be vacant:

6	Inker/Nesmith	EMPTY
5	Kelly	Lewis (??)
4	Michaels	EMPTY
3	Harrison	Lewis (??)
2	Inker/Nesmith	EMPTY
1	Otterman	Jones

Note that you now have every space in the diagram filled. The only possibilities are that Inker and Nesmith may be in either of two spaces and Lewis could be in the space on 3 or the space on 5. Otherwise, the entire diagram is completed and answering the question should be very easy.

Answer (A) must be true, and therefore an incorrect answer for this question, since Inker's only options are 2 or 6, both even-numbered floors. Answer (B) must be true, and therefore an incorrect answer for this question, since both of Lewis' options, either 3 or 5, are above Jones, who must be on 1. Answer (C) similarly is incorrect because the diagram clearly shows that Harrison must be above Otterman. Answer (D) is similar to (A) in that you do not know the exact placement for the Inker family, but it will definitely be somewhere above Otterman. The only remaining statement is (E). Considering this answer, you see that Nesmith could be on either the second floor or the sixth. One of these is above Harrison, but one is below. Because you do not know which of the alternatives is correct, it is possible for the statement in answer (E) to be false. Therefore, (E) is the answer.

5. If the sixth floor is left completely vacant but all other conditions remain true, then which of the following statements could be true?

(A) The Michaels family lives somewhere below the Jones family.

(B) The Inker family lives somewhere below the Harrison family.

(C) Exactly three families live somewhere above the Michaels family.

(D) Exactly three floors will have only one vacant apartment.

(E) Exactly two floors will have no vacant apartments.

The first step for this question is to create a diagram, marking both apartments on the sixth floor as vacant:

6	VACANT	VACANT
5	Kelly	
4	Michaels	
3	Harrison	
2		
1		

Because the sixth floor is vacant, then the Kelly family must be on the fifth floor, which is its only other option, and the Michaels family must be on the fourth floor, one floor below. The other bit of information that you know is that the Otterman—Jones combination still must remain together, and the only spaces now available for this combination are on the bottom two floors. This results in the two following alternatives:

6	VACANT	VACANT			6	VACANT	VACANT
5	Kelly				5	Kelly	
4	Michaels		OR		4	Michaels	
3	Harrison				3	Harrison	
2	Otterman	Jones			2		
1					1	Otterman	Jones

These alternative diagrams show that you have five spaces left, with three names left to use, Inker, Lewis, and Nesmith. Since one of these names will take the completely vacant floor (either 1 or 2), then the remaining two names will share floors with someone. This analysis helps you realize that there will be three floors with two occupants, two floors with only one occupant, and the sixth floor with no occupants. You are now ready to begin considering the answers.

Answer (A) is clearly incorrect because, in each alternative diagram, the Jones family is on either the first or second floor, while the Michaels family is on the fourth floor. Answer (B), placing the Inker family "somewhere below the Harrison family," could be true, since there are vacancies below the Harrison family and there are no limits on where the Inker family could go. As an illustration, the following diagram shows a possible arrangement that would make this statement true:

6	VACANT	VACANT
5	Kelly	
4	Michaels	Nesmith
3	Harrison	
2	Otterman	Jones
1	Inker	Lewis

The above diagram is not the only arrangement; it is just one possibility. But since the question only asks for a statement that "could be true," this one possibility is enough. The answer is (B). Answer (C) is false since the diagram shows that there are only two available apartments, on the fifth floor, that are above the Michaels family. Answers (D) and (E) are incorrect based on the initial analysis above, showing that there will be three floors with two families, two floors with one family, and the sixth floor with nobody. Therefore, the answer is still (B).

DISTRIBUTION PRACTICE QUESTIONS

Directions: Each question or group of questions is based on a passage or set of conditions. In answering some of the questions, it may be useful to draw a rough diagram. For each question, select the best answer given:

An apartment building has seven vacant apartments—one each on the first, second, and fifth floors and two each on the third and fourth floors. Six people, Robert, Sam, Tyler, Usher, Victor, and Wally, live in the apartments according to the following rules:

Each floor must have at least one occupant.
Robert must be on a higher floor than Tyler.
Exactly two people live above Sam.

1. If Sam lives above Tyler, which of the following must be false?

   (A) Sam lives above Robert.
   (B) Usher lives above Victor.
   (C) Wally lives on the first floor.
   (D) Sam and Usher live on the same floor.
   (E) Robert and Victor live on the same floor.

2. Which of the following statements could be true?

   (A) Sam lives on the fourth floor.
   (B) Two people live on the fourth floor.
   (C) Tyler is the only person on the third floor.
   (D) Victor lives on the fifth floor.
   (E) Wally and Usher live on the same floor.

3. If Robert does not live on a higher floor than Sam, then how many different floors could Robert live on?

   (A) 1
   (B) 2
   (C) 3
   (D) 4
   (E) 5

4. If Victor and Wally live above Sam, then which of the following is a complete list of the people who could live on the second floor?

    (A) Robert, Sam
    (B) Robert, Usher, Tyler
    (C) Robert, Sam, Tyler
    (D) Sam, Usher, Tyler
    (E) Robert, Sam, Tyler, Usher

5. If Tyler lives on the same floor with one other person, which of the following could be false?

    (A) Robert lives on the fourth floor.
    (B) Exactly two people live below Tyler.
    (C) Victor and Wally live on different floors.
    (D) Robert lives above Sam.
    (E) Exactly two people live below Sam.

The following information applies to questions 6–9

Tom's bookshelf has four shelves, numbered 1 through 4 from bottom to top. Each shelf has space for three video-taped movies. Tom's movie collection consists of nine movies, *Arthur, Bambi, Cheyenne, David Copperfield, East of Eden, Father of the Bride, Gaslight, Harry & Tonto,* and *Ice Station Zebra*, which he stores as follows:

> Every shelf must have at least one movie.
>
> *Bambi* and *Cheyenne* must be on Shelf 2.
> *David Copperfield* must be on a lower shelf than
>   *Harry & Tonto*.
> Neither *East of Eden* nor *Father of the Bride* may be
>   on an odd-numbered shelf.
> *Arthur* and *Harry & Tonto* must be on the same shelf.

6. Which of the following statements could be true?

    (A) *David Copperfield* is on Shelf 4.
    (B) *Harry & Tonto* is on Shelf 1.
    (C) *Father of the Bride* is on the shelf immediately below
         Cheyenne.
    (D) Shelf 2 has *3* movies.
    (E) *East of Eden* is on the bottom shelf.

7. If *Cheyenne* and *Father of the Bride* are on different shelves, which of the following must be true?

   (A) *David Copperfield* is on a higher shelf than *Arthur*.
   (B) *East of Eden* is on the top shelf.
   (C) *East of Eden* and *Gaslight* are on different shelves.
   (D) *Father of the Bride* is on the top shelf.
   (E) *Arthur* is on the bottom shelf.

8. Which of the following pairs of movies CANNOT be on the same shelf?

   (A) *Father of the Bride* and *Gaslight*
   (B) *Bambi* and ~~*Harry & Tonto*~~ *EAST OF EDEN*
   (C) *Arthur* and *David Copperfield*
   (D) *East of Eden* and *David Copperfield*
   (E) *Cheyenne* and *Ice Station Zebra*

9. Which of the following is a complete list of all the movies that could be on the bottom shelf?

   (A) *David Copperfield, Gaslight,* ~~*Harry & Tonto,*~~ *Ice Station Zebra*
   (B) *Arthur, David Copperfield, Gaslight, Ice Station Zebra*
   (C) *Arthur, East of Eden, Gaslight, Harry & Tonto*
   (D) *Arthur, David Copperfield, East of Eden, Ice Station Zebra*
   (E) *David Copperfield, Father of the Bride, Gaslight, Harry & Tonto*

3. SCHEDULING PROBLEMS

A scheduling problem usually requires you to arrange a schedule of some event or activity. You might be organizing a schedule of performers in a recital, children visiting the doctor, television shows during nights of the week, or any other activities or events that can be placed in some form of "time order." In fact, this idea of "time" is the key to recognizing a scheduling problem. In most other respects, a scheduling problem is very similar to a ranking problem or a distribution problem. However, the idea of "time" makes a scheduling problem special, so you will be working with concepts of certain events occurring "before" or "after" other events. The rules will differ somewhat from the kinds of rules you will have in ranking or distribution problems, but the basic task is still the same: arrange the people or events in the order allowed by the rules. Because of the similarities between scheduling problems and distribution problems, the first three keys for recognition are the same:

1. The items do not fit neatly into a single row, column, or similar arrangement;

2. The number of items does not exactly match the number of spaces; and

3. The problem may directly tell you that you will have two or more rows, columns, etc.

The one additional key for recognition is unique to scheduling problems:

4. The events are arranged in a "time" order, with some events being placed "before" or "after" others.

As with both ranking and distribution problems, scheduling problems are the easiest to solve when you begin with an accurate diagram, marking spaces for the times to be filled for the schedule. First, read the problem carefully and identify how many days or hours or other time units are to be filled. Scheduling problems are similar to distribution problems in that they could both have multiple items for any single row or column of your diagram. The diagram need not always be simply a single straight line.

Consider the following sample problem:

John is starting a new business mowing lawns for people in town. He has seven customers, A, B, C, D, E, F, and G. He must arrange his schedule so that he can mow everyone's lawn once a week. He must plan his schedule as follows:

> *John can only mow lawns from Monday to Friday, and he can do no more than two each day, one in the morning and one in the afternoon.*
> *John mows at least one lawn each day.*
> *A's lawn is so large that it requires an entire day.*
> *Because B and D live on opposite sides of town, John cannot schedule them together on the same day.*
> *John must mow F's lawn on Friday afternoon.*
> *John must mow C's lawn on Tuesday morning.*
> *John can mow G's lawn only in the afternoon, but on any day.*

The first step for this problem, as with a distribution problem, is to decide on the "shape" or "structure" of the diagram. The first rule provides the information to assist you with this step. Your diagram must account for the five days, Monday through Friday, with one space for each morning and one space for each afternoon. Therefore, the diagram structure will look like this:

	Mon	Tue	Wed	Thur	Fri
Morning					
Afternoon					

You are now ready to begin placing the information you know into the spaces of the diagram, making any necessary notes beside or below the diagram to remind you of information that is not specific enough to be placed directly into the diagram. The third and fourth rules are examples of this situation—the information is important, but it does not give you enough specific information to be able to place any of the customers in place in the diagram, so you will just make an abbreviated note below the diagram:

	Mon	Tue	Wed	Thur	Fri
Morning					
Afternoon					

A = any whole day

B/D — must be separate days

The fifth and sixth rules allow you to place F and C directly into their permanent positions. The final rule about G is something you can place to the side of the diagram, showing that G must be in the afternoons:

	Mon	Tue	Wed	Thur	Fri	
Morning		C				
Afternoon					F	—G, any afternoon

A = any whole day

B/D — must be separate days

Now that the initial rules have been incorporated into the initial diagram, the next step is to consider the rules and try to draw any possible conclusions for additional information. The rule about B and D being on separate days is still too broad. However, the rule about A taking an entire day, combined with the rules that C is already placed on Tuesday morning and F is already placed on Friday afternoon, assures you that A cannot be scheduled for Tuesday or Friday. This information can be added to the diagram:

	Mon	Tue	Wed	Thur	Fri
Morning		C			(not A)
Afternoon		(not A)			F

—G, any afternoon

A = any whole day

B/D — must be separate days

LOGIC TIP: It is just as important to note in your diagram certain impossible situations. Whenever you know that a particular item CANNOT be placed into a particular space, make a note of that fact directly in the space, using the "NOT" notation. When you do this, though, be careful that you do not later glance quickly at your diagram and, seeing something written in the space, assume that it is occupied.

You can also note from the initial rules that the problem works with seven customers, and there are ten spaces in the diagram. Because C is already placed in Tuesday morning and F is already placed in Friday afternoon, there are eight remaining spaces for the five remaining customers. Keep in mind that A will require two spaces (morning and afternoon), so, after accounting for A, there will be six remaining spaces for the four remaining customers. As a result, there will always be exactly two empty spaces in the diagram. This information cannot be drawn into the diagram, but it is useful information that is sure to assist you as you answer the questions.

You have now created a diagram that accounts for all the rules and includes all the conclusions that you can draw at this early stage. It is now time to begin considering the questions.

1. Which of the following is a possible list of John's schedule for the mornings from Monday through Friday?

   (A) A, C, B, D, (off)
   (B) (off), C, A, G, D
   (C) (off), C, D, E, A
   (D) B, C, (off), D, E
   (E) G, C, A, E, (off)

This is a standard first question for any problem set. It does not provide any new information and merely asks you to interpret the initial rules to test a series of options. There are two methods of answering a question of this type. You can either work down the list of answers, from (A) to (E), and check each one against all the rules to see if any rules are violated, or you can start with the first of your rules and work your way through the list of rules, eliminating answers as you go whenever you see one that violates the rule you are considering. Both solving alternatives are valid. In some cases, one method may be slightly quicker than the other, but you cannot tell which will be quicker until you begin. The best procedure is to pick one method or the other and then be consistent with it.

In this particular case, the quickest method is to consider the answers in order, because answer (A) will prove to be the correct answer. Answer (A) satisfies the rule about scheduling C for Tuesday morning; it does not include G, who is supposed to be on some afternoon; and by scheduling B and D for two different mornings, there will be no problem with them both being on the same day. Therefore, answer (A) is a possible schedule for the mornings and is the correct answer. Reviewing the other answers will demonstrate a flaw in each one. Answer (B) is incorrect because it schedules G for a morning. Answer (C) is incorrect because it schedules A for Friday, but that is impossible since A requires an entire day, and Friday afternoon is already occupied by F. Answer (D) is incorrect because it does not include A. Because A needs an entire day, there must be a space in the morning schedule for A. Answer (E) is incorrect for the same reason as (B), that G cannot be scheduled for the morning.

2. Which of the following is a possible list of John's schedule for the afternoons from Monday through Friday?

(A) G, C, D, A, F
(B) D, B, G, E, F
(C) E, A, G, (off), F
(D) (off), B, A, D, F
(E) G, (off), A, B, F

This is the same kind of question as the previous one, with the emphasis shifted to the afternoon schedule. Answer (A) is not possible because it includes C in the afternoon schedule, when the diagram shows that C must be in the morning. Answer (B) is incorrect because it does not include A at all; remember that A must be included in both the morning and afternoon schedules. Answer (C) is incorrect because A, who requires a full day, is scheduled on Tuesday. Reviewing the diagram shows that this would overlap with C, who is already scheduled on Tuesday morning. Answer (D) is incorrect because it does not include G, who must be scheduled in the afternoon. The only remaining answer, answer (E), should satisfy all the rules, and it does. G is scheduled in the afternoon, A does not overlap with anyone else, and F is included on Friday afternoon. Therefore, the correct answer is (E).

3. If A is scheduled for Thursday, then which of the following statements must be false?

(A) B and D are scheduled on consecutive days.
(B) C and G are scheduled on consecutive days.
(C) F and G are scheduled on consecutive days.
(D) B and E are scheduled on the same day.
(E) E and G are scheduled on the same day.

The first step is to revise your diagram to add in the new information for this question:

	Mon	Tue	Wed	Thur	Fri	
Morning		C		A		
Afternoon				A	F	—G, any after-noon

B/D — must be separate days

Although this does not seem like much new information, it will be enough to answer the question. You must constantly remember that the test does provide you with enough information to answer the question. This particular question asks for a situation that "must be false." Therefore, any statement that "could be true" will be immediately incorrect. All you have to do is look for ANY POSSIBLE arrangement of individuals in the schedule that would make each statement true. If that is possible, the answer is incorrect and you can move on to the next answer.

The only rule about B and D is that they must be on separate days, but there is nothing preventing them from being on consecutive days. There seems to be so little information at this point that it is hard to realize that anything must be either true or false. When this situation occurs, you can generally be assured that the one correct answer will "stick out like a sore thumb." So do not spend too much time with every answer that seems to have no limitations on it. Therefore, while there is little information about (A), there is no reason at this point to say that it "must be false," so pass over it and check the remaining answers. When you consider all the answers in this way, (A), (B), (D), and (E) all fall into this category. Each statement could be either true or false, since there is so little information provided. Answer (C), however, is a blatantly false statement. Reviewing the diagram shows that A takes the entire day on Thursday and F is on Friday. Therefore, it is impossible for anyone else to be on "consecutive days" with F. So the correct answer is (C).

4. If B and D must be on consecutive mornings, then which of the following statements must be false?

   (A) G and C are scheduled for the same day.
   (B) G and D are scheduled for the same day.
   (C) B is scheduled for Wednesday.
   (D) A is scheduled for Thursday.
   (E) E is scheduled for Monday.

This question still does not provide much information that will allow you to specifically place any of the customers in the schedule, so you must count on just checking the answer. Because this question asks you to find the statement that "must be false," then any statement that could possibly be true will be a wrong answer. All you have to do is test the diagram and see if you can create a schedule that would make the answer true. If you can, that is an incorrect answer and can be eliminated. If you cannot, then just pass over that particular answer and check the others.

Answer (A) places G and C on the same day. This seems possible, since G is in the afternoon and C is in the morning. Considering the diagram, it would be easy to construct a possible schedule to make this true:

	Mon	Tue	Wed	Thur	Fri
Morning	A	C	B	D	
Afternoon	A	G		E	F

—G, any after-noon

B/D — must be separate days

This is not the ONLY possible arrangement with G and C on the same day. But because it is at least possible to make even one such schedule, then Answer (A) is incorrect. Similarly, you can do the same for all the answers except (D), which is the correct answer for the question. If you try to schedule A on Thursday, the diagram becomes the following:

	Mon	Tue	Wed	Thur	Fri
Morning		C		A	
Afternoon				A	F

—G, any after-noon

B/D — must be separate days

Once you place A into the diagram, you can see that the only remaining mornings are Monday, Wednesday, and Friday. However, because for this question you must schedule B and D for consecutive mornings, this diagram is impossible. Therefore, the correct answer must be (D).

SCHEDULING PRACTICE QUESTIONS

> **Directions:** Each question or group of questions is based on a passage or set of conditions. In answering some of the questions, it may be useful to draw a rough diagram. For each question, select the best answer given.

The following information applies to questions 1–6

There were seven students in Downtown High School's driver's education class—Phillip, Sheryl, Wilbur, Louise, Ryan, Annie, and Eddie. Because of safety regulations, the teacher can only take one student at a time during the school week, from Monday through Friday, for either a morning or an afternoon session. When the instructor plans the weekly schedule, the following rules must apply:

Phillip and Sheryl must have their lessons on the same day.
Eddie cannot come on Thursday.
Louise is available only for morning sessions.
Wilbur is available only for afternoon sessions.
Annie is available only Monday morning.

1. Which of the following is a possible list, from Monday to Friday, of morning driver's education students?

   (A) Annie, Eddie, Phillip, Sheryl, Louise
   (B) Annie, Wilbur, Eddie, Phillip, Louise
   (C) Louise, Phillip, Ryan, Annie, Eddie
   (D) Annie, Sheryl, Louise, Eddie, Ryan
   (E) Annie, Eddie, Phillip, Louise, Ryan

2. Which of the following is a possible list, from Monday to Friday, of afternoon driver's education students?

   (A) Annie, Eddie, Sheryl, Wilbur, Ryan
   (B) Wilbur, Sheryl, Louise, Ryan, Eddie
   (C) Eddie, Sheryl, Wilbur, Ryan, nobody
   (D) Phillip, Sheryl, nobody, Ryan, Eddie
   (E) Louise, Wilbur, Eddie, Sheryl, Ryan

3. If the teacher does not want to schedule any lessons on Friday, which of the following could be true?

(A) Annie and Phillip are scheduled for the same day.
(B) Louise and Phillip are scheduled for Tuesday.
(C) Eddie and Ryan are scheduled for Thursday.
(D) Wilbur and Annie are scheduled for Monday.
(E) Ryan is the only student scheduled for Monday.

4. Which of the following pairs of students cannot both have their lessons on the same day?

    I. Eddie and Annie
    II. Phillip and Wilbur
    III. Annie and Louise
    IV. Ryan and Wilbur

(A) I only
(B) II and III
(C) I, II, and III
(D) II and IV
(E) I, III, and IV

5. If Phillip's lesson is Wednesday afternoon, which of the following must be false?

(A) Eddie and Wilbur are scheduled for the same day.
(B) Eddie's lesson is before Ryan's lesson.
(C) Sheryl and Wilbur are scheduled for the same day.
(D) Eddie is scheduled on Monday.
(E) Ryan and Annie are scheduled for the same day.

6. If Phillip is scheduled for Friday morning, which of the following is a complete list of students who could have their driving lesson on Monday?

(A) Annie, Sheryl, Eddie
(B) Louise, Annie, Wilbur, Eddie
(C) Annie, Wilbur, Sheryl, Ryan
(D) Wilbur, Ryan, Annie, Eddie
(E) Wilbur, Louise, Ryan, Annie, Eddie

The following information applies to questions 7–11

A college professor has to schedule oral presentations to be given by the 10 students in his class, Fred, Glen, Harry, Iris, Jane, Kathy, Lewis, Mike, Nathan, and Oscar. The professor will schedule one student in the morning and one in the afternoon on five consecutive days from Monday through

Friday. The following scheduling requirements must be followed:

> Nathan's presentation must be in the morning.
> Harry must give his presentation before Iris does.
> Lewis' presentation must be on Wednesday.
> If Kathy's presentation is in the morning, then she must be scheduled on the same day as Oscar.
> If Oscar's presentation is in the afternoon, then he must be scheduled on the same day as Kathy.
> Glen must be scheduled for Tuesday afternoon.

7. Which of the following is a possible list of the afternoon presentations in order from Monday through Friday?

(A) Jane, Glen, Lewis, Nathan, Kathy
(B) Oscar, Glen, Harry, Jane, Mike
(C) Kathy, Glen, Fred, Jane, Harry
(D) Oscar, Mike, Lewis, Iris, Jane
(E) Jane, Glen, Kathy, Oscar, Iris

8. Which of the following pairs could be scheduled for Friday?

(A) Lewis, morning; Kathy, afternoon
(B) Jane, morning; Oscar, afternoon
(C) Mike, morning; Nathan, afternoon
(D) Iris, morning; Kathy, afternoon
(E) Harry, morning; Mike, afternoon

9. Which of the following pairs cannot be scheduled for the same day?

(A) Harry and Iris
(B) Kathy and Oscar
(C) Lewis and Jane
(D) Mike and Nathan
(E) Glen and Kathy

10. If Kathy and Harry are scheduled for Thursday and Friday morning, respectively, then which of the following must be false?

(A) Lewis is scheduled for Wednesday morning.
(B) Mike is scheduled for Monday afternoon.
(C) Jane is scheduled for Friday afternoon.
(D) Fred is scheduled for Tuesday morning.
(E) Nathan is scheduled for Monday morning.

11. If Kathy and Nathan are scheduled for the same day, then which of the following must be true?

(A) Oscar's presentation must be in the morning.
(B) Mike's presentation must be in the morning.
(C) Lewis' presentation must be in the morning.
(D) Jane's presentation must be in the afternoon.
(E) Iris' presentation must be in the afternoon.

4. CONNECTION PROBLEMS

Also called "networks," the connection problems are not like any other problem type. These problems begin by giving you a series of connections between people, places, or objects. Typically, you will be connecting towns by a series of roads, islands by a series of bridges, or people in offices by the series of jobs they must perform. Sometimes a connection problem will consist of a series of tasks that must be taken in order, leading you from the first step to the completion of some task.

Connection problems are nearly impossible to complete without a good diagram. The diagram for a connection problem will generally look nothing like the diagrams for the ranking, distribution, and scheduling problems that you have seen already. For the most part, those problem types are mostly linear, with the items in the problem appearing in a straight line, either up and down or left to right, while a diagram for a connection problem will often look like a knot of connecting lines, which may not have much meaning until you begin considering the actual questions.

A connection problem is generally easy to identify quickly. The main key to spotting a connection problem is that it will usually contain several more items for you to work with than a ranking, distribution or scheduling problem will use. While those problems typically use between five and seven items, a connection problem can have as many as 10 or more. The second key to identifying a connection problem is a longer list of initial rules. Because the connection problem uses more items and has more rules, it is often the most intimidating of all the problem types. To succeed on a connection problem, the diagram becomes essential. With a good diagram, a connection problem can be very easy.

> **LOGIC TIP:** Once you have identified a problem as a "connection" problem, do not be intimidated by the sheer number of rules and items to use for the problem. Work deliberately and carefully with the rules, drawing the connections that the rules identify. Although the diagram may not make much sense at first, and it appears more confusing than the diagrams for the other problem types, it will all come together in the end.

Consider a sample problem:

A college campus has 10 different buildings, connected by a series of underground tunnels. The tunnels connect the buildings as follows:

> *Building 1 is connected directly to Buildings 2 and 3.*
> *Building 2 is connected directly to Buildings 3 and 4.*
> *Building 4 is connected directly to Buildings 3, 5, and 6.*
> *Building 6 is connected directly to Buildings 3, 7, and 8.*
> *Building 7 is connected directly to Building 8.*
> *Building 8 is connected directly to Buildings 5 and 9.*
> *Building 9 is connected directly to Buildings 5 and 10.*

The best way to handle a connection problem, which can appear very troublesome when you first read the rules, is to begin by drawing the connecting lines. Start with the first rule and work your way along, one step at a time.

The first rule says that Building 1 is connected to Buildings 2 and 3. Show this in the diagram with straight lines connecting 1 to 2 and to 3. Be careful, when you read this, that you do not misread the rule. This first rule does not say that 2 and 3 are connected to each other. It only says that Building 1 is connected to both 2 and 3. So the beginning of your diagram looks like this:

Peterson's Logic & Reading Review

Continue with the second rule, which requires that 2 is connected to 3 and 4. This expands your diagram as follows:

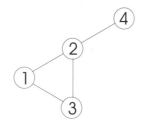

The third rule adds that Building 4 is connected to 3, 5, and 6, as follows:

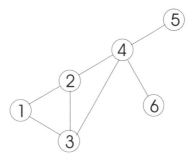

The next rule adds that Building 6 is connected to 3, 7, and 8, as follows:

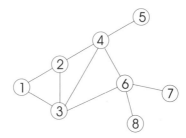

The next rule adds that Building 7 is connected to building 8, as follows:

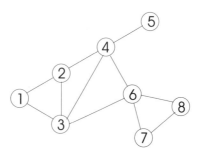

The next rule adds that Building 8 is connected to buildings 5 and 9, as follows:

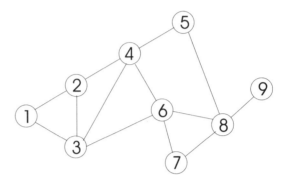

The final rule adds that Building 9 is connected to buildings 5 and 10, as follows:

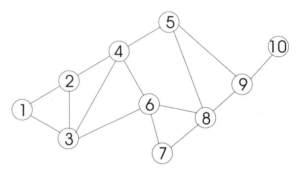

Because this is the final rule, you now have the entire series of connections laid out before you. This series of connections works like a kind of "road map" for answering the questions. The questions for a connection problem will ask about certain "paths" that can be taken from one part of the map to another. Your job will be to navigate your way through these connections.

With this complete "connections map," you are ready to answer the questions.

1. Which of the following is NOT a possible path from Building 1 to Building 10?

    (A) 1-2-4-6-8-9-10
    (B) 1-2-3-6-5-9-10
    (C) 1-3-6-8-9-10
    (D) 1-2-4-5-9-10
    (E) 1-3-6-8-5-9-10

With your complete "connections map," answering a question of this type is a simple matter of beginning with answer (A) and checking each answer to see if the series of

Peterson's Logic & Reading Review

connections remains unbroken. In this case, answer (B) is NOT possible, and is therefore the correct answer, because there is no direct connection between Buildings 6 and 5. Therefore, (B) is the answer. All the other answers could be seen to be possible, and therefore incorrect for this question, just by following the connections map.

2. If the tunnel between Buildings 5 and 9 were closed, then the minimum number of buildings that someone beginning in Building 9 would have to pass through, including the starting and ending buildings, to reach Building 2 is:

(A) 4
(B) 5
(C) 6
(D) 7
(E) 8

For a question such as this one, asking you to find the "minimum" number of connections, the best solution method is "trial and error." Using your final connections map, try to trace the paths from Building 9 to Building 2 to find the shortest path possible. The shortest path would be 9-5-4-2, consisting of four buildings. However, remember that for this question, you are told to assume that the tunnel from 9 to 5 cannot be used. Therefore, from Building 9, the only immediate connection is to Building 8 (or to Building 10, but that goes in the wrong direction and has no other connections, so it can be ignored). From 8, the connections can proceed to 5-4-2, which was the original answer for the minimum. Other options are 9-8-6-4-2 and 9-8-6-3-2. Both of these connections consist of five buildings. There are other buildings that can be added, such as 9-8-7-6-4-3-2, but that makes the connection series longer and defeats the purpose of selecting the "minimum" series of connections. Therefore, it can be seen that the shortest path consists of five buildings, and the answer is (B).

3. A person beginning in which of the following buildings could NOT travel through the tunnels to visit all the buildings on campus without traveling through any tunnel or any building more than once?

(A) 1
(B) 3
(C) 5
(D) 7
(E) 9

This problem can be answered by using the same "trial and error" method that generally works well for other connection questions. Alternatively, a brief review of the diagram and some quick analysis can lead directly to the answer. Looking at the diagram, Building 10 seems to stand out by itself as the only building with only one connection. This creates a kind of "dead end," so that traveling into Building 10 will leave no way out except through the same tunnel. Since this question does not allow passing through the same tunnel or the same building, you can conclude that Building 10 will have to be the final building in the series. If someone were to begin at Building 9, which is the only one connecting to Building 10, that person could either go directly to Building 10, which would end the journey immediately, or go to Building 5 or 8. However, to get back to Building 10, someone who began at Building 9 would have to return to Building 9 before getting to Building 10. This is not allowed, so the correct answer is (E). All the others could be possible, and connections could be found by trial and error.

4. How long is the longest series of connections that consists of alternating even- and odd-numbered buildings?

(A) 5
(B) 6
(C) 7
(D) 8
(E) 9

As with most connection problems, the best method for solving this kind of question is "trial and error," combined with some common sense. The common sense helps you decide where to begin testing the connections. It seems to make the most sense to begin at either end of the diagram, with either Building 1 or Building 10. Following the rule of alternating through odd- and even-numbered buildings and starting at Building 1, you can quickly create the following series of connection, as a sample: 1-2-3-4-5-8-9-10. This series of connections is eight buildings long. It is not necessarily the longest chain that satisfies the requirements, but it is at least a possibility. As a result, you can already eliminate answers (A), (B), and (C), since they are less than eight. Now the real "work" for this question begins, as you analyze your chain and try to figure out if it can possibly be made longer. To do so, begin at Building 1 and see what answers are available. From Building 1, a person could go to either 2 or 3. For this question, 3 is not allowed because both 1 and 3 are odd. So the connection must be from 1 to 2. Then from 2, the answers are 4 or 3. It must be 3, because an odd-numbered building is required to follow Building 2. From 3, the options are 4 or 6, both even, so the connection series could go either way. Beginning with 1-2-3-4, the next steps would have to be 5 and then 8. This much of the chain is forced, 1-2-3-4-5-8. From there, the first answer arises, either 9 or 7, then either 6 or 10. These alternatives lead to two possible chains, 1-2-3-4-5-8-9-10 and 1-2-3-4-5-8-7-6, but they are both eight buildings long. Further analysis of other possibilities, beginning at other buildings, reveals that eight buildings is the length of the longest chain. Therefore, the answer must be (D).

CONNECTION PRACTICE QUESTIONS

Directions: Each question or group of questions is based on a passage or set of conditions. In answering some of the questions, it may be useful to draw a rough diagram. For each question, select the best answer given.

The following information applies to questions 1–5

A city with an extensive train network has two major terminal stations, North Station and South Station. All trains in the city begin at North Station, pass through one or more connecting stations, identified as CS1 through CS7, and end at South Station. The network of stations complies with the following requirements:

> From North Station, trains travel to either CS1 or CS2.
> From CS1, trains travel to either CS2 or CS3.
> From CS2, trains travel to either CS3 or CS4.
> From CS3, trains travel to either CS5 or CS6.
> From CS4, trains travel to either CS6 or CS7.
> From CS5, trains travel to either CS6 or CS7.
> From CS6, trains travel to either CS7 or South Station.
> From CS7, trains travel to South Station.
> All trains travel only in the directions noted above; no train may travel in the opposite direction.

1. Which of the following lists the connecting stations a train may pass through from North Station (NS) to South Station (SS), in order?

    (A) NS,1,2,4,5,6,SS
    (B) NS,2,4,6,SS
    (C) NS,1,3,5,SS
    (D) NS,1,2,3,4,5,6,SS
    (E) NS,1,3,6,4,7,SS

2. Which of the following statements must be true?

   (A) A train will pass through at least four connecting stations from North Station to South Station.
   (B) A train whose first connecting station is CS2 must pass through more connecting stations than a train whose first connecting station is CS1.
   (C) A train whose first connecting station is CS1 must pass through more connecting stations than a train whose first connecting station is CS2.
   (D) A train will pass through no more than six connecting stations from North Station to South Station.
   (E) A train may pass through CS3 or CS7 but not both.

3. Which of the following must be true about a train passing through CS4?

   (A) That train must pass through a total of at least four connecting stations before reaching South Station.
   (B) That train did not pass through CS2.
   (C) That train will not pass through CS5.
   (D) That train will not pass through CS6.
   (E) That train will pass through at least two more connecting stations after leaving CS4 before reaching South Station.

4. Which of the following must be true about a train that passes through exactly three connecting stations between North Station and South Station?

   (A) That train will not pass through both CS1 and CS3.
   (B) That train will not pass through both CS4 and CS7.
   (C) That train will not pass through both CS2 and CS6.
   (D) That train will not pass through both CS1 and CS2.
   (E) That train will not pass through both CS3 and CS6.

5. What is the maximum number of connecting stations that a train can pass through from North Station to South Station if its trip includes CS4?

   (A) 2
   (B) 3
   (C) 4
   (D) 5
   (E) 6

The following information applies to questions 6–10

In a certain party game, a person who gets a red ticket will receive a prize. Everyone receives either a green ticket or a blue ticket when they arrive at the party, and then tickets can be traded as follows:

A green ticket can be traded for a yellow ticket or a brown ticket.

A blue ticket can be traded for a yellow ticket or an orange ticket.

A brown ticket can be traded for a yellow ticket or a gray ticket.

A yellow ticket can be traded for a teal ticket or an orange ticket.

An orange ticket can be traded for a teal ticket or a purple ticket.

A gray ticket can be traded for a red ticket.

A teal ticket can be traded for a gray ticket or a purple ticket.

A purple ticket can be traded for a red ticket or a black ticket.

A black ticket can be traded for a red ticket.

6. Which of the following is an accurate list of the tickets a person could have, in order from beginning to end?

   (A) Green, yellow, purple, black, red
   (B) Green, yellow, teal, gray, red
   (C) Green, orange, purple, red
   (D) Blue, yellow, gray, teal, red
   (E) Blue, yellow, teal, black, red

7. How many different paths exist that consist of exactly five tickets, including the final red ticket?

   (A) 6
   (B) 7
   (C) 8
   (D) 9
   (E) 10

8. A person holding a black ticket may not previously have held a ticket of which color?

(A) Blue
(B) Teal
(C) Gray
(D) Yellow
(E) Green

9. If a person trades a yellow ticket for a teal ticket, which of the following must be false?

(A) That person at one time received or may receive a black ticket.
(B) That person originally received a blue ticket.
(C) That person's last ticket, before trading for red, will be purple.
(D) That person previously received an orange ticket.
(E) That person cannot receive a gray ticket.

10. Which of the following must be true about the shortest path to receiving a red ticket?

(A) The shortest path begins with a green ticket.
(B) The last ticket before red is gray.
(C) The shortest path does not include an orange ticket.
(D) The shortest path consists of three tickets.
(E) The shortest path does not include a yellow ticket.

5. MAPPING PROBLEMS

The final of the five primary Analytical Reasoning question types is the mapping problems. These problems usually require you to arrange certain people or places in a geographic arrangement, usually around some central location. Typical problems will ask you to arrange mountains around a ski lodge, schools around a town hall, or cities around a state capital. You will be given information helping you to place some of the items in relation to the central point, such as "Mountain #1 is north of the ski lodge" or "School A is due east of the town hall." Sometimes you will be given information relating one item to another item, such as "Mountain #3 is somewhere east of Mountain #2." The best diagram for a mapping problem will usually place the central reference point in the middle and then mark off the space into four areas, or "quadrants." You can then place the mountains, schools, cities, etc. around the central point as you receive information about them.

The keys to recognizing that you are working with a mapping problem are:

1. The identification of some central point of reference;

2. An introduction to the problem that tells you that the several items are "located" in some arrangement "around" the central point of reference;

3. The rules for the problem include directional information such as "north," "south," "east," and "west." Other key directions to watch for are key words such as "due north" as opposed to "somewhere north," etc.

> **LOGIC TIP:** When working with a mapping problem, pay close attention to the difference between the directions "north" and "due north." The first one means only that the item that is "north" is SOMEWHERE above (assuming that north points toward the top of the diagram) the other item. However, "due north" means that the two items line up directly in a straight vertical line. Be sure that you read the rules carefully enough to identify these differences.

Consider the following sample mapping problem:

A business has its manufacturing headquarters in the exact center of the state, with ten delivery offices scattered throughout the state. Five delivery offices are north of the headquarters, and five delivery offices are south of the headquarters.

> *Office 1 is due east of Office 2.*
> *Office 4 is somewhere southwest of the headquarters.*
> *Office 6 and Office 7 are both west of the headquarters.*
> *Office 9 is due north of the headquarters.*

This problem is quickly identified as a mapping problem as soon as the first sentence points out that there is a central office and there are ten offices arranged around it. When you continue to read the rules and see all the directional references, the conclusion that this is a mapping problem is strengthened.

As soon as you identify a problem as a mapping problem, the diagram can begin as two crossing lines marking the directions north, south, east, and west. The point at the intersection is the center of your map. In most cases, and in this one,

Peterson's Logic & Reading Review

the center is the location of the main office or other reference point. So this diagram begins as follows:

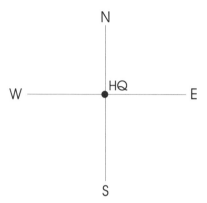

Now work with each of the rules, adding information to the diagram one piece at a time. The first rule is that Office 1 is due east of Office 2. However, this rule does not provide any information to let you place either Office 1 or Office 2 in place around the central headquarters (HQ). So you can only make a note at the bottom of the diagram so you remember the rule as you work through the questions.

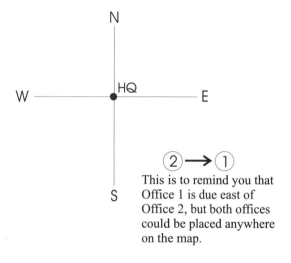

This is to remind you that Office 1 is due east of Office 2, but both offices could be placed anywhere on the map.

The next rule allows you to place Office 4 "somewhere southwest" of the headquarters. This will be in the lower left quadrant of the diagram:

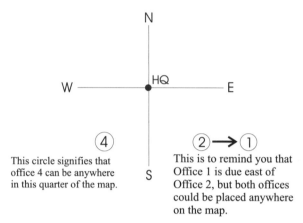

The next rule places both Office 6 and Office 7 somewhere "west" of the headquarters. With this rule, you need to realize that these offices could be placed anywhere north or south of the central horizontal line, as long as they remain west (left) of the central headquarters. This notation is best accomplished with arrows, to remind you that the offices can "move" up or down in your map diagram:

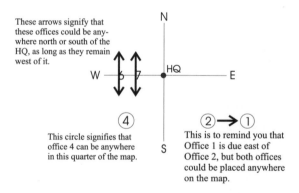

The final rule is perhaps the most specific, placing Office 9 "due north" of the headquarters. This will be represented in the diagram as a position somewhere on the axis directly above the central HQ:

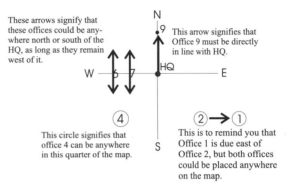

With this complete diagram, you are now ready to begin answering the questions.

1. If Office 4 is north of Office 2, then which of the following statements must be true?

   (A) Office 6 is north of HQ.
   (B) Office 9 is east of Office 8.
   (C) Office 1 is south of HQ.
   (D) Office 2 is north of exactly three other offices.
   (E) Office 7 is east of Office 6.

   The key to this question is in the phrasing of the question, which asks you to find the statement that "must be true." If an answer does not give you enough information to determine that the placement of an office "must be true," then you cannot select it as the answer. You can begin solving this question by working with the diagram and adding the new information to see what additional conclusions you can draw. The new diagram with the new information is as follows:

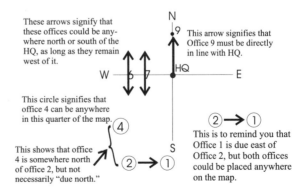

The information added to the diagram shows that Office 4 is somewhere north of Office 2. Also, by keeping Office 2 and Office 1 connected as in the original diagram, you can see that Office 4 is also somewhere north of Office 1. As a result, it is quickly clear that answer (C) is the correct answer, since Office 1 is south of 4 and 4 is south of HQ. The other answers can be seen to be incorrect. The arrows in the diagram show that Office 6 can move north or south of HQ, so answer (A) is incorrect. Answer (B) is incorrect because there are no requirements about the placement of Office 8, so it could be either east or west of Office 9. Answer (D) is a statement that must be false, since there can only be five offices south of HQ (and five offices north of HQ). The diagram shows that there are already three offices south of HQ, and 1 and 4 are either even with or north of 2. Therefore, there cannot be three more that are south of 2. Answer (E) is incorrect because Office 7 could be either east or west of Office 6, as long as it remains west of HQ. The only statement that "must be true" is (C).

2. If Offices 2 and 3 are both due east of Office 9, then which of the following statements must be false?

    (A) Offices 6 and 7 are both southeast of HQ.
    (B) Office 8 is northeast of Office 2.
    (C) Offices 10 and 7 are both south of HQ.
    (D) Offices 4 and 5 are both southwest of HQ.
    (E) Two offices are northwest of Office 9.

Adding the new information for this question to the diagram will place Offices 9, 2, 1, and 3 all in a horizontal row, since Offices 2 and 3 must be due east of Office 9 and Office 1 must be due east of Office 2. You must be careful here to recognize that you do not have enough information to know the exact order of these four offices, except that Office 9 is the furthest west of these four and Office 2 is west of Office 1. Some possible orders of these four offices could be 9-2-1-3, 9-3-2-1, 9-2-3-1, and 9-2-1-3.

Because this question asks you to identify the statement that "must be false," you are looking for a statement that violates any of the initial rules. You can "guess ahead" for this question and guess that the relevant rule is likely to be the one that only allows five offices north of HQ and five offices south of it. Because there are already four offices in a line north of HQ, any answer that places two or more offices north of either 9, 1, 2, or 3 will be incorrect. With this early analysis, you can immediately see that answer (E) must be the false statement, since two offices cannot be northwest of 9 or there would be six offices north of HQ. Therefore, the answer must be (E).

3. Which of the following arrangements of offices is/are possible?

I.   All even-numbered offices north of HQ.
II. All even-numbered offices west of HQ.
III. All odd-numbered offices north of HQ.

(A) I only
(B) II only
(C) III only
(D) II and III
(E) I, II, and III

This is a style of question that requires you to do a two-step analysis. Your first step is to consider each of the Roman numeral statements as an individual "true/false" question. Then, once you have decided which of the first statements are or are not possible, you work with the answers. Considering the initial set of statements, you first need to think about the relationships between certain offices that have already been identified. For example, since Office 9 is already north of HQ and Office 4 is already south of HQ, it will be impossible to have all even-numbered offices north of HQ. Therefore, statement I is false. Comparing this result to the lettered answers, you can immediately eliminate answers (A) and (E), since they both include statement I. Next consider statement II, which would place all even-numbered offices west of HQ. At first, you may be inclined to disregard this as an impossible situation because the diagram shows that Office 7 is one of the offices west of HQ. However, by carefully reading the question, you will realize that there are no limitations to the number of offices that appear either east or west of HQ. Theoretically, it would be allowable to have all ten of the offices west of HQ and none of them east of HQ. Also notice that statement II, says that "all even-numbered offices" are west of HQ; it does not say that "only" even-numbered offices are west of HQ. So by comparing the diagram and the initial rules to statement II, you can see that Offices 4 and 6 are already placed west of HQ, and the remaining even-numbered offices, 2, 8, and 10, have no limitations on them. So statement II could be a possible arrangement, and any correct answer must include II. Therefore, answer (C) is incorrect, and the only possible answers are either (B) or (D). Now consider statement

III, that all odd-numbered offices are north of HQ. Notice in the diagram that Office 1 and Office 2 must be horizontally even with each other ("due east"); then if Office 1 is placed north of HQ, Office 2 will also have to be placed north of HQ. If all other odd-numbered offices are also positioned north of HQ, six offices would be north of HQ, which is not allowed. Therefore, statement III is false, and the correct answer to this question must be (B).

4. Which of the following is NOT a list of offices, in order, that a plane could pass directly over while flying in a straight line traveling northeast?

(A) 4, 6, HQ, 9, 2
(B) 4, 8, 10, 2, 3
(C) 6, 7, 3, 8, HQ
(D) 4, 7, HQ, 3, 2
(E) 6, 7, 8, HQ, 10

This is a standard type of mapping question, which requires you to be able to manipulate the offices on your diagram to see if you can be aware of where various offices can be placed. The key to succeeding with a "straight line" question of this type is flexibility, so that you do not remain too fixed with the initial placements that you gave to various offices in your initial diagram. First, review the initial diagram:

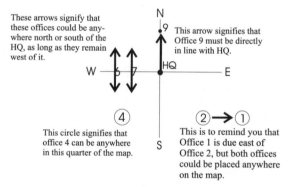

You must realize that even though Offices 6 and 7 were initially placed in the diagram on an even level with each other, the arrows mean that they may move anywhere north or south. Therefore, it is possible for 6 to be south of 7 or 7 to be south of 6. Either one could be north or south of Office 4, even though they both appear to be north of 4 in the initial diagram.

LOGIC TIP: Especially for mapping problems, you must realize that your initial diagram must be flexible. You must always keep in mind the limitations inherent in writing down the items in your map and realize which notes in your map could be moved to other positions.

With these limitations in mind, the best way to solve a "straight line" question like this one is to try to rearrange the offices, within the limitations of the initial rules, to position them in a straight line. Answer (A) suggests the order 4, 6, HQ, 9, 2. Reviewing the diagram shows quickly that HQ and Office 9 are in a direct line from north to south and not northeast. Therefore, for a plane to travel along this path, it would have to travel due north for at least a portion of its trip, which is not allowed. Therefore, (A) is an impossible path and is therefore the correct answer. If you attempt to line up each of the offices for each of the other answers, you will find that each arrangement is possible, even though it may require some fluctuation from your original diagram. This fluctuation does not mean that the rules are changing; it merely means that the rules for most mapping problems are not fixed firmly in position.

Mapping Practice Questions

> **Directions:** Each question or group of questions is based on a passage or set of conditions. In answering some of the questions, it may be useful to draw a rough diagram. For each question, select the best answer given.

The following information applies to questions 1–5

A new planet is going to be colonized by a civilization of space travelers. The planet has enough resources to accommodate only ten cities, with five cities north of the equator and five cities south of the equator. The cities are known only by numbers, from 1 through 10. The planners for the civilization have established the following numbers:

Cities 1 and 2 are in the Northern Hemisphere.
Cities 3 and 4 are in the Southern Hemisphere.
Cities 5 and 6 must be in different hemispheres.
Cities 7 and 8 must be in the same hemisphere.

1. Which of the following is a list of the cities that could be in the Southern Hemisphere?

   (A) 3, 4, 6, 7, 10
   (B) 2, 3, 4, 5, 7
   (C) 3, 4, 5, 8, 9
   (D) 3, 5, 7, 8, 10
   (E) 3, 4, 6, 9, 10

2. If City 7 is in the Northern Hemisphere, which of the following must be true?

   (A) City 6 will be in the Southern Hemisphere.
   (B) City 5 will be in the Northern Hemisphere.
   (C) City 10 will be in the Southern Hemisphere.
   (D) City 9 will be in the Northern Hemisphere.
   (E) City 4 will be in the Northern Hemisphere.

3. Which combination of cities cannot be in the same hemisphere?

   (A) 7 and 10
   (B) 3 and 4
   (C) 2 and 6
   (D) 4 and 8
   (E) 3 and 10

Peterson's Logic & Reading Review

4. How many different combinations are there of cities that could be in the Southern Hemisphere?

   (A) 4
   (B) 6
   (C) 8
   (D) 10
   (E) 12

5. Which of the following must be true?

   (A) City 3 and City 6 must be in the same hemisphere.
   (B) City 4 and City 7 must be in the same hemisphere.
   (C) City 5 and City 8 must be in different hemispheres.
   (D) City 7 and City 8 must be in different hemispheres.
   (E) City 8 and City 9 must be in different hemispheres.

The following information applies to Questions 6–10

The city of Kaptal, the state capital of the state of New-state, is located in the exact center of the state. Newstate has eight other cities, named Simpson, Tunney, Under-wood, Vivlit, Woodsville, Xercia, Youngstown, and Ziffer. The eight cities are laid out around the state of Newstate as follows:

> Simpson and Tunney are both due north of Kaptal.
> Underwood is due east of Tunney.
> Vivlit is south of Kaptal, but not as far south as Youngstown.
> Exactly two cities are west of Kaptal.

6. If Kaptal is northeast of Youngstown, then which of the following must be false?

   (A) Kaptal is northeast of Vivlit.
   (B) Kaptal is south of Woodsville.
   (C) Woodsville and Xercia are west of Simpson.
   (D) Vivlit is southeast of Kaptal.
   (E) Tunney is northeast of Youngstown.

7. If Underwood is due north of Youngstown, then which of the following could be true?

   (A) Vivlit lies in a straight line between Youngstown and Simpson.
   (B) Kaptal lies in a straight line between Underwood and Youngstown.
   (C) Woodsville, Xercia, and Ziffer are all west of Simpson.
   (D) Three cities lie in a straight line between Simpson and Tunney.
   (E) Three cities lie in a straight line between Underwood and Youngstown.

8. A plane flying due east could pass directly over which of the following combinations of cities, in order from farthest west to east?

   (A) Kaptal, Simpson, Woodsville
   (B) Vivlit, Youngstown, Xercia
   (C) Woodsville, Simpson, Tunney
   (D) Simpson, Kaptal, Underwood
   (E) Woodsville, Kaptal, Ziffer

9. If exactly three cities are southeast of Kaptal, which of the following must be true?

   (A) Exactly two cities are northwest of Kaptal.
   (B) No cities are due south of Kaptal.
   (C) No cities are due west of Kaptal.
   (D) Woodsville is west of Underwood.
   (E) Underwood is due north of at least one city.

10. If Woodsville is northwest of Kaptal, which of the following could NOT be the list of cities that are southeast of Kaptal?

   (A) Vivlit and Youngstown
   (B) Vivlit and Xercia
   (C) Vivlit, Xercia, and Youngstown
   (D) Vivlit, Youngstown, and Ziffer
   (E) Vivlit, Xercia, Youngstown, and Ziffer

6. HYBRID PROBLEMS

"Hybrid" is not a specific type of Analytical Reasoning problem. This section is included to make you aware that the five problem types that you have studied to this point are not the only problems that you will see. The creators of the GRE and LSAT are creative enough to make up other kinds of problems. These "other" problems will often contain many of the principles of the five primary problem types and will require many of the same solving methods. When you encounter a problem that does not neatly fall within any one of the five primary categories, you can assume that you are dealing with a hybrid problem. The best way to work with one of these hybrid problems is to apply all the principles that you have already learned. First, try to decide what "structure" for a diagram will work best for the stated problem. Second, work your way through the rules, one at a time, adding information to your diagram and making your notes as concrete as possible. When you have rules that cannot specifically be placed into your diagram, then make a summary note of that rule somewhere near your diagram so that you remain conscious of the requirements of that rule. Finally, when any specific question adds new information, add those notes to your diagram, but remember that the new information applies only to that specific question.

Hybrid Practice Questions

The following information applies to questions 1–6

A chef is preparing sauces using eight different ingredients—H, J, K, L, M, N, O, and P. According to the recipes, the following requirements apply to the use of the ingredients:

If J is used, both K and P must also be used.
M and N must always be used together.
If K is used, at least two of H, J, and O must also be used.
K and N cannot be used together.
M, O, and P cannot all be used in the same dish.
H, L, and P cannot all be used in the same dish.

1. Which of the following is an acceptable combination of ingredients for a sauce?

   (A) H, J, K, O
   (B) H, L, M, P
   (C) L, M, N, P
   (D) K, L, M, O
   (E) M, N, O, P

2. Which of the following CANNOT be included in a sauce that contains M?

   (A) J
   (B) L
   (C) N
   (D) O
   (E) P

3. In a sauce in which J is used, what is the smallest number of additional ingredients that would meet recipe requirements?

   (A) 1
   (B) 2
   (C) 3
   (D) 5
   (E) 6

4. By the addition of exactly one more ingredient, which of the following could make an acceptable combination of ingredients?

   (A) H, L, P
   (B) J, N, M
   (C) K, L, N
   (D) K, M, P
   (E) L, M, O

5. Which ingredient must be omitted from the combination H, J, K, L, P to meet the recipe requirements?

   (A) H
   (B) J
   (C) K
   (D) L
   (E) P

6. Exactly how many ingredients can be used as the only ingredients of a sauce?

   (A) 2
   (B) 3
   (C) 4
   (D) 5
   (E) 6

The following information applies to questions 7–10

Seven people—Carl, Diane, Elvin, Florence, George, Heather, and Ivan—apply to an employment office for job placement. The placement office has exactly seven jobs available in two different stores: The Jeans Place and The Electronics Shop. Each store may take either three or four employees. The employment office also has to consider the following requirements:

Carl and Diane may not work for the same store.
Heather and Florence must work for the same store.
If Diane and Elvin work for the same store, then that store must hire four employees.
George must work for The Electronics Shop.
The Jeans Place may hire only four employees if Diane is one of those employees hired.

7. Which of the following is a possible placement of the employees?

	The Jeans Place	The Electronics Shop
(A)	Diane, Elvin, Carl, Ivan	Florence, George, Heather
(B)	Diane, Heather, Florence	Carl, Elvin, George, Ivan
(C)	Carl, Elvin, Florence	Diane, George, Heather, Ivan
(D)	Diane, Elvin, Ivan	Carl, Florence, George, Heather
(E)	Carl, Elvin, Florence, Heather	Diane, George, Ivan

8. If Diane works for The Jeans Place, then which of the following statements must be true?

(A) Elvin works for The Jeans Place.
(B) Ivan works for The Jeans Place.
(C) Heather may not work for The Electronics Shop.
(D) Florence and Ivan work for the same store.
(E) Ivan and Carl work for the same store.

9. If Heather is one of four people hired by The Electronics Shop, then which of the following could be true?

(A) Carl works for The Electronics Shop.
(B) Florence and Ivan work for the same store.
(C) Diane and Ivan both work for The Jeans Place.
(D) Elvin works for The Electronics Shop.
(E) Elvin and Ivan both work for The Jeans Place.

10. If The Jeans Place hires only three people, then which of the following must be false?

   (A)   Heather and Elvin work for the same store.
   (B)   Elvin works for The Electronics Shop.
   (C)   Ivan works for The Electronics Shop.
   (D)   Florence and Carl work for the same store.
   (E)   Ivan and Elvin work for the same store.

LOGICAL REASONING

Logical reasoning questions appear on the GRE, GMAT, and LSAT (on the GMAT, the questions are generally referred to as "Critical Reasoning" but the questions are the same). These questions require just as much careful reading and analysis as for the analytical reasoning questions, but the style of the questions is different and the method for answering them is different. This section of the book will focus on the primary types of logical reasoning questions that you will face and gives you some hints about the best way to analyze the material.

There are only three primary categories of logical reasoning questions that you must be ready to answer. They are:

1. Additional Fact Questions

2. Hidden Assumption Questions

3. Conclusion Questions

The additional fact questions can further be separated into questions that ask you to "weaken" the argument and questions that ask you to "strengthen" the argument. All three primary categories require generally the same reading and analysis skills, but you must first be able to recognize the type of question in order to be sure that you answer it correctly. The following section will show you how to recognize the three primary question types and how to answer each one. You will then be given sample questions of each type to practice before moving on to full sample test sections.

ADDITIONAL FACT QUESTIONS

The additional fact question focuses on the supporting details of the argument. You are presented with a complete argument and are asked either to weaken or strengthen the argument by considering five multiple-choice statements. These statements are new facts about the argument, which you must accept as true. Some additional fact questions ask for a weakening of argument; others ask you to strengthen what you read.

For example, consider this argument and its five answers:

United Artists' most recent film is based on a best-selling novel and stars Brad Heartthrob. Therefore, the film is expected to do well at the box office.

(A) The film will play only in urban areas.

(B) The producers of the film have cast their next movie without Brad H.

(C) The film is not likely to win an Academy Award.

(D) The book upon which the film is based is a world-wide hit.

(E) Brad H.'s popularity ratings are at an all-time low.

If the question asks you to weaken the argument, you will choose a statement that either weakens a given fact or disputes a hidden assumption and as a consequence makes the conclusion illogical. Answer (E) best weakens this argument by disputing the hidden assumption that Brad H. will attract moviegoers. The conclusion no longer logically follows.

For a strengthening answer, you would choose a statement to bolster a given fact or hidden assumption to support the conclusion. The correct strengthening answer here would be (D), for it elaborates on the fact about the book's popularity, thus supporting the conclusion.

Wrong answers, called *distracters*, usually follow a pattern. They may touch upon the argument only marginally (such as answers A, B, and C), they may accomplish the opposite task (strengthen when you want to weaken), or they may not be the best strengthening or weakening statement (e.g., answer A is not the best weakening statement when compared to E). Try these few questions.

1. The trend in the United States banking industry of several small community banks merging into fewer large, interstate banks has consumers worried about service. Many consumers worry that, as banks become larger and fewer in number, the competition in the banking industry will decrease, and consumers will lose services and will pay higher fees. As a result, many consumers are urging their legislators to enact legislation to limit the size of any individual banking company.

The fears of the consumers discussed in the preceding argument would most be allayed by which of the following facts?

(A) The federal government recently enacted legislation to increase the maximum amounts of deposits that will be insured.

(B) A limitation on mergers between interstate banks could be construed as a violation of the Commerce Clause of the United States Constitution.

(C) Larger banks are able to generate higher profits for their investors with lower levels of risk.

(D) As a bank increases in size, its overhead costs for operation will decrease, and it will be able to improve the services to its consumers.

(E) Large, governmentally operated banks have functioned successfully in other countries for many years without any decrease in services to their consumers and with service fees that are less than many private banks.

The correct answer is (D). The consumers assume that bank mergers will result in higher fees and fewer services. Answer (D) contradicts this assumption and would be the best response for weakening the conclusion. Answer (A) is irrelevant, as nothing in the argument addresses insurance of deposits or federal involvement. Answer (B) is irrelevant because the argument is not concerned with whether or not such mergers are allowable but whether they are a good move for consumers. Answer (C) focuses on investors and not customers. Answer (E) is somewhat informative but is not as directly addressed to this argument as answer (D).

2. Of the graduating students from Governor Smith Academy, a private high school, 93 percent go on to college. From Eastern High, the public high school in the same city, only 74 percent go on to attend college. As a result, many parents with children about to enter high school believe that Governor Smith Academy gives students a better education than they can get at Eastern High School.

Which of the following statements, if true, would cast the most doubt on the conclusion about Governor Smith Academy?

(A) Until 1992, Governor Smith Academy was exclusively a girls' school, but Eastern High School has always been coeducational.

(B) Governor Smith Academy requires students to pass an admissions examination before entering, but Eastern High School admits all applicants who live in the city.

(C) Eastern High School has problems with severe student violence during school hours.

(D) Governor Smith Academy has a higher percentage of students attending Ivy League colleges than any other high school in the state.

(E) Eastern High School receives its funding from local property taxes, while Governor Smith Academy receives funding from tuition costs and from alumni donations.

The correct answer is (B). This argument assumes that the percentage of students moving on to college reflects on the quality of the education at the two high schools. Answer (B) contradicts this assumption by suggesting that the students at Governor Smith Academy may have entered school with better academic abilities than the public school students. Answer (A) is incorrect because nothing in the argument suggests any difference between male and female students. Although student violence might reflect on students' abilities to learn, answer (C) is irrelevant to this particular argument without more information. Answer (D) addresses the end results of the students attending college, but too many other factors could be part of this result. Answer (E) is insufficient without more information in the argument that taxes or funding have anything to do with the quality of the education.

3. Television Advertisement: "Leonardo da Vinci was a genius, and everyone recognizes his art as the greatest in the world. At Acme Art Supply Company, you can get modern, improved art supplies, so you will be able to create works of art even better than Leonardo da Vinci's."

Which of the following statements, if true, most shows the flaws in the claims made in this advertisement?

(A) Leonardo da Vinci, at the time he was painting in the fifteenth century, was sponsored by patrons who provided him with the opportunity to use the best materials then available in the world.

(B) Most of the customers of Acme Art Supply Company are hobbyists who are not professionally trained and who do not realize the value of using professional-quality art supplies.

(C) The art supplies at Acme Art Supply Company are more expensive than similar supplies available at any other supply store in the area.

(D) An art professor from the local community college supplies all of his students with materials from the Acme Art Supply Company.

(E) Even when using supplies from Acme Art Supply Company, many amateur artists create projects that art critics call inferior and childish.

The correct answer is (E). This argument depends on the assumption that the quality of an artist's materials leads directly to the quality of the finished product and that no other factors are involved. Answer (E) shows that even with the best materials, some artists do not create excellent art. Answer (A) is incorrect in that it does not recognize the individual quality of the artist. Answer (B) does not address the quality of the finished product and so is insufficient. Answer (C) is irrelevant because nothing in the argument suggests that the cost of the materials is a factor. Answer (D) is insufficient without additional information about the finished works of art produced by the students involved.

4. While some job loss is inevitable in a changing American economy, the current phase of corporate "downsizing" has reached the level of becoming an epidemic. Many employees are being fired simply to enhance profits for top management and company shareholders. Even so, some economists see improvement in the fact that the total number of new jobs being created is increasing at a steady rate.

Which of the following facts, if true, would show that the economists' view of improvement is incorrect?

(A) The new jobs that are being created come as a result of governmental tax incentives to large corporations.

(B) Corporate downsizing is not actually resulting in higher profits for shareholders as expected.

(C) Many of the new jobs are low-paying entry-level positions that do not provide health-care or pension benefits.

(D) A separate study of corporate shareholders reveals that many of them would be willing to forgo higher profits in order to increase hiring levels.

(E) Other countries are experiencing similar increases in job creation.

The correct answer is (C). The economists assume that creation of any new jobs is a positive sign. Answer (C) questions this assumption by showing that the new jobs may be inadequate to support individuals or families and thereby may not improve the general economy. Answer (A) provides irrelevant information because the conclusion does not depend on the reason for the creation of the new jobs. Answers (B) and (D) are incorrect because the argument does not seem to be concerned with the motivation for downsizing. Answer (E) provides irrelevant information because nothing in the argument suggests that the economies in other countries are related to this issue.

5. High doses of niacin in a person's diet have been shown to raise HDL levels, which doctors call the "good" cholesterol, and to lower levels of triglycerides and LDL, the so-called "bad" cholesterol. As a result of this study, some nutritionists are now recommending diets that are extremely high in niacin.

Which of the following facts, if true, would most question the recommendations of the nutritionists?

(A) The original study was conducted on a sample of hospital patients who initially had dangerously high cholesterol levels.

(B) High doses of niacin have been shown to reduce the clotting factors in blood, thereby reducing a person's ability to heal after receiving minor injuries.

(C) When levels of triglycerides decrease, patients report higher levels of stamina and improved physical endurance.

(D) The doctors reporting the results of the study had once been discredited for falsifying the results of their research.

(E) Other studies have shown that the body eventually reaches a maximum plateau with regard to its LDL level.

The correct answer is (B). The nutritionists assume that people should take in high levels of niacin because niacin shows a positive result in this one study. Answer (B) suggests that high doses of niacin may have a negative effect, despite the positive results of this study. Answer (A) might have an effect, but without further information linking the effect of this information to the result, the information provided is insufficient to weaken the argument. Answer (C) would strengthen, not weaken, the argument. Answer (D) illustrates an "ad homonym" attack by questioning the researchers and not the quality or results of the research. Answer (E) is irrelevant to the argument.

ADDITIONAL FACT PRACTICE QUESTIONS (WEAKENING THE CONCLUSION)

Directions: Each question or group of questions is based on a passage or set of conditions. In answering some of the questions, it may be useful to draw a rough diagram. For each question, select the best answer given.

1. The psychological stress of telling a lie produces certain physiological changes. By using appropriate instruments, the physiological symptoms of lying can be measured and result in reliable lie detection.

   Which of the following, if true, most weakens the above argument?

   (A) Lie detectors are sensitive machines that require constant maintenance.
   (B) Lying is only moderately stress-inducing to some people.
   (C) Lie detector operators must be highly trained and careful.
   (D) Numerous kinds of psychological stress produce similar physiological symptoms.
   (E) Measurement instruments such as lie detectors can be misused and abused.

2. Performing outstanding medical research requires more than a simple talent and more than a simple explanation. A drive to solve problems is clearly a part of it. Also critical is the ability to identify the right questions to ask. Thus, if we are to produce successful medical researchers, our universities must cultivate dedication and creativity rather than merely convey information.

   If true, which of the following would be the strongest objection to the argument of the passage above?

   (A) Researchers have a genuine curiosity about the world.
   (B) Scientific talent is only a small facet of what makes an outstanding researcher.
   (C) The proper function of our universities is not to produce outstanding researchers but to create well-rounded graduates.
   (D) Developing creativity in students is less important for the cultivation of research talent than is instilling a sense of dedication.
   (E) Teachers often cause harm when they attempt to do more than convey information.

3. Unlike the more traditional energy sources of coal, gas, and nuclear energy, energy from the sun produces no major problems. It produces no pollution and requires no transportation from foreign lands. It threatens no one with radiation dangers and is not controlled by powerful corporations. Therefore, we should encourage people to use solar energy.

Which of the following statements, if true, most seriously weakens this argument?

(A) There have been very few studies of solar energy use by households.

(B) The cost of oil and gas could be regulated to make it less costly for home consumption.

(C) The cost of the equipment required to collect enough solar energy for a family of four equals the amount a family now pays for oil, gas, or nuclear energy in one year.

(D) Most critics of solar energy are connected to energy monopolies.

(E) An effective way for families to capture and store solar energy has not yet been developed.

4. Real estate developer: "We expect that the formation of this new corporation to create a business park will make access easier for commuters to new business that we hope will locate in this area. As a result, tax revenues will increase and the quality of life in this area will improve."

Which of the following, if true, would most weaken the developer's conclusion?

(A) The town's crime rate has steadily increased for each of the past three years.

(B) The tax rate for new businesses in this area is higher than in any other community in the state.

(C) High unemployment rates have never been a problem in this town.

(D) People who invest in the new corporation for town development will be motivated by their desire for a positive return on their investments and not by concern for the quality of life in this area.

(E) If new businesses open in this area, new money will be available to improve educational materials for local schools.

ADDITIONAL FACT PRACTICE QUESTIONS (STRENGTHEN THE CONCLUSION)

Directions: Each question or group of questions is based on a passage or set of conditions. In answering some of the questions, it may be useful to draw a rough diagram. For each question, select the best answer given.

1. Scientists have found through experimentation that baby female gorillas who were "nurtured" by inanimate mother substitutes that performed some parenting functions were unable to function as mothers when they had offspring. This teaches us that infants should not be placed in the care of babysitters and day-care centers but should only be raised by their natural mothers.

   The conclusion reached by the author would be strengthened by which of the following?

   (A) The scientists found that the baby gorillas in the experiments were very dependent on each other.
   (B) The gorilla babies in the experiments would only accept food from the scientists, not from the "surrogate" mothers.
   (C) Baby gorillas that had brief but regular exposure to their natural mothers were able to function as mothers later.
   (D) Baby gorillas raised by females other than their own mothers were unable to function as mothers when they had offspring.
   (E) Mature female gorillas that were "raised" by the mother substitutes could be taught many mothering functions when they had offspring.

2. The Department of Agriculture will stop inspecting milk processing plants because no citations have been issued in the past two years.

   If true, which of the following most strengthens the decision?

   (A) Processors will cut corners if the threat of inspection is removed.
   (B) Milk processing is very automated.
   (C) The source of milk is known, so compensation can be had for any problem that occurs.
   (D) The department budget has been cut by 30 percent.
   (E) The industry association has standards that exceed the legal requirements.

3. Particularly disquieting is the gap between the enormous power they wield and their critical ability, which must be estimated as null. To wield power well entails a certain faculty of criticism, judgment, and option. It is impossible to have confidence in men who apparently lack these faculties. Yet it is apparently our fate to be facing a "golden age" in the power of sorcerers who are totally blind to the meaning of the human adventure.

   Which of the following statements, if true, would most accurately reflect the major function of the scientist?

   (A) Scientists must engage in efforts to prolong human life.
   (B) Changes in people's eating habits must be enforced.
   (C) The mystery of how the universe was created must be explained.
   (D) The problems that improve the quality of everyday life must be solved.
   (E) Science and religion must be reconciled.

4. To be beneficent when we can is a duty; and besides this, there are many minds so sympathetically constituted that, without any other motive of vanity or self-interest, they find a pleasure in spreading joy around them and can take delight in the satisfaction of others so far as it is their own work.

Which of the following, if true, would most strengthen the author's definition of sense of duty?

(A) An outgrowth of patriotism is a sense of duty.
(B) The production of one's heredity and environment is embodied in a sense of duty.
(C) A sense of duty is forced upon one by an authority.
(D) A sense of duty is the true source of beneficence.
(E) A sense of duty is acquired through education.

HIDDEN ASSUMPTIONS

To tackle a hidden assumption (HA) question, you must directly face the hidden statements that underlie the argument. Each HA statement meets the following two criteria: it gives you extra information about the existing facts instead of supplying new facts *and* it must be true for the argument to be valid.

For example:

The Republican candidate for governor of State X will get the education vote. More than $200,000 was donated to her campaign fund by the state teachers' union. The same union donated only half that amount to the Democratic candidate's campaign.

You would then be asked to choose the statement that best reveals an assumption underlying the preceding argument.

(A) The Republican candidate is a former teacher.
(B) The Democratic candidate will lose the election.
(C) A donation usually indicates approval of a candidate.
(D) Most teachers have joined the union.
(E) Unions endorse candidates in each election.

An excellent test of an HA is the "negation test:" If you think an answer is an HA, negate it and see if it seriously affects the validity of the conclusion; the right answer should.

For example, suppose you are struggling between answers (C) and (D). If answer (D) were falsified, you would now have the statement "Most teachers have not joined the union." Does that mean that the Republican candidate is now likely not to win the education vote? She may still. Negation of answer (C) gives you, "Donations usually don't indicate approval of a candidate." This negative statement does the most direct harm to the conclusion that the Republican candidate will get teachers' votes; it makes the connection between the facts and conclusion illogical. Answer (C) is correct.

Distracters associated with this question type include answers such as (D), which doesn't support the conclusion enough, as well as irrelevant statements such as (A), (B), and (E); besides being marginal to the problem, these statements also introduce new facts, whereas answer (C) elaborates on the facts given. Try these next questions.

1. In order to ensure a successful vote on the issue of abortion rights, the governor is pressuring the leaders of the state political party to replace several delegates to the national convention. The governor is insisting that certain individuals with a history of voting in favor of abortion rights be replaced with new delegates who have voted against abortion rights in the past. The governor's actions demonstrate that he is making which of the following assumptions?

   (A) Voting on abortion issues is an important part of the national political agenda.
   (B) The current delegates will probably not share the governor's views on such issues as the national budget or federal spending limits.
   (C) The proposed new delegates will continue to vote on abortion issues in the same way that they have voted in the past.
   (D) The national delegation will not have an opportunity to vote on any issues other than abortion rights.
   (E) Governors of other states will be making similar changes to their states' delegations, so the issue of abortion rights will be guaranteed to be decided as this governor desires.

The correct answer is (C). The governor is choosing new delegates based upon their past voting records. This shows the assumption that they will continue to vote the same way, so answer (C) is the best answer. Answers (A) and (D) are incorrect because the importance of the issue is not made part of this argument; this argument is based upon the fact that the governor is making these decisions for whatever reason he chooses. Answer (B) is irrelevant to this particular argument because nothing in this argument mentions the budget issues. Answer (E) is incorrect because there is nothing in the argument to suggest that activities in other states have anything to do with this governor's actions.

2. To travel on public transportation from City Hall to the convention center, the most direct route requires passengers to ride the Blue Bus line to Center Street, collect a token at Center Street station, then ride the subway to Middle Street. This weekend there will be a big political rally, so the city should hire extra token vendors for the Center Street station. The conclusion for the preceding argument depends upon which of the following assumptions?

   (A) The mayor will be working at City Hall this weekend and will need to use public transportation to go to the convention center.

   (B) There is no way to get from City Hall to the convention center without going through the Center Street station.

   (C) The political rally will draw thousands of people to the city from all parts of the state.

   (D) Because of the political rally, traffic at the Center Street station will increase.

   (E) The city's public transportation system does not allow passengers to buy tokens in advance.

The correct answer is (D). This argument concludes that additional token vendors are necessary as a result of the rally. Answer (D) shows the best assumption, that the rally will increase use of the Center Street station, where token vendors will be required. Answer (A) is incorrect because there is no reason to believe that the mayor has anything to do with this particular rally. Answer (B) is incorrect because the argument merely says that the route discussed is the "best" route, not the "only" one. Answer (C) is probably the second-best answer, because it suggests that the traffic on public transportation will increase, but (D) is better because it makes this statement directly. Answer (E) is not directly related to the argument without making the connection directly to the Center Street station.

3. The newspaper just reported that a man won this year's national baking contest for the first time in its history. The contest has used both male and female judges for many years. This must have been the first year that the contest was open to male participants. Which of the following is an assumption upon which the speaker's conclusion is based?

   (A) The newspaper has never before reported the results of the national baking contest.
   (B) Male judges are more likely to vote for a male contestant than for a female contestant.
   (C) Men have tried to enter the national baking contest for several years but have been denied.
   (D) Men are generally superior to women and would be able to beat them in any kind of competition.
   (E) Men are better bakers than women and could win this contest every year.

   The correct answer is (E). The speaker considers that a man won in the first year that men were allowed to enter and assumes that men could win this contest any time they enter. Answer (E), therefore, is the best answer. Answer (D) is similar, but it goes too far beyond the argument. Answers (A), (B), and (C) do not address the result of this contest and are therefore irrelevant.

4. Today is Tuesday and yesterday was Monday. Therefore, tomorrow will be Wednesday. This speaker's conclusion depends on which of the following assumptions?

   (A) Wednesday is the day that precedes Thursday.
   (B) Tuesday always follows Monday.
   (C) If, in any given week, Tuesday follows Monday, then Wednesday will follow Tuesday.
   (D) Every week consists of seven days arranged in a particular order.
   (E) The speaker always schedules a certain meeting to occur on Wednesday.

   The correct answer is (C). This appears to be a simple argument because it presents a relatively common issue, the days of the week, but analysis may be complicated. Answers (A), (B), and (D) are all true statements, using the standard calendar, but they do not directly address this as a logical argument. Only answer (C) provides information that could be a hidden assumption for this argument, linking the information in the premise with the conclusion. Answer (E) is irrelevant because nothing in the argument suggests any connection to the speaker's meeting schedule.

5. In the animal world, when any species becomes overpopulated, naturalists observe that the animals begin fighting among themselves and become cannibalistic. Sociologists have been reporting for years that the human population of the world is growing at an uncontrollable rate, and the world's cities will be overpopulated in about ten years. As a result, human societies will begin experiencing a global breakdown and we can expect an international war within the next ten years. Which of the following statements represents a hidden assumption upon which the preceding argument depends?

(A) Human social behaviors follow the same patterns as the behaviors of animals.

(B) Major cities do not always have adequate budgets to provide resources for all their residents.

(C) Naturalists and sociologists use the same research methods in studying their subjects and reporting results.

(D) The study that showed cannibalistic patterns in animals studied only carnivorous animals.

(E) The population of the world has doubled in the past five years, and its rate of growth will increase even faster in the future.

The correct answer is (A). This argument begins with information about animal behavior and then makes a conclusion about human behavior. Thus, the best assumption is one that connects human behavior to the observed animal behavior. Answer (B) is incorrect because nothing in the argument considers cities' budgets. Answer (C) is close but is not as good an answer as (A) because it does not address the conclusion reached. Answer (D) might question the validity of the result of the animal study, but it does not make any connection to the human behavior. Answer (E) is incorrect because it makes no connection between the animal study and human behavior.

HIDDEN ASSUMPTION PRACTICE QUESTIONS

Directions: Each question or group of questions is based on a passage or set of conditions. In answering some of the questions, it may be useful to draw a rough diagram. For each question, select the best answer given.

1. Nursing home residents have the right to refuse treatment. Forcing a resident to take sedatives, unless that person threatens the well-being of others, is a clear affront to human dignity, an illegal invasion of privacy, and an intolerable violation of the individual's right to think and make decisions about one's own welfare.

   A major assumption in this argument is that:

   (A) residents in nursing homes are no threat to the well-being of others
   (B) treatment in nursing homes is clearly harmful to residents
   (C) sedating drugs should not be used as a treatment in nursing homes
   (D) nursing home residents are capable of making decisions about their own welfare
   (E) the privacy rights of most residents of nursing homes are not protected

2. A lone hijacker is holding a plane full of passengers hostage with a handgun. If the passengers rise up and rush the hijacker, one or two might be killed or wounded but the group would certainly overwhelm and disarm the hijacker and save the lives of most hostages and the plane. Is it the case, therefore, that each hostage is responsible for the loss of his or her life and the loss of the plane should the group not attack the hijacker? No, because in a hostage situation, attacking a hijacker would be a heroic act, and so no individual is at fault for not acting.

   The author logically depends on which of the following to reach her conclusion?

   (A) In a hostage situation, only those who risk death can be considered heroes.
   (B) Hijacking is a risk that passengers assume when they board a plane.
   (C) Hijackers are desperate and unstable people.
   (D) Effective group action requires an established structure to be in place.
   (E) In a hostage situation, no victim can be justly blamed for failing to act heroically.

3. Dr. Burns: If the medicine arrives today, the baby will be saved.

Dr. Mills: No, if the medicine arrives tomorrow, it will be just as good for the baby.

Dr. Mills' reaction to Dr. Burns' assertion indicates that she understood Dr. Burns to mean that:

(A) nothing but medicine will save the baby
(B) if medicine arrives today, it will not arrive tomorrow
(C) today is the only day that medicine can arrive
(D) medicine arriving tomorrow will be of no use
(E) medicine will save the baby only if it comes today

4. The ethereal state of the Lotophagai of Greek history was thought to result from eating the narcotic in the lotus fruit. But modern research with rats has shown that the smell of the fruit produces the sleepy, dreamy condition that identified the lotus eaters.

This statement assumes that:

(A) eating the narcotic in the lotus fruit has no effect on people
(B) the fragrance of the lotus enhances the narcotic effect of the fruit
(C) rats and humans are affected by the lotus fragrance in the same way
(D) the effect produced by eating the lotus fruit is greater than that produced by smelling the fruit
(E) it is the fragrance of the lotus fruit that is addictive rather than the narcotic

5. Mr. Wall teaches six high school classes each weekday. Professor Wall, his wife, teaches two courses each semester at the university. Professor Wall is in class 6 hours per week, and Mr. Wall is in class 5 hours each day. Professor Wall is paid 40 percent more than her husband. These differences are reasonable when the expectations for research of the two people are taken into account.

This description and explanation assumes that:

(A) university teaching demands more research than high school teaching

(B) university teaching requires more education than does high school teaching

(C) equal pay for equal work does not apply in academic environments

(D) student contact hours for the Walls are similar

(E) university course preparation is more demanding than high school course preparation

6. For the first time in this century, the most recent national census shows that towns with populations under 10,000 are growing more rapidly than cities of more than 1 million. This confirms that people prefer human scale environments to rich, high-density environments.

The above argument assumes that:

(A) the populations of large cities are declining

(B) the environmental quality of cities is declining

(C) financial opportunities are the primary reason people live in large cities

(D) people find more financial opportunities in large cities than in small towns

(E) there are more rich people today than ever before

Peterson's Logic & Reading Review

7. A mother told her daughter, "You lie too much. You cannot be believed. When you start telling me the truth, I will start believing you."

Which of the following is assumed by the mother's statement?

(A) The mother has explained what is wrong about lying.
(B) The mother has determined that her daughter knows what a lie is.
(C) The mother knows when the daughter has been truthful.
(D) The mother is routinely truthful with her daughter.
(E) The mother believes her daughter ultimately will tell the truth.

8. Officials reviewing conditions of a local police station are considering whether major structural renovations are required. "The chances are good that a police officer will be killed or injured by a prisoner because of the cramped space and poor design of the holding cells," one official concluded. The official's conclusion is based most upon which of the following assumptions?

(A) In crowded conditions, dangerous criminals will have more access to weapons and closer contact with police officers.
(B) All criminals who are brought to this particular holding cell are violently dangerous and present a serious threat to safety.
(C) Storage of and access to police files will be more efficient if the planned renovations are accomplished.
(D) Police officers will be able to perform their public duties more effectively if they are provided with new office spaces.
(E) Holding prisoners in small, cramped holding cells is unconstitutional because it constitutes cruel and inhuman punishment.

9. Light bulbs that emit lower-intensity light save energy by requiring less electricity. Therefore, if homeowners use only low-intensity light bulbs, their electric bills will decrease. Which of the following represents a necessary assumption for the above argument?

(A) Homeowners are always concerned with lowering their utility bills.
(B) By lowering electricity use, homeowners can help decrease pollution levels in their communities.
(C) Low-intensity light bulbs are less expensive than more standard light bulbs.
(D) The low-intensity light bulbs are as effective in providing light as standard light bulbs.
(E) Low-intensity light bulbs have been shown to create less stress on eyes, and people using low-intensity light bulbs have fewer medical problems.

CONCLUSION QUESTIONS

At times, arguments will be missing their conclusion. A series of facts, along with unstated hidden assumptions, will lead to the final statement, which you then must supply. Sound arguments are linear in that you can usually predict in what general direction the facts are headed. You may also consider the conclusion to be an inference: you are inferring the conclusion from the specific statements and associated HA.

Consider the following argument:

The newest book by England's favorite political satirist has received warm praise from critics. In addition, there is a strong market in the U.K. for political satire.

You are now asked to choose the statement that best completes this series of facts.

(A) Political satire transfers well to other countries.
(B) The author of this book is a member of Parliament.
(C) People read book reviews before making purchases.
(D) Such a book will be banned by the current Tory government.
(E) The book will do well in British bookstores.

Although a series of facts does not usually have just one possible conclusion, there is only one best conclusion in the given answers. The best answer here would be one that follows the path the facts are taking but goes one step beyond the facts by making a more general statement. The answer is (E).

Peterson's Logic & Reading Review

Distracters may read too much into the facts. In the preceding example, statement (D) is an answer that steps too far from the given facts; you cannot reach the conclusion from the facts alone. Another sort of distracter introduces more detail instead of making the leap to a conclusion; examples of this are answers (A), (B), and (C). Now try these:

1. A consumer watchdog group recently reported the results of a study surrounding the deregulation of the U.S. banking industry, which has allowed for more mergers between banks and has allowed banks more freedom in setting their interest rates for their customers. The report shows that customers now have access to higher savings interest rates and lower borrowing interest rates. At the same time, banks are reporting record profits.

   From the results of this study, what can be concluded about the effect of deregulation of the American banking industry?

   (A) Deregulation has hurt the banking industry by limiting the number of options allowed to the customers of small, local banks.

   (B) Deregulation has been a success because it has given the banks the ability to raise their interest rates and force their customers to pay the highest rates possible.

   (C) As a result of the deregulation of the banking industry, investments in other industries will increase, resulting in a stronger economy nationwide.

   (D) Deregulation has been a success because it allows both the banks and their customers to realize savings and profits at the same time.

   (E) Because deregulation has lowered the interest rates that customers will have to pay, many banks will be driven out of business in the near future.

The correct answer is (D). The information given in the argument shows that banks have benefited from deregulation by collecting higher profits, and customers have benefited by receiving better interest rates for both saving and borrowing. The best answer, then, is (D), which reports both of these results. Answer (B) has the correct result, that deregulation has been a success, but it gives reasons that contradict the premises provided in the argument. Answers (A), (C), and (E) all go too far beyond the scope of the provided information and therefore do not make acceptable conclusions.

2. A report from the head of the city's school department reveals that the school department had a large surplus in its health insurance account at the end of 1994. The same report showed that at the end of 1995 the school department suffered a deficit of $300,000 in the same account. Despite this decline, the school department reported no significant changes in costs over the two-year period studied.

What can be concluded from the results of this report?

(A) The school department's budget for health costs is excessively high.

(B) More teachers were provided with health insurance payments during 1995 than in 1994.

(C) The costs related to operating the school department's health insurance program must have increased dramatically from 1994 to 1995.

(D) The health insurance account received less funding in 1995 than it did in 1994.

(E) The health insurance budget will show an even greater deficit in 1996 than it did in 1995.

The correct answer is (D). The premises of this argument show that while costs remained constant for this two-year period, the final budget decreased. From this, a logical conclusion would be (D), that the budget received less funding to start with in 1995 than in 1994. Answer (A) may or may not be true, but there is not enough information in the argument to make this decision. Answers (B) and (C) contradict the premise that costs remained constant. Answer (E) may be a reasonable inference for the future, but without additional information about the 1996 budget, it stretches too far beyond the information provided and is not as good a response as (D).

3. In a game of Monopoly™, if a player owns a hotel on Boardwalk, he must own both Boardwalk and Park Place. If he owns a hotel in Marvin Gardens, he must own Marvin Gardens and either Boardwalk or Park Place. If he owns Park Place, he also owns Marvin Gardens.

If the player described above does not own Park Place, which of the following conclusions may be drawn?

(A) The player owns a hotel on Boardwalk.

(B) The player owns a hotel in Marvin Gardens but does not own a hotel on Boardwalk.

(C) The player owns Marvin Gardens and Boardwalk but does not own a hotel on either property.

(D) The player does not own a hotel in Marvin Gardens.

(E) The player does not own a hotel on Boardwalk.

The correct answer is (E). This is a direct "if-then" argument. Answer (A) is incorrect because the first sentence of the argument required Park Place in order to own a hotel on Boardwalk. This same reasoning explains why answer (E) must be correct. (In fact, notice that (A) and (E) are direct opposites of each other; one of them must be true!) Answers (B) and (C) could both be true but cannot be concluded from the information given. Answer (D) is incorrect because the player could still own a hotel in Marvin Gardens by owning Boardwalk instead of Park Place.

4. As the temperature of a solution of water and chemical X increases, the reactivity of chemical X also increases. As the temperature of a mixture of chemical X and chemical Y increases, the reactivity of chemical Y increases but the reactivity of chemical X remains constant. As the temperature of a solution of water and chemical Y increases, the reactivity of chemical Y remains constant.

From the above information, what conclusion may be drawn?

(A) A change in temperature has no effect on the reactivity of chemical Y.
(B) A change in temperature has no effect on the reactivity of chemical X.
(C) When combined, chemical X and chemical Y display different reaction levels than when studied separately.
(D) When combined with chemical X, chemical Y demonstrates the same reactive properties as it does when it is studied alone.
(E) A change in temperature produces a greater effect on chemical Y than it does on chemical X.

The correct answer is (C). Answers (A), (B), and (D) are all incorrect because the premises show that both chemical X and chemical Y display changes in reactivity when combined. Answer (C) is the best answer because it reflects this change. Answer (E) is incorrect because nothing in the argument addresses the degree of the changes of either chemical.

5. *Advertisement:* Seven out of ten municipal employees choose Green Arrow Underwriters as their health insurance provider.

From the information provided in this advertisement, what further conclusion may be drawn?

(A) Green Arrow Underwriters has the cheapest premium rates of any insurance company available.

(B) All other health insurance providers, excluding Green Arrow Underwriters, provide services to less than 50 percent of the municipal employees.

(C) Municipal employees need less health insurance coverage than employees in other industries.

(D) Green Arrow Underwriters provides more valuable services and better customer assistance than any of its competitors.

(E) Except for Green Arrow Underwriters, the health insurance industry is suffering a decline in the rate of obtaining new customers.

The correct answer is (B). This is a very short statement, so there is not much that can be concluded. Answers (A), (C), (D), and (E) all state conclusions that require information outside the scope of the information provided. Only answer (B) remains limited to the known material. If Green Arrow provides coverage to "seven out of ten"—i.e., 70 percent—the rest of the industry can only cover the remaining 30 percent. Therefore, answer (B) is a reasonable conclusion.

CONCLUSION PRACTICE QUESTIONS

> **Directions:** Each question or group of questions is based on a passage or set of conditions. In answering some of the questions, it may be useful to draw a rough diagram. For each question, select the best answer given.

1. Price and wage controls are the only way to control inflation. But wage controls limit worker spending, which, in turn, results in reduced corporate profits if price controls are in place.

   Assume the above statements are true. Which of the following statements also must be true if corporate profits are not decreasing?

   (A) If there is inflation, wage controls are not in place.
   (B) If there is inflation, it is not being controlled.
   (C) Workers have less money to spend.
   (D) Price controls are in effect.
   (E) Wage controls are in effect.

2. People who do not understand the laws of probability often explain random happenings as the work of supernatural forces. Those people would be much less likely to believe in the supernatural if they had knowledge of statistical probability.

   The author of the above would agree most with which of the following?

   (A) Supernatural forces must obey the laws of probability.
   (B) There is a scientific explanation for every occurrence.
   (C) Phenomenology is a valid form of understanding.
   (D) Knowledge of the laws of probability reduces the likelihood of a person believing in the supernatural.
   (E) Natural causes produce random happenings.

3. If they get customers to believe that earlier patrons have given large tips, cosmetologists can get larger tips from them. However, if cosmetologists give the impression that they are wealthy, their customers will not tip them at all.

Which of the following draws the most reliable conclusion from the passage?

(A) Wealthy people should not be cosmetologists.

(B) If a cosmetologist is wealthy, he or she will not usually receive big tips.

(C) If customers feel that a cosmetologist is not wealthy, they will tip generously.

(D) Customers often give tips according to their perceptions of the cosmetologist and of the actions of other customers.

(E) Patrons are not usually influenced by the quality of the service provided by the cosmetologist when they determine the amount of their tips.

4. Even though art need not have an intellectual appeal, neither is it something that immediately can be appreciated without previous experiences that have deepened one's capacity for appreciation. So it follows that to get full enjoyment from art, people must commit considerable time and effort to developing their ability to observe and understand art.

The point of the argument in the above paragraph is that:

(A) the enjoyment of art has little to do with the intellect

(B) viewing art does not always result in an increase of a person's appreciation

(C) art has a universal appeal

(D) the ability to enjoy art often requires preparation

(E) art that is enjoyed usually deepens a person's capacity for appreciation

5. The different types of speech therapy based on experience produce virtually the same rates of success. While practitioner proponents of each type of therapy assert that their procedure is different from the others, studies of the results achieved by every one of these treatments show no significant differences in effectiveness.

It can be best inferred from the statement above that:

(A) there are few differences among the different types of speech therapies considered

(B) the speech therapies discussed are less effective than other types of treatment

(C) the differences among the various speech therapies considered are not causally relevant to their effectiveness

(D) practitioner proponents differ substantially in their conceptions of therapeutic success

(E) practitioner proponents ignore the connection between therapeutic experience and effectiveness

6. Five separate applications of the pesticide failed to rid the area of the mites. Only the most resistant of the mites survived each application. When the surviving mites reproduced, their offspring resisted the pesticide more effectively than did the parents.

Which of the following conclusions can best be drawn from the statement above?

(A) Normally, more pesticide-resistant mites tend to mate with less resistant mites.

(B) The mites that survived each exposure grew more pesticide resistant with each application.

(C) The pesticide applications did not coincide with the mating season of the mites.

(D) The pesticide was formulated to kill the mites in one application.

(E) Resistance to the pesticide is passed from parent to offspring.

7. Singularity saves politicians from having to take infinite variations into account when they establish rules and regulations for diverse populations. A single set of rules and regulations fits all.

The main point of this commentary is that:

(A) it is good when people are similar to one another
(B) the identification of variations among people is difficult
(C) rules and regulations cannot take diverse populations into account
(D) it is easier to treat a country's population as though it is homogeneous
(E) dealing with similar populations similarly is not just

8. Compared to a carnivore, an herbivore needs relatively few pounds of plants as food to be able to produce a pound of protein. Since carnivores feed on both herbivores and other carnivores, the accumulated consumption of thousands of pounds of plants is needed for a carnivore to produce a pound of protein.

This argument is best completed by which of the following?

(A) Herbivores produce protein faster than carnivores.
(B) A pound of carnivore protein has more food value than a pound of herbivore protein.
(C) The impact of people on plant resources would be much less if they substituted chicken for tuna in their diets.
(D) Carnivores' diets consist of more plants than meat.
(E) Chickens are a cheaper source of food than tuna.

9. Well-designed clothing was once described as the hallmark of a stylish person. We agree, and our clothing is designed for stylish people. Their lifestyles are well defined. They do everything in good taste. And they search out well-designed clothing as the guarantee of good workmanship.

This advertisement is intended to suggest which of the following conclusions?

(A) Well-designed clothing defines a lifestyle.
(B) Good taste is important in clothing design.
(C) Workmanship guarantees good design.
(D) Purchasers of this brand of clothing will be stylish.
(E) Appearance is the hallmark of purchasers of this brand of clothing.

LOGIC INSTRUCTION ANSWERS AND EXPLANATIONS

RANKING ANSWERS AND EXPLANATIONS

Questions 1–5

This is a simple ordering type of question, with eight spaces to fill with eight people. The initial rules allow you to create the following initial diagram:

8	7	6	5	4	3	2	1
Donna (?)			Eddie			Donna (?)	NOT Frank

Also: [Frank/Gary] _____ _____ [Gary/Frank]

(Iris/Hanna) together or (Hanna/Iris) together

1. The correct answer is (D). The best approach to a question of this type is to check each answer against the initial rules until you find that a rule is broken. Then disregard that answer and move to the next one. Answer (A) is incorrect because Iris and Hanna must be adjacent to each other. Answer (B) is incorrect because Frank may not be first. Answer (C) is incorrect because Donna must be either second or last. Answer (D) is the correct answer. Answer (E) is incorrect because two students must be between Frank and Gary.

2. The correct answer is (C). Put Gary in place in the eighth position, and then fill in as much as you can. Because Gary is eighth, then Donna must be second. The next limitation is that Frank must be at least two spaces from Gary, so Frank cannot be sixth or seventh; he cannot be fifth or second because those spaces are taken; and he is not allowed to be first. So Frank will have to be either third or fourth. This leaves sixth and seventh as the only two adjacent spaces for Iris and Hanna. As a result, the diagram looks like this:

8	7	6	5	4	3	2	1
Gary	Hanna/ Iris	Iris/ Hanna	Eddie	(Frank?)	(Frank?)	Donna	

Comparing this diagram to the answer choices makes it obvious that (C) is the correct answer. Answers (A), (B), and (E) all COULD be true, but nothing requires that they MUST be true. Answer (D) must be false.

3. The correct answer is (E). Requiring two people between Frank and Gary and recognizing that Eddie is in fifth place allows the following five possibilities:

8	7	6	5	4	3	2	1
	Gary		Eddie	Frank			
	Frank		Eddie	Gary			
		Gary	Eddie		Frank		
		Frank	Eddie		Gary		
			Eddie	Frank			Gary

With these possibilities in mind, attempt each of the answers to find the one that does not work. All of them are possible except answer (E). By requiring Donna to be second and Hanna to be third, Iris would have to be fourth in order to be next to Hanna. However, there is no possible arrangement in the table above that has BOTH spaces 3 and 4 available. So answer (E) is impossible and is therefore the correct answer.

4. The correct answer is (A). If Gary is fourth, Frank would have to be first, seventh, or eighth in order to leave at least two spaces between Gary and Frank. Frank cannot be first, so he must be either seventh or eighth. If Iris is in front of Donna, then Iris would have to be first if Donna were second; but this is impossible because Iris and Hanna must be together. So Donna cannot be second and must therefore be eighth. As a result, Frank must be seventh. Iris and Hanna, in either order, can be first and second or second and third. The remaining people, Barry and Carol, can be either first or sixth. This all results in the following:

8	7	6	5	4	3	2	1
Donna	Frank	Barry/ Carol (?)	Eddie	Gary	Iris	Hanna	Carol/ (?)
Donna	Frank	Barry/ Carol (?)	Eddie	Gary	Hanna	Iris	Carol/ Barry (?)
Donna	Frank	Barry/ Carol (?)	Eddie	Gary	Carol/ Barry (?)	Iris	Hanna
Donna	Frank	Barry/ Carol (?)	Eddie	Gary	Carol/ Barry (?)	Hanna	Iris

In every option, Barry and Carol are the only possible people to be in the sixth position. Therefore, the answer is (A).

5. The correct answer is (B). If Iris and Hanna are the only people between Frank and Gary, then this group of four people—Iris, Hanna, Frank, and Gary—must all be placed together in some order. The only position with four consecutive places is places 1 through 4. Because Frank cannot be first, then Gary must be first and Frank must be fourth. Iris and Hanna will be either second or third, in either order. Eddie must always be fifth. Donna must be last because the second position is taken by Iris or Hanna. Barry and Carol could be sixth or seventh, in either order. Therefore, the only positions that can change are second and third, between Iris and Hanna, and sixth and seventh, between Barry and Carol. This creates the following different lineups:

8	7	6	5	4	3	2	1
Donna	Barry	Carol	Eddie	Frank	Iris	Hanna	Gary
Donna	Carol	Barry	Eddie	Frank	Iris	Hanna	Gary
Donna	Barry	Carol	Eddie	Frank	Hanna	Iris	Gary
Donna	Carol	Barry	Eddie	Frank	Hanna	Iris	Gary

Therefore, the correct answer is (B).

Questions 6–10

This is a simple ordering type of question, with eight cities to place in order. The initial rules allow the following initial diagram:

first	second	third	fourth	fifth	sixth	seventh	eighth
Ft. Lauderdale (?)	Ft. Lauderdale (?)	Honolulu	Ft. Lauderdale (?)				

Also: (Boulder/Cleveland) or (Cleveland/Boulder) in order
Alexandria < Gary

6. The correct answer is (B). Answers (A) and (E) are incorrect because Alexandria must come before Gary. Answer (B) is the correct answer. Answer (C) is incorrect because Honolulu must be third. Answer (D) is incorrect because Boulder and Cleveland must be together.

7. The correct answer is (D). The initial diagram shows that Honolulu and Ft. Lauderdale cannot be last. Also, because Alexandria must be visited before Gary, then Alexandria cannot be last. All of the other five cities could possibly be last, so the correct answer is (D).

8. The correct answer is (D). Putting Alexandria into the diagram in first place results in the following:

first	second	third	fourth	fifth	sixth	seventh	eighth
Alexandria	Ft. Lauderdale (?)	Honolulu	Ft. Lauderdale (?)				

Because Boulder and Cleveland must be visited consecutively, neither one could be second, since there would not be room for the other one. Therefore, Boulder and Cleveland may be visited fourth (if Ft. Lauderdale is visited second) or later. As a result, answer (D) is the correct answer, since Ft. Lauderdale must always be visited before Cleveland. All of the other answers COULD be true, but it is not required that they MUST be true.

9. The correct answer is (D). Because Ft. Lauderdale must be one of the first four, because Honolulu must be third, and because Boulder and Cleveland must be visited consecutively, then Boulder and Cleveland, in either order, must be the first two cities visited. The first four places, therefore, are as follows:

first	second	third	fourth	fifth	sixth	seventh	eighth
Boulder/ Cleveland	Cleveland/ Boulder	Honolulu	Ft. Lauderdale				

Of the remaining four cities, the only requirement is that Alexandria must be visited before Gary. Therefore, Gary cannot be fifth. Any of the remaining three cities, Alexandria, Dallas, and East Lansing, could be fifth, so the answer is (D).

10. The correct answer is (C). Because this question does not add any new information, refer back to the initial diagram:

first	second	third	fourth	fifth	sixth	seventh	eighth
Ft. Lauderdale (?)	Ft. Lauderdale (?)	Honolulu	Ft. Lauderdale (?)				

Try to "fit" each of the answers to see if any could work. If any answer could work, then it is an incorrect answer. Answer (C) is the only one that must be false. In order for Boulder to be visited immediately before Ft. Lauderdale, Ft. Lauderdale would have to be second and Boulder first. But this would not allow Boulder and Cleveland to be visited consecutively, as required. So answer (C) must be false and is therefore the correct answer.

DISTRIBUTION ANSWERS AND EXPLANATIONS

1. The correct answer is (E). If Sam is above Tyler, then Tyler must be on either the first or second floor. Also, because Robert must be above Tyler, Robert may be on any floor except the first floor. All of the answers are possible except answer (E), since there is no floor, according to the initial diagram, with two remaining possible apartments for Robert and Victor to be on the same floor. The fourth floor must have one vacancy, and the third floor already has Sam living in one of the two apartments.

2. The correct answer is (D). Answers (A), (B), and (C) are clearly incorrect from the initial diagram. Answer (E) is incorrect because there is no floor remaining with two open apartments. Answer (D) is the only statement that could be true.

3. The correct answer is (B). Notice that this problem does not say that Robert is necessarily on a lower floor than Sam, just that he is not higher. Therefore, Robert could be on floors 3, 2, or 1. However, because Robert must be on a higher floor than Tyler, Robert could never live on the first floor. As a result, Robert could live on either the second or the third floor, so the answer is (B).

4. The correct answer is (B). If Victor and Wally are on the top two floors and Sam is on the third floor, then only Robert, Usher, and Tyler remain as possible candidates for the second floor. Any of them could live on that floor, so the answer is (B).

5. The correct answer is (A). The only place where Tyler could live on the same floor with another person is on the third floor with Sam. If that is true, then Robert must be on either the fourth or the fifth floor, and the diagram would look like this:

5	Robert/Victor/Wally (?)	
4	Robert/Victor/Wally (?)	VACANT
3	Sam	Tyler
2	Victor/Wally (?)	
1	Victor/Wally (?)	

Notice that Victor or Wally could be in any of the apartments on 1, 2, 4, or 5 since there are few requirements on them. Reviewing the answers, the one statement that could be false is answer (A), since Robert could be on either the fourth or the fifth floor. All remaining statements must be true.

Questions 6–9

This is another "distributed ordering" problem, with multiple items possibly being placed on each shelf. The initial diagram can look like this:

Shelf 4		*East of Eden* (?)
		Father of the Bride (?)
Shelf 3		
Shelf 2	*Bambi* *Cheyenne*	*East of Eden* (?)
		Father of the Bride (?)
Shelf 1		

Also: *David Copperfield < Arthur + Harry & Tonto*

6. The correct answer is (D). Answer (A) is incorrect because *David Copperfield* must be below *Harry & Tonto*, so it cannot be on the top shelf. Answer (B) is incorrect since the same reason prevents *Harry & Tonto* from being on the bottom shelf. Answer (C) is incorrect because *Father of the Bride* cannot be on the shelf below *Cheyenne*, because that would be an odd-numbered shelf. Answer (D) is the correct answer, which could be, but does not have to be, true. Answer (E) is incorrect because *East of Eden* cannot be on an odd-numbered shelf.

7. The correct answer is (D). The initial diagram shows that *Father of the Bride* can only be on shelf 2, together with *Cheyenne*, or on shelf 4. Therefore, if it is on a different shelf from *Cheyenne*, it must be on the top shelf, so answer (D) is the correct answer. Answers (A) and (E) must both be false because *Arthur* must be higher than *David Copperfield*. Answers (B) and (C) could be either true or false.

8. The correct answer is (C). Reviewing the initial rules reveals that *Arthur* must be on the same shelf as *Harry & Tonto*, and *Harry & Tonto* must be higher than *David Copperfield*. Therefore, *Arthur* must be higher than *David Copperfield*. As a result, answer (C) must be correct. All other pairs could be placed together.

9. The correct answer is (A). This question is best answered by first considering all the movies that CANNOT be on the bottom shelf. *Harry & Tonto* and *Arthur* cannot be on the bottom shelf, because they must both be higher than *David Copperfield*. Therefore, answers (B), (C), and (D) must all be incorrect. *Father of the Bride* and *East of Eden* cannot be on the bottom shelf because they must be on even-numbered shelves. Therefore, answer (E) is incorrect. The remaining movies could all be on the bottom, so (A) is the correct answer.

Scheduling Answers and Explanations

The initial rules set up the following:

	Mon	Tue	Wed	Thur	Fri	
Morning	Annie					} Louise
Afternoon						} Wilbur
				Not Eddie		

1. The correct answer is (E). Check each answer against the rules to see which cause conflicts. Answer (A) is incorrect because Phillip and Sheryl must have their driving lesson on the same day and therefore cannot both appear in the morning. Answer (B) is incorrect because Wilbur can appear only in the afternoon. Answer (C) is incorrect because Annie's lesson must be on Monday. Answer (D) is incorrect because Eddie cannot have his lesson on Thursday. Answer (E) is correct because it satisfies all the rules.

2. The correct answer is (C). This question needs the same approach as the previous question. Answer (A) is incorrect because Annie must have her driving lesson in the morning. Answer (B) is incorrect because Louise must have her lesson in the morning. Answer (C) is correct because all of the rules are satisfied by this arrangement. Sheryl and Phillip can still have their lessons on the same day, Louise can have her lesson any morning, Wilbur is scheduled for the afternoon, and Eddie is not scheduled for Thursday. Answer (D) is incorrect because Phillip and Sheryl must appear on the same day. Answer (E) is incorrect because Louise must appear in the morning.

3. The correct answer is (D). Answer (A) is incorrect because Phillip and Sheryl must be scheduled for the same day, so Phillip and Annie cannot be on the same day. Answer (B) is incorrect for the same reason. Answer (C) is incorrect because Eddie is not available on Thursdays. Answer (D) is the correct answer because Annie's lesson must be Monday morning and Wilbur's must be any afternoon. Answer (E) is incorrect because Annie's lesson must be on Monday morning.

4. The correct answer is (B). The first couple, Eddie and Annie, could be together, both on Monday. The second couple, Phillip and Wilbur, cannot be on the same day because Phillip and Sheryl must be on the same day. The third couple, Annie and Louise, cannot be on the same day because Annie must be Monday morning and Louise must also be in the morning. The fourth couple, Ryan and Wilbur, have no limitations and may be together. Therefore, the correct answer is (B), answers II and III.

5. The correct answer is (C). If Phillip's driving lesson is on Wednesday afternoon, then Sheryl's lesson must be on Wednesday morning. As a result, answer (C) must be false, since Sheryl and Wilbur cannot be on the same day. The other answers are all possible, though not necessarily true.

6. The correct answer is (D). If Phillip is on Friday, then Sheryl must also be on Friday. Therefore, neither of them can be on Monday. So answers (A) and (C) are incorrect. Because Annie must be Monday morning, the correct answer must include Annie. However, because Louise must also be in the morning, she cannot be on Monday, since Monday morning is already taken by Annie. Therefore, the correct choice cannot include Louise. As a result, answers (B) and (E) are incorrect, and answer (D) must be the correct answer.

7. The correct answer is (B). Check each of the answers against the initial rules to see which answers are not permitted. Answer (A) is incorrect because Nathan must be in the morning, not the afternoon. Answer (B) is the correct answer. Answer (C) is incorrect because this would place Harry last on Friday afternoon, which would have Iris' presentation coming earlier. Answer (D) is incorrect because Glen must be on Tuesday afternoon. Answer (E) is incorrect because if Oscar's presentation is in the afternoon, then Kathy must be scheduled for that morning.

8. The correct answer is (D). Answer (A) is incorrect because Lewis' presentation must be sometime on Wednesday, not Friday. Answer (B) is incorrect because scheduling Oscar for the afternoon would require Kathy to be on the same day. Answer (C) is incorrect because Nathan must be scheduled for the morning. Answer (D) is possible and is therefore the correct answer. Answer (E) is incorrect because scheduling Harry's and Mike's as the last two presentations would mean that Iris' presentation precedes Harry's.

9. The correct answer is (E). Glen and Kathy cannot be scheduled for the same day because Glen must be Tuesday afternoon, forcing Kathy into Tuesday morning. However, if Kathy is in the morning, then Oscar must be scheduled for the same afternoon, which would be impossible here. All other pairs are possible.

10. The correct answer is (C). If Kathy is on Thursday morning, then Oscar must be on Thursday afternoon. Because Iris must follow Harry, placing Harry on Friday morning means Iris must be on Friday afternoon. Therefore, answer (C) is impossible and "must be false." All other answers could be true.

11. The correct answer is (A). If Kathy and Nathan are on the same day, that means that Nathan is in the morning (because of the initial rules) and Kathy is in the afternoon. Also, because of the rules relating to Oscar and Kathy, Oscar cannot be scheduled for an afternoon, or else he would require Kathy to be on the same day. Therefore, answer (A) must be true, since Oscar must be scheduled for the morning. All of the other answers could be either true or false.

CONNECTION ANSWERS AND EXPLANATIONS

1. The correct answer is (B). Answers (A) and (D) are incorrect because there is no connection between CS4 and CS5. Answer (B) is the correct answer. Answer (C) is incorrect because there is no connection between CS5 and South Station. Answer (E) is incorrect because a train cannot travel backwards from CS6 to CS4.

2. The correct answer is (D). Because the question asks for a statement that "must be true," any answer that "could be false" is incorrect. Answer (A) could be false because it is possible to travel from North Station to South Station by passing through only three connecting stations: CS2–CS4–CS7. Answers (B) and (C), which are reverse statements of each other, are incorrect because it is possible for paths beginning with CS1 or CS2 to both have the same number of connecting stations, such as CS1–CS3–CS6–SS and CS2–CS3–CS6–SS. Answer (D) is the correct answer, because the longest path possible connects six connecting stations: CS1–CS2–CS3–CS5–CS6–CS7. It is impossible to include CS4 in this list. Answer (E) is incorrect because it IS possible for a train to pass through both CS3 and CS7, as in the six-station list just recited: CS1–CS2–CS3–CS5–CS6–CS7.

3. The correct answer is (C). The analysis of this "must be true" question is very similar to the previous question. Just test each answer to find the wrong answer choices that "could be false." Answer (A) could be false because a three-station connection of CS2, CS4, and CS7 is possible. The same list shows that answer (B) could be false. Answer (C) is the correct answer, since CS4 goes only to CS6, which goes only to South Station or CS7, or to CS7, which in turn goes only to South Station. Answer (D) is incorrect because a train from CS4 can clearly go to CS6. Answer (E) is incorrect because a train leaving CS4 could go only to CS6 or CS7 and then to South Station.

4. The correct answer is (D). The only paths that pass through exactly three connecting stations are:

   CS1–CS3–CS6
   CS2–CS3–CS6
   CS2–CS4–CS6
   CS2–CS4–CS7

   Based on these combinations, the one answer that lists a combination that the train cannot pass through is (D), since there is no combination that includes both CS1 and CS2.

5. The correct answer is (D). The longest path that includes CS4 is CS1–CS2–CS4–CS6–CS7. Therefore, the correct answer is (D).

Questions 6–10

This is a "network" problem. The best approach is to read each of the initial rules individually and use them to draw a diagram of arrows connecting the various items. The diagram then helps in easily answering the questions. A diagram for this problem appears as follows:

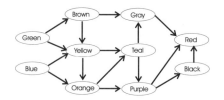

6. The correct answer is (B). Test each of the answers against the diagram above to see which answer follows the allowed system of arrows. The only one that is possible is answer (B). Answer (A) is incorrect because there is no connection from yellow to purple. Answer (C) is incorrect because there is no connection from green to orange. Answer (D) is incorrect because there is no connection from yellow to gray. Answer (E) is incorrect because there is no connection from teal to black.

7. The correct answer is (C). A problem like this requires "trial and error," trying all possible combinations to make paths of five tickets. The possible paths are:

1	green	yellow	teal	gray	red
2	green	yellow	teal	purple	red
3	blue	yellow	teal	gray	red
4	blue	yellow	teal	purple	red
5	blue	orange	teal	gray	red
6	blue	orange	teal	purple	red
7	blue	yellow	orange	purple	red
8	blue	orange	purple	black	red

Therefore, there are eight combinations, so the answer is (C).

8. The correct answer is (C). Use the diagram to trace each of the answers and try to reach the black ticket. The only answer that cannot connect is the gray ticket, so the answer is (C).

9. The correct answer is (D). Because the question asks for the statement that "must be false," test each answer to see if it "could be true." Any answer choice that "could be true" will be incorrect and can be eliminated. Answer (A) is incorrect because it is possible to trade a yellow ticket for a teal ticket, then trade for purple and eventually black. Answer (B) is incorrect because it is possible to begin with a blue ticket and trade directly for a yellow and then a teal ticket. Answer (C) is incorrect because it is possible to trade the yellow ticket for teal, and then purple, then red. Answer (D) is the correct answer because it is impossible to receive an orange ticket BEFORE a yellow. Answer (E) is incorrect because it is possible to trade a yellow ticket for a teal ticket and then trade for a gray ticket.

10. The correct answer is (E). The first step here is to determine the shortest path (or paths) by "trial and error" and then use the results to check the answers. There are two different paths that include only four tickets: (1) green, brown, gray, red and (2) blue, orange, purple, red. Using this information, answer (A) is incorrect because one of the possible paths does not begin with a green ticket. Answer (B) is incorrect because in path (2) above, the last ticket does not have to be gray. Answer (C) is incorrect because it is possible for the shortest path to contain an orange ticket. Answer (D) is incorrect because the shortest path consists of four, not three, tickets. Answer (E) is correct because neither of the shortest path options contains a yellow ticket.

Mapping Answers and Explanations

Questions 1–5

This is a modified example of a "mapping" problem, where the only requirements are whether certain cities are north or south of a dividing line (the equator). Based on the initial rules, the following diagram can be created:

| NORTH | 1 | 2 | 5 or 6 | (7 and 8) OR (9 and 10) |
| SOUTH | 3 | 4 | 6 or 5 | (9 and 10) OR (7 and 8) |

It is evident that 9 and 10 must be in the same hemisphere, even though this is not directly required by the rules, because each hemisphere must have five cities.

1. The correct answer is (E). Use the diagram to see which of the answers is possible and which are not. Answers (A), (B), and (C) are incorrect because 7 and 8 are not together. Answer (D) is incorrect because this arrangement would put city 4 into the Northern Hemisphere, which is not allowed. Only answer (E) is possible.

2. The correct answer is (C). Looking at the diagram above, it is evident that cities 9 and 10 must be in the opposite hemisphere from cities 7 and 8. Therefore, if 7 is in the Northern Hemisphere, then both 9 and 10 must be in the Southern Hemisphere. Therefore, answer (C) is the correct answer. Answers (A) and (B) could be either true or false; answers (D) and (E) must both be false.

3. The correct answer is (A). For the same reasons discussed in the two previous questions, the combination of 7 and 10 is impossible, so answer (A) is the correct answer. All other combinations could be placed together.

4. The correct answer is (A). Looking at the initial diagram, there are only two ways to make choices: either 5 or 6 and either the combination of 7 and 8 or the combination of 9 and 10. Because there are two choices of two items each, the total number of possible combinations is four, so the answer is (A). The four combinations are (1) 3-4-5-7-8, (2) 3-4-6-7-8, (3) 3-4-5-9-10, and (4) 3-4-6-9-10.

5. The correct answer is (E). Because the combinations of 7 and 8 and 9 and 10 must be in separate hemispheres, the answer is (E), separating cities 8 and 9. Answers (A), (B), and (C) could be either true or false; answer (D) must be false.

Questions 6–10

The best initial approach to this question is to draw a "map" or diagram of the initial rules. In this case, the initial rules result in the following diagram:

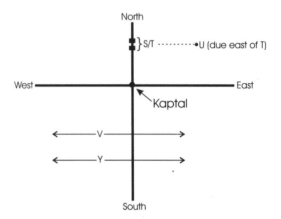

6. The correct answer is (C). If Kaptal is northeast of Youngstown, that means that Youngstown is one of the two cities that is west of Kaptal. Only one other city may also be west of Kaptal. Therefore, answer (C), which places two other cities west of Kaptal, must be false. Each of the other statements could be either true or false.

7. The correct answer is (A). Underwood is already northeast of Kaptal because Tunney is due north of Kaptal and Underwood is due east of Tunney. Because Youngstown is south of Kaptal, placing Youngstown due south of Underwood would make Youngstown southeast of Kaptal. The diagram would look like this:

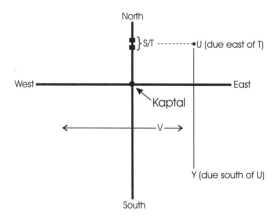

Reviewing the diagram shows that answer (A) could be true and is therefore the correct answer, because Vivlit could be placed southeast of Kaptal in a position that puts it between Youngstown and Simpson. Answer (B) is incorrect because Underwood and Youngstown both have to be somewhere east of Kaptal; therefore, Kaptal cannot be in a straight line between them. Answer (C) is incorrect because it would have three cities west of Kaptal, which is not allowed. Answer (D) is incorrect because it would result in having five cities due north of Kaptal (E, F, and the three between them) and two cities (Underwood and Youngstown) east of Kaptal. Only one city would remain, but two cities must be west of Kaptal. Answer (E) is incorrect for the same reason.

8. The correct answer is (E). The answer to this question will be determined by considering the answers and eliminating any choices in which the cities given are already defined to be at least partially north or south of each other, since the plane is flying due east. Answer (A) is incorrect because Simpson is due north of Kaptal. Answer (B) is incorrect because Youngstown is located somewhere south of Vivlit. Answer (C) is incorrect because Simpson and Tunney are both somewhere due north of Kaptal, so one of them must be north of the other. Answer (D) is incorrect because Simpson must be due north of Kaptal and Underwood must be somewhere northeast of Kaptal. Answer (E) is the only possible combination, because no information is given that would limit the location of Woodville or Ziffer.

9. The correct answer is (B). If exactly three cities are southeast of Kaptal, and three other cities (Simpson, Tunney, Underwood) are already placed somewhere due north or northeast of Kaptal, only two other cities would remain, because the total is eight cities. The rules require that these two cities be somewhere west of Kaptal. Answer (A) could be either true or false, since the two cities could be northwest or southwest of Kaptal. Answer (B) is the correct answer, because the remaining cities must be somewhere west of Kaptal. Answer (C) is incorrect because either or both of the remaining two cities could be due west, or they could be northwest or southwest. Answer (D) is incorrect because Woodville could be one of the cities that is placed southeast of Kaptal and could be east of Underwood. Answer (E) is incorrect because nothing requires that the three "southeast" cities must be due south of Underwood.

10. The correct answer is (E). The initial rules require that exactly two cities are somewhere west of Kaptal. This question places Woodville northwest of Kaptal, so exactly one other city must appear somewhere west of Kaptal. Cities Simpson, Tunney, and Underwood are already either due north or east of Kaptal, so they cannot appear anywhere west of it. That leaves only Vivlit, Xercia, Youngstown, and Ziffer. Any of those cities, taken alone, COULD be southeast of Kaptal, but if all of them together appear southeast, as suggested in answer (E), then only Woodville would appear west of Kaptal, violating the initial rules. Therefore, at most, only three of those remaining four cities can be southeast of Kaptal.

Hybrid Answers and Explanations

Questions 1–6

Ingredients

H J K L M N O P

M ——must—— N | If   Then | M —⁄— O —⁄— P

K ——no—— N | J   K and P | H —⁄— L —⁄— P

Cannot be together

K ⟨ H / J / O

This is a hybrid type of problem, one that cannot readily be assigned to one of the six major categories already discussed. This specific problem is of a type sometimes referred to as a "combination" or "selection" problem. Your task is to consider the eight ingredients and the possible combinations that can be made according to the rules. The rules for this kind of "combination" problem do not easily lend themselves to a diagram. The best you can do is make a series of "symbolic notes" to summarize the information. For example, the first rule, "If J is used, both K and P must also be used," can be symbolized as:

If J → J, K, P

The other rules can similarly be symbolized as follows:

Rule	Symbol
1. If J is used, both K and P must also be used.	If J → J, K, P
2. M and N must always be used together.	M ↔ N
3. If K is used, at least two of H, J, and O must also be used.	If K → H, J, O (at least 2)
4. K and N cannot be used together.	K ≠ N
5. M, O, and P cannot all be used in the same dish.	M, O, P—not all 3
6. H, L, and P cannot all be used in the same dish.	H, L, P—not all 3

The symbols for this type of problem are not as completely helpful as, for example, the diagram in a ranking problem, but these symbols can help you understand the rules and simplify your job of reviewing them.

1. The correct answer is (C). The first question, as with most first questions for Analytical Reasoning problems, asks you to pick out the one acceptable combination. The best approach is to begin with answer choice A and work your way down the list, checking each list against the rules. In this case, answer (A) is incorrect because using J requires the use of both K and P, but P is not included in the list. Answer (B) is incorrect because the last rule says that H, L, and P cannot all be used together. Answer (C) is the correct answer because it satisfies all the rules. (If you were really taking the test, you would stop your analysis here and move on to the next question.) Answer (D) is incorrect because M and N must be used together, according to the second rule. Answer (E) is incorrect because the fifth rule prohibits using M, O, and P together.

2. The correct answer is (A). The best approach for this question is to scan the rules for any relationships or combinations that either include or exclude M. The first rule tells you nothing about M, so you can skip over it for now. The second rule requires that N must be included with M, so, according to the way the question is asked, answer (C) can be eliminated. The third rule says nothing directly about M, so it can be ignored for now. The fourth rule, "K and N cannot be used together," also appears to say nothing about M. However, if you recall that M and N must be used together, this rule has the same effect as telling you that K cannot be used with M. So you look at the answers to select K as the answer, but it is not one of the choices. However, now you can focus on rules addressing K as well as M. If you return to the first rule, you see that any combination using J must also include K, and since K cannot be used with M, then J also cannot be used with M, since using J would require using K, and you would have a contradiction of rule 4. Therefore, the correct answer is (A).

3. The correct answer is (C). As with the previous question, the first step in solving this question is to review the rules for any requirements about J and then expand from there. Only the first rule makes any direct statement about J, requiring that the sauce also includes K and P. The sauce is already up to three ingredients, J, K, and P. Carefully read the question and note that it does not ask for the number of ingredients in the sauce but the number of "additional" ingredients, so if

the complete list is J, K, and P, the number of "additional" ingredients is two. Therefore, answer (A) must be incorrect. Now look for rules with requirements about K and P. The third rule requires that if K is used, at least two others from the list H, J, and O must also be used. Because you are already using J, you must add either H or O. (Note that you could possibly add BOTH H AND O, but since the question is asking for the minimum number of ingredients, you only want one.) Now the minimum list of TOTAL ingredients is up to four, J, K, P, and either H or O, so the number of "additional" ingredients is up to three. Therefore, answer (B) must be incorrect. At this point, none of the rules adds any information or requirements that would force the addition of any more ingredients. Therefore, the minimum number of "additional" ingredients is three, so the answer is (C).

4. The correct answer is (E). Solving this question is similar to the first question, with the added twist that there is one ingredient missing from each list. Even so, you can still work with the information given and figure out what combinations are not allowed. For example, answer (A) is not acceptable, regardless of the added ingredient, because the list includes H, L, and P. This combination is not acceptable because, according to the final rule, H, L, and P cannot all be used together. Now examine answer (B). Because the list already includes J, the first rule requires that the complete list must also include K and P, neither of which is already on the list. However, the question only allows you to add ONE more ingredient, so this combination is unacceptable, and (B) is incorrect. Answer (C) is incorrect, regardless of the added ingredient, because it includes both K and N, which cannot be used together. Answer (D) is incorrect for a reason similar to the reason used in eliminating (B). Because the list includes K, the third rule requires that "at least two of H, J, and O must also be used." Since none of these is on the list already, you would have to add two of them, which is not allowed. Now, as a test-taking strategy, because all four answers (A) through (D) have been eliminated, the answer must be (E). Considering answer (E) briefly does not quickly show any problems, so you should select it as the answer and move on to the next problem.

5. The correct answer is (D). This question is, in a way, the "opposite" of the preceding question. You are given a list of five ingredients—H, J, K, L, and P—and you are to remove only one of them. You can quickly see that, by removing one ingredient at a time, you get five possible combinations:

J, K, L, P	(remove H)
H, K, L, P	(remove J)
H, J, L, P	(remove K)
H, J, K, P	(remove L)
H, J, K, L	(remove P)

Now consider these five combinations and find the one that is acceptable. The first and second combinations are not acceptable because, since K is included, the third rule requires that your list must also include two of H, J, and O. The third combination is not acceptable because it includes H, L, and P, which may not all be used together, based on the final rule. The fourth combination appears to be acceptable, suggesting that L is the one to be removed. But before selecting this conclusively, consider the final combination. The final combination is not acceptable because it includes J without including P, which the first rule would require. Therefore, the ingredient to remove is L, so the answer must be (D).

6. The correct answer is (C). To answer this question, work through the list of the eight ingredients and check each one to see if it requires the use of any others. Starting with H, there are no requirements that anything else must be included. Note that there are some statements that include H, such as the third and the last rules, but these both include H only as options with other ingredients. They do not require that other ingredients must be used with H, so H could be used alone. Now move on to J. The first rule requires that if J is used, then J must be used together with K and P, so J cannot be used alone. Now move on to K. The third rule requires that if K is used, then others are needed with it, so K cannot be used alone. Now move on to L. There are no rules about L, so it appears to be allowable by itself. The next two items on the list of ingredients, M and N, must be used together according to the second rule, so they negate each other. The final two ingredients, O and P, could be used alone, since there are no rules requiring anything else to be used with them. Therefore, the list of ingredients that could be used alone consists of H, L, O, and P, for a total of four. The answer is (C).

7. The correct answer is (B). Answer (A) is incorrect because Diane and Carl may not work for the same store. Answer (C) is incorrect because Heather and Florence must work for the same store. Answer (D) is incorrect because if Diane and Elvin work together, then that store must hire four people. Answer (E) is incorrect because The Jeans Place may not hire four people without hiring Diane.

8. The correct answer is (C). If Diane works for The Jeans Place, then Carl and George must both work for The Electronics Shop, since Carl and Diane may not work together, and George must always work for The Electronics Shop. Heather and Florence, who must work together may not work for The Electronics Shop, since that would give The Electronics Shop four employees without having Diane. As a result, The Jeans Place will have Diane, Heather, and Florence, and The Electronics Shop must have George and Carl. Elvin and Ivan will then be split, with either one working for The Jeans Place and the other one working for The Electronics Shop. This analysis requires that answer (C) is the only statement that must be true. The other statements either must be false or could be either true or false.

9. The correct answer is (E). If Heather works for The Electronics Shop, then Florence must also work for The Electronics Shop. George, as always, must also work for The Electronics Shop. That leaves one more employee to be hired by The Electronics Shop, with the remaining three to work for The Jeans Place. Diane and Carl cannot both work for The Jeans Place because they are not allowed to work together. Diane and Elvin cannot both work for The Jeans Place because if they were put together, then The Jeans Place would have to have four employees. The only way to separate Diane from both Carl and Elvin is to have Diane work for The Electronics Shop and Carl, Elvin, and Ivan work for The Jeans Place. This analysis shows that answer (E) is the only statement that could be true.

10. The correct answer is (A). The best way to approach a question like this one is to test each answer choice to determine if it is possible to make each answer be true; if so, then it is not a statement that must be false, and it is therefore an incorrect answer. Answer (A) is the correct answer because there is no way to arrange Heather and Elvin so that they work for the same store. It is important

to notice, first, that Heather must work together with Florence. Therefore, Heather, Elvin, and Florence would have to be placed as a group. If these three people work for The Jeans Place and if The Jeans Place is hiring only three people, then the remaining four employees would all have to work for The Electronics Shop. This is impossible since Diane and Carl may not work together. The second check is to determine if Heather, Elvin, and Florence could work for The Electronics Shop. Since George must also work for The Electronics Shop, then the remaining three employees must work for The Jeans Place, and Carl and Diane are again thrown together. Therefore, answer (A) must be false. The other four statements could be either true or false.

Additional Fact (Weakening the Conclusion) Answers and Explanations

1. The correct answer is (D). The argument links together the "psychological stress" connected with lying and the "physiological changes" that the instruments measure. This argument assumes that all "physiological changes" will point to the lying. Answer (A) is incorrect because the maintenance of the machine is not part of the argument. Answer (B) is incorrect because the level of the stress, whether severe or moderate, is not part of the argument. Answer (C) is incorrect because nothing in the argument addresses the level of training of the machine operators. The statement may be true, but it is not directly related to this particular argument. Answer (D) directly connects both the psychological stress and the physiological symptoms, so it appears to be the answer. Check answer (E) just to see if it may be better. Answer (E), however, is incorrect because, although it makes a statement that could otherwise be true, the statement is not directly connected to the argument. The answer, therefore, is (D).

2. The correct answer is (C). In considering this question, it is important to note a few particular key changes in language use. Note that in the first sentence of the argument, the discussion is about "outstanding" researchers, while in the final sentence, the conclusion is about "successful" researchers. The key to the question, therefore, appears to have something to do with this shift between "outstanding" researchers and "successful" researchers. The requirements

of dedication and creativity presented in the first half of the argument are requirements for "outstanding" researchers, while the conclusion says "we are to produce successful medical researchers." Answer (C) is the one that best states this contradiction between outstanding and successful, or "well-rounded." Answer (A) is wrong because, although it may be a true statement, it does not address the problem. Answer (B) is wrong for the same reason and because it focuses only on the "outstanding researcher." Answers (D) and (E) are other examples of sentences that may be true but are irrelevant.

3. The correct answer is (E). This argument centers only on the positive effects of solar energy. When the question asks for a statement to weaken the argument, you are looking for a statement that will show a negative effect of using solar energy. Answer (A) does not say anything directly negative about using solar energy, so it is incorrect. Answer (B) does not say anything at all about solar energy. Answer (C), which discusses the costs of collecting solar energy, at least addresses the correct topic, and suggests that solar energy may be no better than the other energy forms, but you should continue checking the other answers to see if there is a better selection. Answer (D) does not say anything directly about solar energy itself but instead attacks the critics of solar energy. Answer (E) suggests that, although solar energy may be a good idea in theory, it cannot be used practically. Answer (E) is a better answer than (C) because it more directly undermines the argument that solar energy should be encouraged.

4. The correct answer is (B). The argument assumes that businesses will want to locate in this town. Answer (B) provides evidence of a reason that may keep them away, despite the formation of the new corporation. Answers (A) and (C) provide information about the town, but that information does not directly address the question of whether businesses will locate in the town. Answer (D) is irrelevant because it addresses the motivations of the investors but not the businesses themselves. Answer (E) discusses a positive result of the new corporation but does not address the actual question of attracting businesses.

ADDITIONAL FACT (STRENGTHENING THE CONCLUSION) ANSWERS AND EXPLANATIONS

1. The correct answer is (D). The argument makes the point that parenting skills are lost if babies are not raised by their mothers. Answer (D) restates this point by saying that baby gorillas raised by females other than their mothers were unable to function as mothers when they had their own offspring. Answer (A) is irrelevant to the argument because the argument does not discuss the relative dependencies between the babies. Answer (B) is incorrect because it mentions only a small part of the problem of "functioning" as a mother. Answer (C) is incorrect because, although it seems to strengthen the role of mothering, it does not directly stick to the topic of surrogate mothers. Answer (E) is incorrect because it adds a fact that goes beyond the scope of the argument, the idea of additional teaching after the gorillas mature. Therefore, the best answer is (D).

2. The correct answer is (E). The argument seems to suggest that the Department of Agriculture assumes its inspections are unnecessary because of the lack of citations. Therefore, you are looking for a statement that directly connects the inspections to the citations. Only answer (E) accomplishes this by suggesting that, with the higher standards of the industry association, no citations would ever be issued and inspections would be unnecessary. The other answers are all statements that, although they may be true, do not address the topic of the argument.

3. The correct answer is (D). The question asks about the "major function of scientists." Answers (B) and (C) are statements that are entirely irrelevant to the question, not addressing the function of the scientist at all. Answer (E) suggests a connection between science and religion, but it does not directly address the function of the scientist, as requested in the question. This leaves answers (A) and (D), which both provide "functions" for the scientist. The choice is between "efforts to prolong human life" in answer (A) and "improve the quality of everyday life" in answer (D). The final statement in the argument, alluding to the "human adventure," suggests more the "everyday life" as opposed to prolonging life. Therefore, the better answer is (D).

4. The correct answer is (D). The argument presents a position that being beneficent is a duty, but is one that people choose to do on their own, "spreading joy around them." Answer (A) is incorrect because, although the argument addresses a person's "duty," there is nothing about patriotism. Answer (B) is incorrect because the phrase "production of one's heredity and environment" is not defined or relevant to the question. Answer (C) is incorrect because it directly contradicts the argument that a person would exercise a sense of duty voluntarily. Answer (E) is incorrect because education is not a topic of the argument, so even though the statement may be true, it is irrelevant. The best answer, therefore, is (D).

HIDDEN ASSUMPTION ANSWERS AND EXPLANATIONS

1. The correct answer is (D). To answer a "hidden assumption" question, you first must determine the conclusion of the argument and then look for an answer selection that leads to that conclusion. In this question, the conclusion appears in the first sentence, that "nursing home residents have the right to refuse treatment." The argument goes on to discuss the "individual's right to think and make decisions." You are therefore looking for a statement that has some bearing on the individual's thinking, decision making, and "right to refuse treatment" as the assumption. Only answer (D) accomplishes this, by repeating the idea that nursing home residents are "capable" of making decisions. Therefore, this must be the answer. All the other statements may or may not be true statements, but they do not address the topics of decision making, thinking, and refusing or accepting treatment.

2. The correct answer is (E). The argument here illustrates certain activity that it describes as "heroic" and then concludes that "no individual is at fault for not acting," implying that heroic activities are not expected at all times. The correct answer, therefore, must be a statement that says something about heroic activities. Answers (B), (C), and (D) are quickly eliminated as not mentioning the heroic activity at all. Answer (A) gives a definition of heroic activity, but it does not address the expectation of heroic activity, which is the conclusion of the argument. Answer (E) is a better answer, repeating that heroic activity is not expected.

3. The correct answer is (E). The two statements by the doctors show that Dr. Burns believes the medicine must

come today in order to save the baby and that no other alternative will save the baby. The emphasis is on the arrival of the medicine and the saving of the baby. Answer (A) is close but is incorrect because it says nothing about the date of arrival of the medicine. Answers (B), (C), and (D) all mention the arrival of medicine but say nothing about saving the baby. Answer (E) is the only one that combines the arrival of the medicine with the saving of the baby. Therefore, the answer must be (E).

4. The correct answer is (C). The first sentence of the argument makes a statement about humans, while the second sentence mentions research with rats. For the conclusion to be supported, there must be an assumption that rats and humans have similar reactions. This is exactly what answer (C) says, so (C) is the best answer. The other statements all may or may not be true, but they do not directly address the key to the argument.

5. The correct answer is (A). The argument sets up a contrast between high school teaching, which consists of more time actually teaching, and university teaching, which requires less teaching time. The conclusion, however, claims to justify paying the university professor more because of research expectations. The correct statement regarding the assumption must be a statement that accurately combines the elements of research and teaching, showing the contrast between the high school and university levels. Answer (A) adequately does this and is the correct answer. Answer (B) shows the contrast between the two levels but does not focus on the research. Answer (C) ignores the topic completely. Answers (D) and (E), like (B), do not focus on the research aspect of the argument. The best answer is (A).

6. The correct answer is (D). The argument contrasts small towns, as "human-scale environments," to large cities, which it calls "rich, high-density environments." This assumes that the large cities are richer than small towns. The answer that makes this connection directly is answer (D), which suggests that there are more "financial opportunities" (i.e., "richer") in large cities than in small towns. None of the other statements connect the issues of the argument as well or as directly as (D) does.

7. The correct answer is (C). In the statement, the mother implies that she knows when her daughter is or is not telling the truth. This is exactly the statement of answer (C), the best answer. Answer (A) is incorrect because it focuses on the mother's actions or statements and not those of the daughter. Answer (B) is incorrect because whether the daughter "knows" what a lie is does not directly address whether the daughter will or will not continue to tell lies. Answer (D), like answer (A), focuses on the mother's actions instead of the daughter's. Answer (E) is incorrect because the mother's belief about the future is irrelevant. The best answer is (C).

8. The correct answer is (A). The police official assumes that the cramped space will somehow contribute to attacks by prisoners. Answer (A) provides information that supports this assumption. Answer (B) goes too far beyond the scope of the argument because it is not necessary to assume that "all" criminals are dangerous. Answers (C), (D), and (E) are irrelevant to the issue of attacks on police officers.

9. The correct answer is (D). This argument assumes that homeowners can receive as much useful light using the same number of low-intensity bulbs as they can with standard bulbs. If, on the other hand, the bulbs were half as bright and required homeowners to use twice as many bulbs, then electric costs may not actually decrease. Answer (D) repeats this necessary assumption. Answer (A) seems an obvious truth, but it addresses a homeowner's motivation rather than the actual effect of using the low-intensity bulbs. Answers (B) and (E) address other effects of using the special bulbs but say nothing about electric bills. Answer (C) addresses lowering the cost of purchasing bulbs but not of using them.

CONCLUSION ANSWERS AND EXPLANATIONS

1. The correct answer is (B). The argument tells you that controlling inflation implies implementing wage controls, which in turn limit (i.e. "reduce") spending, which also reduces corporate profits. The question then asks you to consider that corporate profits are NOT decreasing. You can work backwards along the line of reasoning and see that if corporate profits are not decreasing, then spending must not be decreasing, and wage controls must not be in effect, so, therefore, inflation cannot be controlled. The best answer, the one that stays most closely to this line of reasoning, is answer (B), which connects the inflation to the idea of control. The other statements are all parts of the argument, but answer (B) is the best direct combination of the elements of the conclusion.

2. The correct answer is (D). The argument discusses the connection between the laws of probability and a belief in supernatural forces. The correct answer must connect these two parts of the argument. Answers (A) and (D) are the only statements that fit this requirement. Of these two, answer (D) is better because it stresses the "knowledge" of the laws of probability and the effect of that knowledge on a belief in supernatural activity. Answer (A) mentions the supernatural forces but does not say anything about a person's understanding of probability. The "understanding" or "knowledge" is the key to the conclusion, so the best answer is (D).

3. The correct answer is (D). The argument says two things about tips to cosmetologists—first, that patrons' tips are based on beliefs about other patrons, and second, that tips are based on beliefs about the cosmetologist's own wealth. Answer (D) is the best statement that combines the perceptions about these two elements, the other customers and the cosmetologist's own wealth. Answer (A) is incorrect because it too simply limits one of the issues. Answer (B) is incorrect because it mentions only the actual wealth and not the perception of wealth, which is really the key issue. Answer (C) is incorrect because it states the argument backward, which is not logically valid. Answer (E) is incorrect because, although it may be a true statement, it does not address the topics of the argument.

4. The correct answer is (D). The argument suggests that "previous experiences" aid in the appreciation of art and that "considerable time and effort" are necessary to understand art. Therefore, you are looking for a statement that connects the appreciation of art with the education or learning that leads to appreciation. Answer (A) is incorrect because it seems to negate this statement. Answer (B) is incorrect because it also, to a lesser degree, seems to contradict statements contained in the argument. Answer (C) is incorrect because it makes a statement that may be true but is irrelevant to this particular argument about education and appreciation. Answer (D) is the best answer because it combines the appreciation ("ability to enjoy") with the education ("preparation"). Answer (E) is incorrect because it states the idea of the argument in reverse.

5. The correct answer is (C). The argument says that different types of therapy produce the same results. The conclusion from this is that the type of therapy used will not affect the success of the result. In choosing an answer, you are looking for a statement that combines the consideration of the different therapy types with the fact that the result is the same for all. Answer (A) is incorrect because it does not mention the effectiveness of the result, only the types of therapy. Answer (B) is incorrect because it addresses only the effectiveness but ignores the fact that there are different types of therapy. Answer (C) correctly combines the different types of therapy with the effectiveness of the result. Answer (D) is irrelevant. Answer (E) adds a new element, the practitioner's experience, which is irrelevant to this argument. The best answer, therefore, is (C).

6. The correct answer is (E). The final statement of the argument says that the "offspring resisted the pesticide more effectively than did the parents." This presents the crux of the argument, that the ability to resist the pesticide is a genetic factor that is passed from parent to offspring. This is exactly the statement contained in answer (E). The other answers are all statements that may or may not be true, but they do not state the conclusion as clearly or as directly as (E).

7. The correct answer is (D). The argument does not say that "singularity" is either a good or bad concept, only that it "saves" effort for politicians, thereby making their jobs easier. Answer (A) is incorrect because it makes an unjustified judgment statement that similarity is "good." Answers (B) and (C) are incorrect because nothing in the problem says that identifying variations is difficult, even though it recognizes that the politicians' jobs would be made still easier without such a task. Answer (D) is the best answer because it recognizes that the key to the argument is the "ease" of the job. Answer (E) is incorrect because, like answer (A), it makes a judgment statement about whether certain activity is "just," but such a conclusion is not related to the problem.

8. The correct answer is (C). The main point of this argument is that herbivores produce protein more efficiently than carnivores. This is shown in the first sentence, that herbivores can create a pound of protein by using less intake than carnivores need. The correct answer choice, therefore, would be a statement that directly connects an herbivore with a carnivore. Answer (A) is close but incorrect because the argument focuses on efficiency, not on speed. Answer (B) is incorrect because nothing in the argument mentions the "food value," so this statement adds information that is outside the scope of the argument. Answer (C) is the best answer, directly juxtaposing the chicken (herbivore) with the tuna (carnivore). Answer (D) is incorrect because it ignores discussion of the efficiency of herbivores (and because it makes a statement that directly contradicts general knowledge of the definition of "carnivore"). Answer (E) is incorrect because the price of any type of food is not part of this argument.

9. The correct answer is (D). The beginning of this argument stresses the idea of a "stylish" person. The answer, therefore, should be a statement that contains the idea of stylishness. The only answer that mentions this concern is answer (D), which is the correct answer. The other answers are all statements that may be true statements, but they are not directly related to the argument as closely as statement (D).

Part III

PRACTICE TESTS

Now that you have reviewed all of the material in the previous section, it's time to test yourself on how much you actually learned. The five tests below are generic tests and contain all of the question types that you've reviewed. If you have the time, take each test on a separate day, but check your answers immediately following your completion of each test so that the material will be fresh in your mind. If you are successful on these tests, it means that you have truly understood the material in this book. On the other hand, if you had more than 10 percent wrong, then it makes sense to go back and review the previous chapters. A complete understanding of this material should bode well for you on any of the graduate exams: GRE, GMAT, and LSAT.

PRACTICE TEST 1

The following passage applies to Questions 1–5

Six people—Graham, Helen, Irving, Johnny, Kevin, and Louise—enter an elevator on the ground floor, with higher floors numbered 1 through 6. The elevator passengers select their floors and the elevator begins rising. Whenever the elevator stops, someone gets off. Nobody else gets on the elevator at any time. Everyone will exit the elevator on one of the six numbered floors, but no more than two will get off at any one floor. The following rules are true:

Graham gets out before Johnny.
If Helen leaves the elevator on Level 3, then Graham will also get out on Level 3.
Irving gets out on either Level 1 or Level 6.
Johnny and Kevin will not get out at the same floor.

1. If all six people get out on separate floors, then which of the following could be the order in which they leave the elevator, from first to last?

   (A) Graham, Johnny, Helen, Kevin, Louise, Irving
   (B) Johnny, Helen, Graham, Louise, Kevin, Irving
   (C) Helen, Graham, Johnny, Kevin, Irving, Louise
   (D) Graham, Louise, Kevin, Helen, Johnny, Irving
   (E) Irving, Helen, Louise, Johnny, Kevin, Graham

2. If Graham gets out on Level 4, which of the following is a complete list of people who could get out on Level 3?

   (A) Johnny and Louise
   (B) Kevin and Louise
   (C) Helen and Louise
   (D) Helen and Kevin
   (E) Helen, Johnny, Kevin, and Louise

3. If Graham and Irving leave the elevator together, which of the following statements must be true?

   (A) Kevin and Louise get out together.
   (B) David gets out alone.
   (C) Helen gets out at Level 4.
   (D) Graham gets out at Level 1.
   (E) Nobody gets out at Level 3.

4. If nobody gets out of the elevator on either Level 1 or Level 2, which of the following could be true?

   (A) Graham and Irving get out on Level 4.
   (B) Helen and Johnny get out on Level 3.
   (C) Graham and Johnny get out on Level 6.
   (D) Kevin gets out alone on Level 5.
   (E) Louise gets out alone on Level 6.

5. If Helen and Irving each get out of the elevator alone, which of the following must be true?

   (A) Irving gets out on Level 6.
   (B) Johnny and Kevin get out on Level 3.
   (C) Helen does not get out on Level 3.
   (D) Graham gets out first.
   (E) Kevin and Louise both get out on Level 5.

6. Sixty-five percent of the graduating class of Hamilton High School, a public high school in the middle of the city, will go on to attend college after graduation. The Harris Academy High School, an expensive private school in the same area, will send approximately 95 percent of its graduates to college. Many parents, realizing this information, believe that sending their children to Harris Academy High School will mean that their children will get a better education than they would get at Hamilton High School.

Which of the following statements, if true, would most indicate the flaws in the parents' reasoning?

(A) Until 1992, Harris Academy High School was exclusively a girls' school, but Hamilton High School has always been coeducational.

(B) Harris Academy High School requires students to pass an admission examination before entering, but Hamilton High School admits all applicants who live in the city.

(C) Hamilton High School has problems with severe student violence during school hours.

(D) Harris Academy High School has a higher percentage of students attending Ivy League colleges than any other high school in the state.

(E) Hamilton High School receives its funding from local property taxes, while Harris Academy High School receives funding from tuition costs and from alumni donations.

7. A poll of all voters in the state shows that only 9 percent of all people who voted were younger than 25 years old. Based on this result, many people have drawn the conclusion that young Americans are not as interested in voting as older generations are. This conclusion becomes troublesome when considered in contrast to the percentages of young people who participate in other activities.

Which of the following statements, if true, would most seriously weaken this author's conclusion?

(A) The number of voters in the state under the age of 25 has increased for each of the past five years.

(B) The average age of all voters in the state is 60 years old.

(C) Of all people in the state who are old enough to vote, only 13 percent are younger than 25 years old.

(D) Most of the voters in the state are registered as either Democrats or Republicans, but the winning candidate is an Independent.

(E) The total number of voters this year was the lowest it has been in 10 years.

8. Educational research has demonstrated a positive correlation between high scores on a certain standardized admission test and a student's probability of graduating from college. Over the past 10 years, more girls from New England high schools have graduated from college than from any other part of the country. Therefore, girls from New England high schools must be the group of students with the highest scores on the standardized admission test.

The structure of the argument above is most like the structure of which of the following arguments?

(A) Most modern famous musicians get their start in very good high school music programs. More great jazz trumpeters have come from New Orleans than any other part of the country. Therefore, one can conclude that high schools in New Orleans have the best music programs.

(B) More famous chefs work in San Francisco than in any other major city in the United States. As a result, one can conclude that San Francisco has more cooking schools than any other major city in the country.

(C) Students from New England attend Ivy League universities more than state universities, while students in the Midwest are more likely to attend state universities. Therefore, the students in New England must have higher standardized test scores.

(D) The states in the southern half of the United States are less likely to have snow than the states in the northern half of the country. Therefore, most Olympic skiers must have lived in the northern half of the country.

(E) Women who have had two or more children are much less likely to develop medical problems late in life than women who have had no children. As a result, if the population continues to increase, the average age of women in the country will also increase.

The following passage applies to Questions 9–14

Seven people, Steve, Tom, Unger, Violet, Willy, Xania, and Yolanda, are riding the late train home after work. They all leave the train at different stops, according to the following conditions:

> Steve leaves the train before Unger.
> Violet and Tom both leave after Unger.
> Willy leaves the train third.

9. Which of the following could be the order in which passengers leave the train, from first to last?

(A) Steve, Xania, Willy, Violet, Yolanda, Unger, Tom

(B) Yolanda, Steve, Unger, Violet, Tom, Willy, Xania

(C) Xania, Steve, Willy, Unger, Yolanda, Tom, Violet

(D) Tom, Xania, Willy, Steve, Unger, Yolanda, Violet

(E) Xania, Yolanda, Willy, Steve, Tom, Unger, Violet

10. All of the following could be the order in which the passengers leave the train, from first to last, EXCEPT:

(A) Steve, Xania, Willy, Unger, Yolanda, Violet, Tom

(B) Xania, Yolanda, Willy, Steve, Unger, Tom, Violet

(C) Yolanda, Steve, Willy, Xania, Violet, Tom, Unger

(D) Xania, Yolanda, Willy, Steve, ~~Henry~~ Unger, Violet, Tom.

(E) Steve, Unger, Willy, Tom, Xania, Violet, Yolanda

11. Which of the following could never be the last one off the train?

(A) Tom
(B) Unger
(C) Violet
(D) Xania
(E) Yolanda

12. Which of the following is a complete list of everyone who could NOT be the first person off the train?

(A) Tom, Unger, Violet
(B) Steve, Tom, Unger
(C) Steve, Tom, Unger, Violet
(D) Tom, Unger, Violet, Willy
(E) Tom, Unger, Violet, Willy, Xania

13. If Willy leaves the train before both Unger and Xania, which of the following statements must be true?

(A) Xania leaves the train last.
(B) Yolanda leaves the train after Steve.
(C) Tom and Xania both leave the train after Unger.
(D) Tom and Violet both leave the train after Yolanda.
(E) Steve leaves the train first.

14. If Steve is not the first person to leave the train, which of the following statements must be false?

(A) Unger leaves the train before Willy.
(B) Tom leaves the train after Xania.
(C) Xania leaves the train before both Willy and Yolanda.
(D) Willy leaves the train before both Tom and Violet.
(E) Tom leaves the train last.

The following passage applies to Questions 15–18

Six people, Alan, Betty, Charles, David, Elmer, and Faith, compete in a cooking contest at the county fair. Their finishing positions at the end of the contest are as follows:

Alan finishes neither first nor last.
Betty finishes ahead of both Charles and David.
Elmer finishes in third place.

15. Which of the following could be the finishing order of the six contestants, from first place to last?

(A) Betty, Faith, Elmer, Alan, David, Charles
(B) Betty, Elmer, Charles, David, Alan, Faith
(C) Alan, Faith, Elmer, Betty, Charles, David
(D) Faith, Charles, Elmer, Betty, Alan, David
(E) Betty, Faith, Elmer, Charles, David, Alan

16. All of the following could be a complete and accurate list of the finishing order of the six contestants EXCEPT:

    (A) Betty, Faith, Elmer, Alan, David, Charles
    (B) Betty, Alan, Elmer, Faith, Charles, David
    (C) Faith, Alan, Elmer, David, Charles, Betty
    (D) Faith, Betty, Elmer, Alan, Charles, David
    (E) Betty, David, Elmer, Charles, Alan, Faith

17. Which of the following is a complete and accurate list of all contestants who could finish first?

    (A) Betty or Elmer
    (B) Betty or Faith
    (C) Betty, Charles, or David
    (D) Betty, Charles, or Faith
    (E) Betty, Charles, David, or Faith

18. Which of the contestants could finish either first or last?

    (A) Betty
    (B) Charles
    (C) David
    (D) Elmer
    (E) Faith

The following passage applies to Questions 19–22

An office director is selecting employees to attend two different combinations of meetings at a conference, Meeting Package A and Meeting Package B. Each Meeting Package must have four members, selected from a group of five accountants, Ed, Frank, Gina, Holly, and Ilsa, and five managers, Lisa, Marvin, Nancy, Oliver, and Paula. In selecting Meeting Package members, the director must follow these guidelines:

> Each Meeting Package must have exactly four employees.
>
> No employee may be chosen for both Meeting Packages at the same time.
>
> Meeting Package A may not have more managers than accountants.
>
> Meeting Package B may not have more accountants than managers.
>
> Ed and Lisa may not be chosen for the same Meeting Package.
>
> Frank may only be chosen for Meeting Package A.
>
> If Gina is chosen for Meeting Package A, then Holly must be chosen for Meeting Package A.
>
> If Holly is chosen for Meeting Package B, then Gina must be chosen for Meeting Package B.
>
> If Paula is chosen for either Meeting Package, then Ilsa may not be chosen for either Meeting Package.

19. Which of the following could be a complete and accurate list of the employees chosen for the two Meeting Packages?

	Meeting Package A	Meeting Package B
(A)	Ed, Ilsa, Nancy, Oliver	Frank, Holly, Gina, Paula
(B)	Ed, Holly, Marvin, Nancy	Lisa, Gina, Oliver, Paula
(C)	Gina, Marvin, Oliver, Frank	Ilsa, Lisa, Nancy, Holly
(D)	Frank, Lisa, Marvin, Nancy	Ed, Gina, Oliver, Paula
(E)	Ilsa, Frank, Nancy, Oliver	Ed, Marvin, Gina, Holly

20. If Holly is chosen for Meeting Package B, which of the following must be true?

(A) Lisa must be chosen for Meeting Package B.
(B) Lisa and Marvin must both be chosen for Meeting Package B.
(C) Paula may not be chosen for Meeting Package A.
(D) Ed may not be chosen for Meeting Package B.
(E) Lisa may not be chosen for Meeting Package A.

21. If Ed is not chosen for either Meeting Package, then which of the following MUST be chosen?

    I. Lisa
    II. Holly
    III. Frank
    IV. Nancy

(A) I and II
(B) I and III
(C) I, II, and IV
(D) II, III, and IV
(E) I, II, III, and IV

22. Who may NOT be chosen for Meeting Package B together with Holly?

(A) Gina and Nancy
(B) Marvin and Oliver
(C) Ed and Paula
(D) Paula and Lisa
(E) Lisa and ~~Nancy~~ Nancy

23. An advertisement on a billboard displays the message to passing motorists, "Honk if you don't use Blind-O Window Cleaner." Based on this advertisement, which of the following statements can be concluded?

(A) A driver who reads the sign and then honks in response to it must not use Blind-O Window Cleaner.
(B) A driver who does not use Blind-O Window Cleaner will not honk after reading the sign.
(C) Based on this advertisement, it is impossible to determine a motorist's use of Blind-O Window Cleaner if that motorist does not honk after reading the sign.
(D) If a driver uses Blind-O Window Cleaner, he or she will not honk after reading the sign.
(E) A driver who reads the sign and then does not honk must not use Blind-O Window Cleaner.

24. In 1994, Tom bought a new foreign-import automobile. In 1996, the electrical system in Tom's car developed severe problems that required expensive repairs. Now Tom has concluded that the manufacturer of his automobile makes cars of inferior quality, and he refuses ever to buy another car from that manufacturer again.

Which of the following statements represents Tom's major assumption?

(A) Once a car's electrical system breaks down, it can never be repaired adequately so that it functions as well as it did before the problem occurred.

(B) Cars are not built as well in 1996 as they were in 1994.

(C) Domestic cars are more reliable than import cars.

(D) The problems that occurred to Tom's car are representative of what will happen with all cars from the same manufacturer.

(E) From one year to the next, manufacturers do not usually make complete changes in the electrical systems they put in the cars they make.

25. Two Congressmen were both elected in the same year. Since their election, Representative Smith has always voted exactly the same as Representative Brown on every issue. Representative Brown has just been recalled by his district and will be replaced by newly elected Representative Jones. Therefore, it is clear that Representative Smith should also be recalled and replaced.

Which of the following statements, if true, would most strengthen the above argument?

(A) Representative Smith has radical ideas that are very different from the views of the great majority of the voters in his district.

(B) Representative Smith is a Republican, but Representative Brown is a Democrat.

(C) Representative Smith and Representative Brown were both elected from the same district.

(D) Representative Smith and Representative Brown were elected from different districts.

(E) Representative Smith's age is closer to the average age of the voters in his district than Representative Brown's is to the age of the voters in his own district.

PRACTICE TEST 2

The following passage applies to Questions 1–5

Six newspapers, the *Globe*, the *Tattler*, the *Imprint*, the *Newsmag*, the *Spectator*, and the *Dialer*, compete for subscription customers in a large city. The following information has been found to be true about the circulation of the six newspapers:

The *Tattler* has more subscribers than any other newspaper.

The *Imprint* has more subscribers than the *Globe*.

The *Newsmag* has more subscribers than at least two other papers.

Whenever the *Imprint* gets more subscribers than the *Spectator*, then the *Dialer* will also have more subscribers than the *Spectator*.

No two newspapers ever have the same number of subscribers.

1. Which of the following is a possible listing of the six newspapers in order from fewest subscribers to most?

    (A) *Globe, Newsmag, Spectator, Imprint, Dialer, Tattler*
    (B) *Imprint, Dialer, Spectator, Globe, Newsmag, Tattler*
    (C) *Newsmag, Spectator, Dialer, Globe, Imprint, Tattler*
    (D) *Spectator, Dialer, Newsmag, Globe, Imprint, Tattler*
    (E) *Dialer, Spectator, Newsmag, Globe, Imprint, Tattler*

2. Which of the following newspapers could have the fewest subscribers?

    I.   *Spectator*
    II. *Globe*
    III. *Newsmag*
    IV. *Dialer*

    (A) I and II
    (B) II and III
    (C) I, II, and III
    (D) I, III, and IV
    (E) I, II, and IV

3. If *Spectator* has more subscribers than *Dialer*, then which of the following statements must be true?

    (A) *Globe* has the fewest subscribers.
    (B) *Newsmag* has more subscribers than exactly three other newspapers.
    (C) *Spectator* has more subscribers than *Imprint*.
    (D) *Spectator* has the second most subscribers.
    (E) *Dialer* has the third most subscribers.

4. If the *Globe* has the fourth most subscribers, then which of the following statements could be false?

    (A) *Dialer* has the fifth most subscriptions.
    (B) *Spectator* has the fewest subscriptions.
    (C) *Newsmag* has more subscriptions than *Globe*.
    (D) *Imprint* has more subscriptions than any paper except *Tattler*.
    (E) *Imprint* has more subscriptions than *Dialer*.

5. If only two newspapers had lower circulations than *Imprint*, all of the following could be true EXCEPT:

(A) *Newsmag* has the second most subscriptions.

(B) *Globe* has the fewest subscriptions.

(C) *Globe* has more subscriptions than *Dialer*.

(D) *Globe* has more subscriptions than *Newsmag*.

(E) *Newsmag* has fewer subscriptions than *Spectator*.

Questions 6 and 7 are based on the following statements:

Since the late 1970s, the rate of inflation in the United States has declined at an impressive rate. However, over the same period of time, incidents of violent crime in the nation's largest cities have been growing worse, with the number of murders and assaults increasing steadily. In order to solve this problem, the Federal Reserve needs to act immediately to return our inflation rate to the same level we had in 1979.

6. Which of the following does the author assume in making the above argument?

I. The crime rate in the nation's largest cities is inversely related to the nation's inflation rate.

II. Inflation is the unwanted result of a number of economic factors and has many negative effects on consumers.

III. The Federal Reserve has the ability to take certain actions, and those actions can affect the nation's inflation rate.

(A) II only

(B) I and II

(C) I and III

(D) II and III

(E) I, II, and III

7. Which of the following statements, if true, would most seriously weaken the above argument?

(A) Recent legislation passed by Congress removes the powers of the Federal Reserve to act alone without approval of the President.

(B) In 1985, both the nation's inflation rate and the crime rate were higher than they are now and higher than they were in 1979.

(C) Crimes that occur in New York City are generally more violent and more repugnant to society than crimes that occur in more rural communities.

(D) The inflation rate declined faster in the 1980s than it has in the 1990s.

(E) In some parts of the country, serious crime is almost nonexistent and has never been a problem.

8. Many states have recently passed versions of a law commonly referred to as "Megan's Law." This law requires individuals who have been convicted of sexual abuse of women or children to notify the local police and certain other agencies upon moving into a new community. As a result of this law, we can now expect repeat offenses of such sexual abuse to decrease significantly.

Which of the following statements could proponents of "Megan's Law" use to reinforce the conclusion of this argument?

(A) Children do not usually fabricate reports of sexual abuse, so the conviction rate for identified suspects in this area is much higher than for other crimes.

(B) Sociologists have conducted studies that show that people generally prefer not to live in communities where they know that convicted criminals may be living.

(C) Experimental programs requiring people convicted of drunk driving to use special license plates identifying them have resulted in much lower rates of repeat drunk driving offenses.

(D) When members of a community are informed of the identity of someone convicted of sex-related crimes, those community members become more careful to protect their children and to avoid contact with that person.

(E) Nationally, the rate of child abuse has been steadily declining since the mid-1980s.

The following passage applies to Questions 9–14

Main Street runs from west to east through the business district of downtown Applebury. In one block of Main Street, there are five buildings on the north side of the street, numbered from 1 to 5 consecutively from west to east, and five buildings on the south side of the street, numbered from 6 to 10 consecutively from west to east. The zoning commission for Applebury has to place seven stores, named ABC Learning, Bell Bottom Jeans, Cat Supplies Plus, Danny's Hobbies, Everything's Roses, Frank's Auto, and "Gotta Dance" Studio, in the shops on Main Street according to the following conditions:

> ABC Learning and Cat Supplies Plus may not be on the same side of the street.
>
> Neither Cat Supplies Plus nor Everything's Roses may be adjacent to Frank's Auto.
>
> Bell Bottom Jeans and Danny's Hobbies must be on opposite ends of the same side of the street.
>
> Danny's Hobbies and Everything's Roses are both in odd-numbered buildings.
>
> Frank's Auto is in Building 7.

9. Which of the following could be a list of stores on the north side of Main Street, from Building 1 to Building 5?

   (A) Everything's Roses, "Gotta Dance" Studio, empty, ABC Learning, Danny's Hobbies

   (B) "Gotta Dance" Studio, Cat Supplies Plus, empty, ABC Learning, Everything's Roses

   (C) Bell Bottom Jeans, ABC Learning, Cat Supplies Plus, empty, Danny's Hobbies

   (D) Danny's Hobbies, empty, Cat Supplies Plus, "Gotta Dance" Studio, Bell Bottom Jeans

   (E) empty, Danny's Hobbies, empty, "Gotta Dance" Studio, Everything's Roses

10. Which of the following could be a list of stores on the south side of Main Street, from Building 6 to Building 10?

    (A) "Gotta Dance" Studio, Frank's Auto, ABC Learning, empty, Cat Supplies Plus

    (B) Bell Bottom Jeans, Frank's Auto, ABC Learning, "Gotta Dance" Studio, Danny's Hobbies

    (C) ABC Learning, Frank's Auto, empty, empty, Cat Supplies Plus

    (D) Danny's Hobbies, Frank's Auto, "Gotta Dance" Studio, Everything's Roses, ABC Learning

    (E) "Gotta Dance" Studio, Frank's Auto, Cat Supplies Plus, empty, ABC Learning

11. If neither Building 6 nor Building 8 is left vacant, which of the following statements must be true?

    (A) ABC Learning is in Building 6.

    (B) Cat Supplies Plus is in Building 10.

    (C) There are more vacant buildings on the north side of Main Street than on the south side.

    (D) Building 9 is left vacant.

    (E) Building 10 is left vacant.

12. If Everything's Roses and Frank's Auto are on opposite sides of the street, then which of the following statements must be false?

    (A) Building 3 is left vacant.

    (B) ABC Learning is in Building 8.

    (C) Building 9 is left vacant.

    (D) Cat Supplies Plus is in Building 10.

    (E) Bell Bottom Jeans is in Building 5.

13. If ABC Learning and Frank's Auto are on opposite sides of Main Street, then which of the following statements could be false?

    (A) Cat Supplies Plus is on the south side of Main Street.

    (B) Everything's Roses is in Building 9.

    (C) Either Building 6 or Building 8 is left vacant.

    (D) At most, two stores on the north side are left vacant.

    (E) ABC Learning is in a lower-numbered store than Cat Supplies Plus.

14. Which of the following situations is/are impossible under the given conditions?

    I.   All stores on the north side of Main Street may be occupied.

    II.   All stores on the south side of Main Street may be occupied.

    III.   All even-numbered stores may be occupied.

(A) I only
(B) II only
(C) III only
(D) I and II only
(E) II and III only

The following passage applies to Questions 15–18

Six students of foreign languages, Annie, Betty, Clinton, Dennis, Edmund, and Frieda, are seated together. They do not all speak the same language, but enough of them speak the same languages that they can translate for each other.

    Annie and Dennis speak only English, French, and Spanish.
    Betty speaks only English, French, and Swedish.
    Clinton speaks only German and Spanish.
    Edmund speaks only Spanish.
    Frieda speaks only Swedish.

15. Which language is spoken by the most students?

(A) English
(B) French
(C) German
(D) Spanish
(E) Swedish

16. Which of the following students could talk to each other without a translator?

(A) Annie and Frieda
(B) Betty and Clinton
(C) Betty and Edmund
(D) Edmund and Frieda
(E) Betty and Frieda

17. Who could act as a translator for a conversation between Betty and Clinton?

    I.   Annie
    II.   Dennis
    III.   Edmund
    IV.   Frieda

(A) I only
(B) I and II
(C) I, II, and III
(D) II, III, and IV
(E) I, II, and IV

18. If Clinton and Frieda wish to talk to each other, what is the fewest number of translators they would need?

(A) 0
(B) 1
(C) 2
(D) 3
(E) 4

The following passage applies to Questions 19–22

At a summer camp, the campers play a game called "Capture the Flag." To play the game, the campground is divided into two halves by a border line that runs from north to south, cutting the camp exactly in half. Team A is on the west side of the line, and Team B is on the east side of the line. A total of 10 safe bases, called "outposts," are evenly divided between the two teams on their own side of the dividing line and are placed as follows:

Outposts 1, 2, and 3 belong to Team A.

Outposts 4, 5, and 6 belong to Team B.

Outpost 1 is farther north than any other outpost.

Outpost 6 is farther south than any other outpost.

Outpost 7 is farther west than any other outpost.

Outpost 10 is farther east than any other outpost.

Outpost 5 is due east of Outpost 2.

19. Which of the following could be a complete list of Team A's outposts?

   (A) 1, 2, 3, 4, 10
   (B) 1, 2, 5, 7, 9
   (C) 1, 2, 3, 5, 7
   (D) 1, 2, 3, 7, 9
   (E) 1, 2, 3, 9, 10

20. Which of the following could be a complete list of Team B's outposts?

   (A) 4, 5, 7, 9, 10
   (B) 4, 5, 6, 8, 10
   (C) 4, 5, 6, 7, 9
   (D) 4, 5, 6, 8, 9
   (E) 4, 5, 6, 7, 8

21. If Outpost 8 is the northern most outpost on its side of the border, then which of the following must be false?

   (A) Outpost 8 is farther north than Outpost 2.
   (B) Outpost 3 is south of Outpost 8.
   (C) Outpost 8 is east of Outpost 5.
   (D) Outpost 8 belongs to Team A.
   (E) Outpost 9 belongs to Team A.

22. If exactly three outposts are north of Outpost 7, then which of the following could be true?

   (A) Outpost 8 and Outpost 9 belong to the same team.
   (B) Outposts 2 and 8 are north of Outpost 7.
   (C) Outposts 4 and 5 are north of Outpost 7.
   (D) Outposts 1 and 5 are north of Outpost 8.
   (E) Outpost 7 is the northern most outpost on its side of the border.

23. Polling data collected from a broad range of people living in this country has allowed sociologists and societal anthropologists to conclude that special circumstances, usually arising from financial desperation, sometimes cause unethical or illegal behavior in individuals who otherwise would not undertake such activities. Small-business men on the verge of bankruptcy may skim cash or withhold payments to the IRS, for example.

Which of the following can be concluded from the above statement?

(A) Bankruptcy is a bad situation, which people should try to avoid at all costs.

(B) An otherwise lawful citizen who has become recently unemployed may turn to robbery as a method of raising money.

(C) The federal budget is compiled each year based on an assumption that the IRS does collect all the money that is required by the current federal tax code.

(D) Business ethics is a subject that should be taught to all students in business schools throughout the country.

(E) Desperation is a psychological problem that can be cured by attending regular therapy sessions with a counselor.

24. Fossil collections in various archaeological retrieval sites around the world have shown scientists that the first creatures resembling modern man originally appeared on earth between 3 million and 4 million years ago. The species called *Homo erectus* first appeared approximately 2 million years later and survived, scientists believe, until about 1 million years ago. It is easy to see, therefore, that the species identified as "neanderthals" must have appeared sometime more than 1 million years ago.

Which of the following statements does the author of the above passage assume?

(A) Fossil collecting is the most efficient method for determining details about the history of the human species on Earth.

(B) Carbon dating is an effective and scientifically accurate method of measuring the age of human fossils.

(C) *Homo erectus* is an ancestor of the current human species of *Homo sapiens*.

(D) Neanderthals and *Homo erectus* are both ancestor species of today's common man.

(E) *Homo erectus* and the neanderthals both lived on Earth at the same time.

25. An effective resume, containing accurate information and clearly presented details about a person's education and business experience, is often the best method of obtaining a job in sales. Many job applicants, however, have the bad habit of sending a resume with no cover letter at all. As a result, their resumes are frequently discarded without being considered at all.

Which of the following statements, if true, would most weaken the conclusion of the above statement?

(A) A survey of people in charge of hiring sales personnel reveals that most of them never read letters of introduction accompanying resumes.

(B) A career in a sales position is very limiting and affords the employee very little ability to grow or improve.

(C) A resume is not always required when applying for a job in a sales-related field.

(D) Many personnel offices prefer to meet applicants directly before considering their qualifications for employment.

(E) Some studies have shown that resumes copied onto colored paper result in higher rates of success than resumes copied onto plain white paper.

PRACTICE TEST 3

The following passage applies to Questions 1–5

A city park is designed with limited walkways to direct visitors to certain points of interest. After traveling from one location to another, visitors may not travel backward to the previous area. Everyone will enter the park at either the Waterfall or the Sandbox. After entering the park, the following possibilities arise:

From the Waterfall, visitors may go to the Petting Zoo or the Swingset. From the Sandbox, visitors may go to the Swingset or the Softball Field. From the Swingset, visitors may go to the Petting Zoo, the Softball Field, or the Picnic Area.

From the Petting Zoo, visitors may go to the Softball Field or the Exit. From the Softball Field, visitors may go to the Picnic Area, the Parking Lot, or the Exit. From the Picnic Area, visitors may go to the Parking Lot or the Exit. From the Parking Lot, visitors must go to the Exit.

1. If a visitor enters the park at the Waterfall, which of the following statements must be true?

   (A) The visitor will visit the Sandbox.
   (B) The visitor will not visit the Picnic Area.
   (C) The visitor will visit the Swingset before the Softball Field.
   (D) The visitor will visit at least two different areas.
   (E) The visitor will visit at most five different areas.

2. If a visitor enters the park at the Sandbox, what is the maximum number of different areas the visitor may visit?

   (A) 3
   (B) 4
   (C) 5
   (D) 6
   (E) 7

3. If the visitor goes to the Picnic Area last before exiting, which of the following statements must be false?

   (A) The visitor entered at the Sandbox.
   (B) The visitor will not visit the Petting Zoo.
   (C) The visitor will visit the Softball Field.
   (D) The visitor will not visit the Softball Field.
   (E) The visitor will visit the Parking Lot.

4. If a visitor is at the Softball Field, which of the following statements could be true?

   (A) The visitor may visit three more areas after the Softball Field.
   (B) The visitor may visit four more areas after the Softball Field.
   (C) The visitor may visit both the Parking Lot and the Picnic Area.
   (D) The visitor has already visited four different areas.
   (E) The visitor has already visited both the Swingset and the Picnic Area.

5. Which of the following is a possible listing of areas visited, in order from first to last?

   (A) Waterfall, Swingset, Petting Zoo, Softball Field, Parking Lot
   (B) Waterfall, Petting Zoo, Swingset, Picnic Area, Parking Lot
   (C) Waterfall, Softball Field, Swingset, Picnic Area, Parking Lot
   (D) Sandbox, Swingset, Picnic Area, Softball Field, Parking Lot
   (E) Sandbox, Softball Field, Picnic Area, Parking Lot, Petting Zoo

6. Michael always takes his dog out for a walk in the morning before sunrise unless the sun rises before 6:00 a.m. Steve does not walk his own dog before Michael does if Michael walks his dog before sunrise.

On a day when the sun rises at 5:30 a.m., which of the following must be true?

(A) Michael will walk his dog before sunrise.
(B) Steve will not walk his dog in the morning.
(C) Steve will not walk his dog before Michael does.
(D) Michael will not walk his dog before sunrise.
(E) Michael and Steve will both walk their dogs at the same time.

7. More people are going out to eat than ever before. This must be true, since the number of Greek restaurants in major cities in the United States has increased in recent years.

For the above conclusion to be correct, which of the following assumptions must be true?

(A) The increase in the number of Greek restaurants does not coincide with a decrease in other restaurants.
(B) The number of restaurants in any major city remains relatively constant.
(C) Greek restaurants are more popular nationwide than any other ethnic restaurant.
(D) Unemployment rates have declined, so more people can afford to go out to eat.
(E) New restaurants open only when existing restaurants are filled to their capacity.

8. Famous sports figures can earn several million dollars each year in royalties and license agreements for endorsing products. The salary of the Chief Justice of the United States is only $200,000 each year, although the Chief Justice's term of office is unlimited. Based on this information, the Chief Justice can never earn more than a sports figure.

Which of the following statements, if true, would most weaken the above argument?

(A) No law prevents the Chief Justice from endorsing any products.
(B) Not all product endorsements for which people sign contracts are actually used in the sale of merchandise.
(C) The Chief Justice's term is unlimited.
(D) Congress determines the Chief Justice's salary by law.
(E) Some sports figures are more famous than others.

Peterson's Logic & Reading Review

The following passage applies to Questions 9–14

Six different students—Adam, Ben, Carl, David, Edgar, and Frank—compete in a "homework race" in which the student with the most completed homework assignments is said to finish the race first and the student with the fewest completed homework assignments is said to finish the race last. The other students are ranked between first and last according to the number of completed homework assignments. The following statements are all true about the results of the homework race:

> Ben finished either immediately before or immediately after David.
> Edgar finished third.
> Adam did not finish last.
> There were no ties.

9. Which of the following is a possible order of the students, from first to last?

(A) Adam, Edgar, Ben, David, Frank, Carl

(B) Ben, David, Edgar, Frank, Carl, Adam

(C) David, Adam, Edgar, Ben, Carl, Frank

(D) Frank, Adam, Edgar, David, Carl, Ben

(E) Carl, Adam, Edgar, Frank, David, Ben

10. All of the following are possible orders of the students, from first to last, EXCEPT:

(A) Adam, Ben, David, Edgar, Carl, Frank

(B) Carl, Frank, Edgar, Adam, David, Ben

(C) Frank, Adam, Edgar, Ben, David, Carl

(D) David, Ben, Edgar, Frank, Adam, Carl

(E) Ben, David, Edgar, Carl, Adam, Frank

11. If Adam finishes fifth, which of the following must be true?

(A) Frank must finish either first or last.

(B) Carl must finish either second or fourth.

(C) David must finish either first or second.

(D) Ben must finish either first or third.

(E) Edgar must finish last.

12. If Edgar finishes before Ben, which of the following must be false?

(A) Adam finishes first.

(B) Adam finishes fifth.

(C) Carl finishes second.

(D) Frank finishes second.

(E) Carl finishes last.

13. Which of the following is a complete list of all students who could finish last?

(A) Carl, Frank

(B) Ben, David, Frank

(C) Ben, Carl, Edgar, Frank

(D) Ben, Carl, David, Frank

(E) Adam, Ben, Carl, David, Frank

14. If David finishes first, which of the following could be true?

(A) Carl and Frank finish before Adam.

(B) Edgar finishes before Ben.

(C) Adam finishes before Ben and Frank.

(D) Frank finishes before Adam and Carl.

(E) Carl finishes before Adam and Edgar.

The following passage applies to Questions 15–18

Eight children, Kathy, Leroy, Marion, Nate, Ophelia, Peter, Quint, and Robert, are seated in two rows in an auditorium. Four children are in the front row, and four children are in the back row. The seats in each row are numbered 1 through 4 from left to right. The following statements are all true about the seating arrangement:

Kathy must sit in the front row.
Leroy may not sit either directly next to or directly in front or in back of Marion.
Ophelia and Peter must sit somewhere to the right of Kathy.
Quint must sit in Seat 2 of the back row.

15. All of the following are possible presentations of the seating arrangement EXCEPT:

	Front Row	**Back Row**
(A)	Kathy, Marion, Nate, Peter	Robert, Quint, Ophelia, Leroy
(B)	Leroy, Kathy, Ophelia, Robert	Nate, Quint, Marion, Peter
(C)	Kathy, Marion, Nate, Robert	Leroy, Quint, Ophelia, Peter
(D)	Kathy, Peter, Leroy, Robert	Nate, Quint, Marion, Ophelia
(E)	Marion, Kathy, Peter, Nate	Robert, Quint, Ophelia, Leroy

16. If Marion sits in Seat 2 in the front row, then which of the following must be false?

(A) Nate is in Seat 1 in the second row.

(B) Peter and Ophelia both sit directly next to Quint.

(C) Kathy is in Seat 1 in the front row.

(D) Leroy sits in the back row.

(E) Robert and Kathy both sit in the front row.

17. If Ophelia and Peter sit next to each other in the front row, then all of the following could be true EXCEPT:

(A) Leroy sits directly in front of Quint.

(B) Marion sits directly in back of Ophelia.

(C) Quint sits directly in back of Kathy.

(D) Robert sits between Kathy and Ophelia.

(E) Marion and Leroy sit left of Quint.

18. If Kathy and Nate are both in Seat 3s, then which of the following could be false?

(A) Richard is in Seat 1 in the front row.
(B) Peter is in Seat 4 in either row.
(C) Leroy is in Seat 2 in the front row.
(D) Kathy is in the front row.
(E) Nate and Quint are in the same row.

The following passage applies to Questions 19–22

A secret code consists only of combinations of the numbers from 1 through 5. All words in the code must meet the following requirements:

> Any code word must have at least three numbers but no more than five numbers.
>
> Code words do not need to use different numbers unless otherwise required below.
>
> All code words must begin with the number 1.
>
> 4 may not be the last number in a code word.
>
> If 5 is the last number in a code word, then the word must have at least one 4.
>
> If 2 is the second number in a code word, then 2 must also be the last number.
>
> The number 1 can only appear once in a code word.

19. Which of the following is a possible code word?

(A) 1 3 3 2
(B) 1 4 1 4
(C) 1 2 2 3
(D) 4 1 3 5
(E) 1 3 5 5

20. Which numbers may not be the only numbers used in a three-number code word?

(A) 1 and 2
(B) 1, 2, and 4
(C) 1, 2, and 5
(D) 1 and 5
(E) 1 and 3

21. How many different three-number code words can be made using only the numbers 1, 2, and 3?

(A) 2
(B) 3
(C) 4
(D) 5
(E) 6

22. If a word ends with the number 5, which of the following must be true?

(A) The word must contain at least four numbers.
(B) 2 is not the second number.
(C) 3 is not the third number.
(D) 1 is the fourth number.
(E) 4 appears twice in the word.

23. Any movie starring Robert Redford will win an Academy Award, but no movie starring Robert Redford will ever earn more than $5 million from ticket sales. Some movies that earn more than $5 million from ticket sales are directed by Steven Spielberg.

Which of the following conclusions must be true, based on the above statements?

(A) No movie directed by Steven Spielberg will win an Academy Award.

(B) Some movies directed by Steven Spielberg may star Robert Redford.

(C) Some movies earning more than $5 million in ticket sales may star Robert Redford.

(D) No movie starring Robert Redford will win an Academy Award.

(E) All movies directed by Steven Spielberg will win an Academy Award.

24. Frederic Chopin is the greatest piano composer who ever lived. After all, more different musical variations have been based on the "Prelude in A," Chopin's most famous piano theme, than on any other musical theme ever written.

Which of the following assumptions is indicated in the above argument?

(A) Only musical Preludes are used as the basis for other composers' musical variations.

(B) Only composers whose compositions become the subject for musical variations can be considered "great."

(C) Chopin's "Prelude in A" is a more famous musical composition than Handel's "Theme in G."

(D) No great musical compositions have ever been written by Spanish composers.

(E) Frederic Chopin wrote music because he wanted to become famous.

25. Whenever the national budget exceeds $8 trillion the government spends $2 billion on travel expenses. Whenever the government spends $2 billion or more on travel expenses, then the President's activities are too visual to the public, too many reports are released to the press, and the President gets impeached. Before 1998, no President had been impeached since 1865, which was 133 years ago.

Which of the following statements must be true?

(A) In 1865, the national budget was at least $8 trillion.

(B) The President will be impeached again in 2131, which is 133 years from now.

(C) The government needs to spend at least $2 billion on travel expenses each year.

(D) In 1980, the government may have spent more than $2 billion on travel expenses.

(E) The national budget in 1940 was less than or equal to $8 trillion.

PRACTICE TEST 4

The following passage applies to Questions 1–5

A college building has eight empty spaces in a five-floor building to assign to certain classes: two spaces on the first floor, two on the second floor, one on the third floor, two on the fourth floor, and one on the fifth floor. The dean of the college has to assign class space to three history classes—Ancient Asia, Babylon Times, and Confucius at Work—and to three business classes: Special Stocks, Turnovers & Mergers, and Unstable Markets. The dean must follow these rules in assigning class space:

No floor may remain completely unoccupied.

No two history classes may be on the same floor.

Two business classes may not be on adjacently numbered floors.

Ancient Asia may not be on the first or fifth floor.

Confucius at Work and Special Stocks must both be on the same floor.

1. Which of the following statements could be true about the arrangement of classes in the building?

   (A) Confucius at Work and Ancient Asia are on the second floor.
   (B) Unstable Markets and Ancient Asia are on the first floor.
   (C) Special Stocks and Unstable Markets are on the second floor.
   (D) Babylon Times and Confucius at Work are on adjacent floors.
   (E) The business classes are on even-numbered floors only.

2. Which of the following classes could share a floor with Unstable Markets?

   I. Ancient Asia
   II. Babylon Times
   III. Turnovers & Mergers

   (A) I only
   (B) II only
   (C) I and II
   (D) II and III
   (E) None of the above

3. If the business classes are on odd-numbered floors only, which of the following statements could be true?

   (A) Ancient Asia and Babylon Times are both on the fourth floor.
   (B) Turnovers & Mergers is on the fifth floor.
   (C) Unstable Markets is on the first floor.
   (D) Ancient Asia and Babylon Times are on adjacent floors.
   (E) Turnovers & Mergers and Confucius at Work are on adjacent floors.

4. If Confucius at Work is on the first floor, which of the following must be false?

   (A) A business class is on the fourth floor.
   (B) A history class is on the fourth floor.
   (C) Ancient Asia is on the fourth floor.
   (D) Babylon Times and Confucius at Work are on adjacent floors.
   (E) Unstable Markets is on the fifth floor.

5. Which of the following is a complete list of all the classes that could be on the second floor?

   (A) Ancient Asia, Babylon Times
   (B) Ancient Asia, Babylon Times, Turnovers & Mergers
   (C) Ancient Asia, Turnovers & Mergers, Unstable Markets
   (D) Ancient Asia, Babylon Times, Confucius at Work, Special Stocks
   (E) Ancient Asia, Babylon Times, Confucius at Work, Special Stocks, Unstable Markets

6. "Acquire" is a game that is based loosely on the stock market and related investment issues. Therefore, the best professional stock brokers should always win when playing "Acquire."

Which of the following statements, if true, would most weaken this conclusion?

(A) Knowledge of stock trading laws and practices is helpful in playing "Acquire."

(B) "Acquire" is a game that has been continuously produced for more than 30 years.

(C) Stock brokers are usually too busy to have time for playing games.

(D) The rules and strategies of "Acquire" are all fully explained in a rule book that accompanies the game.

(E) More children than adults play "Acquire."

7. Archaeologists at the University of South America have concluded that all species of dinosaurs that inhabited any parts of South America died at least 3 million years ago. The Southern Andes iguana is a species of animal that has existed continuously on the Earth for more than 5 million years. It is well established that South American dinosaurs and the Southern Andes iguana never lived on the Earth at the same time.

Based on the results of the studies reported above, which of the following must be true?

(A) South American dinosaurs became extinct at least 5 million years ago.

(B) The conclusion of the archaeologists at the University of South America is incorrect.

(C) If South American dinosaurs and Southern Andes iguanas had lived together on the Earth, the dinosaurs would have eaten the iguanas.

(D) South American dinosaurs and Southern Andes iguanas may have existed together on the Earth but in different locations.

(E) Southern Andes iguanas have been extinct longer than South American dinosaurs have.

8. Fewer inches of rain have fallen in the Midwest this year than in any other year since 1917. Usually, residents of the Midwestern states spend a total of $20 million each year for flood insurance and recovery. Therefore, this year's flood-related costs for the Midwestern states must be less than $20 million.

Which of the following, if true, would most weaken the above argument?

(A) The Midwestern states have had many more individual rainfalls and rainstorms this year than usual.

(B) In the South, the states do not budget any money at all for flood recovery.

(C) The global greenhouse effect is the cause of this year's low rainfall total.

(D) Every individual determines for himself or herself how much money to spend on flood insurance.

(E) In 1917, the combined flood recovery budget for the residents of the Midwestern states was only $10,000.

The following passage applies to Questions 9–14

A piano teacher provides private lessons for seven different children—Albert, Billie, Chuckie, Dolly, Ellis, Felicia, and George. The piano teacher teaches one child at a time, from Monday through Friday, for either a morning or an afternoon session. When the teacher plans her weekly schedule, the following rules must apply:

> Albert and Billie must have their lessons on the same day.
> George cannot come on Thursday.
> Dolly is only available for morning sessions.
> Chuckie is only available for afternoon sessions.
> Felicia is only available Monday morning.

9. Which of the following is a possible list, from Monday to Friday, of students for morning lessons?

   (A) Felicia, George, Albert, Billie, Dolly
   (B) Felicia, Chuckie, George, Albert, Dolly
   (C) Dolly, Albert, Ellis, Felicia, George
   (D) Felicia, Billie, Dolly, George, Ellis
   (E) Felicia, George, Albert, Dolly, Ellis

10. Which of the following is a possible list, from Monday to Friday, of students for afternoon lessons?

    (A) Felicia, George, Billie, Chuckie, Ellis
    (B) Chuckie, Billie, Dolly, Ellis, George
    (C) George, Billie, Chuckie, Ellis, nobody
    (D) Albert, Billie, nobody, Ellis, George
    (E) Dolly, Chuckie, George, Billie, Ellis

11. If the tutor does not want to schedule any lessons on Friday, which of the following could be true?

    (A) Felicia and Albert are scheduled for the same day.
    (B) Dolly and Albert are scheduled for Tuesday.
    (C) George and Ellis are scheduled for Thursday.
    (D) Chuckie and Felicia are scheduled for Monday.
    (E) Ellis is the only student scheduled for Monday.

12. Which of the following pairs of students cannot both have their lessons on the same day?

    I. George and Felicia
    II. Albert and Chuckie
    III. Felicia and Dolly
    IV. Ellis and Chuckie

    (A) I only
    (B) II and III
    (C) I, II, and III
    (D) II and IV
    (E) I, III, and IV

13. If Albert's lesson is Wednesday afternoon, which of the following must be false?

    (A) George and Chuckie are scheduled for the same day.
    (B) George's lesson is before Ellis's lesson.
    (C) Billie and Chuckie are scheduled for the same day.
    (D) George is scheduled on Monday.
    (E) Ellis and Felicia are scheduled for the same day.

14. If Albert is scheduled for Friday morning, which of the following is a complete list of students who could have their lesson on Monday?

    (A) Felicia, Billie, George
    (B) Dolly, Felicia, Chuckie, George
    (C) Felicia, Chuckie, Billie, Ellis
    (D) Chuckie, Ellis, Felicia, George
    (E) Chuckie, Dolly, Ellis, Felicia, George

The following passage applies to Questions 15–18

A television network divides its viewing area into four quadrants: Quadrant I contains the entire area northeast of the main broadcast tower, Quadrant II contains the entire area southeast of the main broadcast tower, Quadrant III contains the entire area southwest of the main broadcast tower, and Quadrant IV contains the entire area northwest of the main broadcast tower. The network consists of eight different stations, known as Station A through Station H. To maximize the network's broadcast range, the eight stations are arranged around the main broadcast tower as follows:

Every quadrant must contain at least one station but may have no more than three stations.

Quadrant IV must have at least two stations.

Station A and Station B may not be in the same quadrant.

Station C must be in Quadrant II.

Station D may not be north of Station C.

Stations E and F must be in the same quadrant.

Station H must be somewhere south of Station A.

15. If Station C is the only station in Quadrant II, then which of the following must be true?

    (A) Station E and Station F are in Quadrant I.
    (B) Station B is in Quadrant IV.
    (C) Station D is in Quadrant III.
    (D) Station A is in Quadrant IV.
    (E) Station H is in Quadrant I.

16. If Quadrant I has three stations, then which of the following could be true?

    (A) Quadrant III has three stations.
    (B) Station E is in Quadrant II.
    (C) Station A and Station F are in Quadrant III.
    (D) Station D and Station H are in the same quadrant.
    (E) Station D and Station E are in Quadrant III.

17. If every quadrant has exactly two stations, then which station could be in the same quadrant as Station D?

    I. A
    II. C
    III. E
    IV. G

(A) I only
(B) I and II
(C) II and III
(D) II, III, and IV
(E) I, II, and IV

18. If Quadrant I and Quadrant II each have only one station, then which of the following must be false?

(A) The two quadrants north of the broadcast tower have as many stations as the two quadrants south of the broadcast tower.
(B) Station D is in Quadrant IV.
(C) Station E and Station F are in Quadrant III.
(D) Station H is in Quadrant I.
(E) Exactly four stations are south of the broadcast tower.

The following passage applies to Questions 19–22

Seven college students, Carl, Diane, Elvin, Florence, George, Heather, and Ivan, apply to a college training office for placements in internships with government offices. The training office has exactly seven internships available in two different government offices, The Senate Legal Office and The Supreme Court Library. Each office may take either three or four students. The training office also has to consider the following requirements:

Carl and Diane may not work for the same office.
Heather and Florence must work for the same office.
If Diane and Elvin work for the same office, then that office must hire four students.
George must work for The Supreme Court Library.
The Senate Legal Office may only hire four students if Diane is one of those students.

19. Which of the following is a possible placement of the students?

	The Senate Legal Office	The Supreme Court Library
(A)	Diane, Elvin, Carl, Ivan	Florence, George, Heather
(B)	Diane, Heather, Florence	Carl, Elvin, George, Ivan
(C)	Carl, Elvin, Florence	Diane, George, Heather, Ivan
(D)	Diane, Elvin, Ivan	Carl, Florence, George, Heather
(E)	Carl, Elvin, Florence, Heather	Diane, George, Ivan

20. If Diane works for The Senate Legal Office, then which of the following statements must be true?

(A) Elvin works for The Senate Legal Office.
(B) Ivan works for The Senate Legal Office.
(C) Heather may not work for The Supreme Court Library.
(D) Florence and Ivan work for the same office.
(E) Ivan and Carl work for the same office.

21. If Heather is one of four people placed at The Supreme Court Library, then which of the following could be true?

    (A) Carl works for The Supreme Court Library.
    (B) Florence and Ivan work for the same office.
    (C) Diane and Ivan both work for The Senate Legal Office.
    (D) Elvin works for The Supreme Court Library.
    (E) Elvin and Ivan both work for The Senate Legal Office.

22. If the Senate Legal Office only takes three people, then which of the following must be false?

    (A) Heather and Elvin work for the same office.
    (B) Elvin works for The Supreme Court Library.
    (C) Ivan works for The Supreme Court Library.
    (D) Florence and Carl work for the same office.
    (E) Ivan and Elvin work for the same office.

23. All blue cars have tailfins. Nothing that is blue has ever traveled to the bottom of the ocean.

    Based on the above statements, which of the following may logically be concluded?

    (A) Only things with tailfins have traveled to the bottom of the ocean.
    (B) All things with tailfins are blue.
    (C) Some cars have not traveled to the bottom of the ocean.
    (D) All cars have tailfins.
    (E) Some cars are not blue.

24. David killed Goliath with only a single stone. If David had taken with him a supply of a hundred stones, then he would have been able to defeat the entire opposing army.

    Which of the following, if true, would most strengthen the above argument?

    (A) Goliath was the most difficult member of the opposing army to defeat.
    (B) The opposing army would have advanced too quickly for David to have the opportunity to use more than 10 stones.
    (C) Goliath was significantly larger and more powerful than David.
    (D) David was significantly larger and more powerful than Goliath.
    (E) The opposing army had fewer than 100 soldiers.

25. A guard dog from Acme Dogs will assume an alert position and will begin barking every time she hears the footsteps of a person walking toward the owner's house. Therefore, anyone with a guard dog from Acme Dogs should feel very secure at home because the dog will warn the owner if an intruder approaches.

    This conclusion makes which of the following assumptions?

    (A) A dog from Acme Dogs would provide good protection after an intruder enters the house.
    (B) A dog from Acme Dogs will hear any intruder who approaches.
    (C) A dog from Acme Dogs has received special training as a guard dog.
    (D) The speaker lives in a dangerous area.
    (E) Some intruders may not be people.

PRACTICE TEST 5

The following passage applies to Questions 1–5

A television network executive is responsible for scheduling television programming for the time period from 8:00 p.m. until 10:00 p.m. each night, Monday through Friday. Each night, the network will broadcast two 1-hour television programs during this time period. To fill these spaces, the executive has three 1-hour variety shows, three 1-hour comedy shows, and four 1-hour drama shows. The programming must follow these guidelines:

> Two shows of the same type may not be scheduled for the same night.
>
> Two variety shows may not be scheduled on consecutive nights.
>
> If a drama show is scheduled for 8:00 on any night, then a comedy show may not be scheduled for the same night. If a variety show is scheduled for 8:00 on any night, then a drama show may not be scheduled for the same night.

1. Which of the following is a possible schedule listing for the 8:00 time slot from Monday through Friday?

   (A) Variety, Drama, Comedy, Comedy, Variety
   (B) Variety, Variety, Comedy, Drama, Comedy
   (C) Comedy, Drama, Variety, Comedy, Variety
   (D) Variety, Comedy, Drama, Comedy, Drama
   (E) Drama, Comedy, Variety, Drama, Drama

2. Which of the following statements about the television schedule could be true?

   (A) A drama is scheduled for 8:00 on Tuesday.
   (B) A variety and a drama are both scheduled on Monday.
   (C) A variety and a comedy are both scheduled on Tuesday.
   (D) A drama and a variety are both scheduled on Thursday.
   (E) A comedy and a drama are both scheduled on Friday.

3. If a drama is scheduled for 9:00 on Tuesday, then which of the following must be true?

   (A) A comedy is scheduled for 8:00 on Thursday.
   (B) A variety is scheduled for 9:00 on Monday.
   (C) A comedy is scheduled for 8:00 on Monday.
   (D) A drama is scheduled for 8:00 on Tuesday.
   (E) A variety is scheduled for 8:00 on Friday.

4. If a comedy is scheduled on Wednesday, then which of the following must be false?

(A) A variety is scheduled for 8:00 on Wednesday.

(B) A comedy is scheduled for 8:00 on Tuesday.

(C) A variety is scheduled for 9:00 on Friday.

(D) Tuesday and Friday have the same schedule.

(E) Monday and Friday have the same schedule.

5. If the same type of show is scheduled for 8:00 on Tuesday, Wednesday, and Thursday, then which of the following could be true?

(A) A variety is scheduled for 8:00 on Monday.

(B) Monday and Wednesday have identical schedules.

(C) Monday and Friday have identical schedules.

(D) A comedy is scheduled for Friday.

(E) At least one variety show is scheduled for 8:00.

6. The belief in an organized religion is one of the indications of an advanced society. Anthropologists have recently discovered evidence that tribes of people living in Asia 7 million years ago buried people together with small statues of common animals and with certain tools and utensils. Therefore, these tribes can be considered the earliest advanced society to have existed.

Which of the following assumptions is part of the above argument?

(A) Organized religion began in Asia.

(B) The ancient tribes in Asia worshiped common animals.

(C) Burying people together with tools and utensils is an indication of a belief in an organized religion.

(D) Animals that existed in Asia 7 million years ago are now extinct.

(E) Only an advanced society would be able to create statues of animals.

7. Every year, the members of the school board PTA select a new Student Representative. If the school board PTA selects a senior as the Student Representative, then the PTA will give the high school money for a spring musical. However, the school board PTA has already given the school money for a spring musical.

If all the statements in the above argument are true, which of the following conclusions must also be true?

(A) The PTA should not select a senior as the Student Representative.

(B) The PTA already has given enough money to the high school.

(C) The current Student Representative is a junior.

(D) If the PTA does not give any additional money to the high school, then the PTA must not have selected a senior as its Student Representative.

(E) If the PTA gives more money to the high school this year, then its Student Representative must be a senior.

8. The Acme Company just announced publicly that it is going to enter into a stock merger with Wonder Corp. It is commonly known that stock prices for any given company usually rise when information about a pending merger involving that company becomes public.

If the stock prices for Acme Corp. decline after the announcement, what conclusion can be inferred?

(A) The price of stocks in Acme Company is too high for the average investors.

(B) Wonder Corp. has only a limited number of stocks available for sale.

(C) The merger between Acme Company and Wonder Corp. creates a major conglomerate with a monopoly on the market, whose stocks are no longer desirable.

(D) The merger between Acme Company and Wonder Corp. can only be accomplished after long periods of negotiations between executives from each company.

(E) The announcement of the merger between Acme Company and Wonder Corp. became public on the same day that the government announced a decrease in prime lending rates.

The following passage applies to Questions 9–14

A travel agency is organizing visits to several cities across North America. One plan offers tourists a travel package to visit eight different cities—Jacksonville, Kingman, Lexington, Montreal, New York, Ottawa, Philadel-

phia, and Quincy. Tourists may visit the eight cities in any order, but their selections must follow these general rules:

> Each travel package must include all eight cities, but each city may be visited only once.
> A traveler must visit New York either immediately before or immediately after visiting Montreal.
> Lexington may not be the last or the first city visited.
> If Kingman is visited before Ottawa, then at least one other city must be visited between Kingman and Ottawa.
> Quincy must be the fourth city visited in any travel package.

9. Which of the following could be a complete list of cities visited, in order from first to last?

(A) Jacksonville, Kingman, Lexington, Montreal, New York, Ottawa, Philadelphia, Quincy

(B) Lexington, Kingman, Montreal, Quincy, Ottawa, New York, Jacksonville, Philadelphia

(C) Philadelphia, Kingman, Ottawa, Quincy, Montreal, New York, Lexington, Jacksonville

(D) Kingman, Jacksonville, Ottawa, Quincy, New York, Montreal, Lexington, Philadelphia

(E) Ottawa, Kingman, Lexington, Jacksonville, Quincy, Philadelphia, Montreal, New York

10. If the tourist begins his or her visit in New York, which of the following statements must be true?

(A) Kingman is visited before Ottawa.
(B) Kingman is visited before Quincy.
(C) Jacksonville is visited after Montreal.
(D) Philadelphia may not be the last city on the list.
(E) Quincy is visited before Ottawa.

11. If Kingman is the second city on the tour, then which of the following statements must be false?

(A) Ottawa is visited after Quincy.
(B) Jacksonville is visited first.
(C) Montreal is visited before New York.
(D) Philadelphia and Lexington are the last two cities visited.
(E) Quincy is visited after New York.

12. If Jacksonville is the seventh city on the tour, which of the following is a complete list of all cities that could be last?

(A) Kingman, Ottawa, Philadelphia
(B) Jacksonville, Kingman, Montreal
(C) Kingman, Lexington, Ottawa, Philadelphia
(D) Kingman, Montreal, New York, Ottawa, Philadelphia
(E) Kingman, Lexington, Montreal, New York, Ottawa, Philadelphia

13. If Kingman is visited seventh, then which city could be visited last?

(A) Jacksonville
(B) Lexington
(C) Montreal
(D) New York
(E) Ottawa

14. If Quincy is visited immediately after Ottawa, then which of the following statements must be false?

(A) Kingman is visited first.
(B) Lexington is visited immediately after Quincy.
(C) Jacksonville and Montreal are the first two cities visited.
(D) New York is visited after Ottawa.
(E) Philadelphia and Lexington are the first two cities on the tour.

The following passage applies to Questions 15–18

A major department store chain plans to build seven new outlet stores. The Administrative Office for the department store chain is in the exact center of the store's market area, and the seven new outlet stores, which will be called OS ("Outlet Store") 1 through OS 7, must be placed in the county as follows:

OS 1 must be built somewhere north of the Administrative Office.

OS 2 must be built due south of OS 1.

OS 4 must be built somewhere southeast of the Administrative Office.

OS 5 must be built due east of OS 4.

OS 6 and OS 7 must both be built somewhere west of the Administrative Office.

15. All of the stores could be built some-where northwest of the Administrative Office EXCEPT which of the following?

    (A) OS 2
    (B) OS 3
    (C) OS 5
    (D) OS 6
    (E) OS 7

16. If OS 6 is built somewhere southwest of the Administrative Office, then which of the following statements must be true?

    (A) OS 7 is somewhere southwest of the Administrative Office.
    (B) OS 6 is somewhere south of OS 2.
    (C) OS 4 is somewhere north of OS 6.
    (D) The Administrative Office is somewhere north of OS 7.
    (E) OS 1 is somewhere north of OS 6.

17. If OS 4 is built due east of OS 2, then which of the following statements must be false?

    (A) OS 2 is somewhere west of OS 5.
    (B) OS 5 is somewhere west of OS 1.
    (C) OS 3 is somewhere south of OS 2.
    (D) OS 4 is somewhere south of OS 1.
    (E) OS 2 is somewhere north of OS 6.

18. If exactly three stores are built east of the Administrative Office, then which of the following statements could be false?

    (A) OS 3 is somewhere east of the Administrative Office.
    (B) OS 2 is somewhere west of OS 5.
    (C) OS 7 is somewhere west of OS 3.
    (D) OS 6 is somewhere south of OS 7.
    (E) OS 1 is somewhere west of the Administrative Office.

The following passage applies to Questions 19–22

Nine buildings in a city's downtown area are connected by a series of overhead walkways. The city engineer's map of the city identifies the buildings simply with the letters R, S, T, U, V, W, X, Y, and Z. Anyone visiting these buildings must begin the visit at Building R. From there, the other buildings may be visited via a series of overhead walkways, connecting the buildings as follows:

> Walkways connect Building R to Buildings S, T, and W.
> A walkway connects Building S to Building U.
> Walkways connect Buildings S and T to Building X.
> Building W is connected to Buildings T, V, and Z.
> Building X is connected to Building Z.
> Buildings X and Z are connected to Building Y.

19. Without visiting any building more than once, what is the maximum number of buildings a person can visit?

    (A) 5
    (B) 6
    (C) 7
    (D) 8
    (E) 9

20. If a visitor must travel from Building R to Building Y by crossing the fewest number of walkways, which of the following statements must be true?

(A) The visitor will visit Buildings S and X.

(B) The visitor may visit Building U or Building V, but not both.

(C) The visitor may not visit Building Z.

(D) If the visitor goes to Building T, he or she must then go to Building W.

(E) If the visitor goes to Building W, he or she must then go to Building Z.

21. If a visitor wants to travel to both Building U and Building V, which of the following must be false?

(A) The visitor will go to every building except Building T.

(B) The visitor will go to Building S only once.

(C) The visitor will visit no building more than once.

(D) The visitor will not visit Building Y.

(E) The visitor will visit at least six different buildings.

22. If a new walkway is built connecting Building V to Building Z, then which of the following could be true?

(A) A visitor may visit all the buildings without visiting any building more than once.

(B) The shortest path from Building R to Building Y includes Building V.

(C) A visitor may visit Building V immediately after Building T.

(D) A visitor may go from Building V to Building U by crossing no more than three walkways.

(E) A visitor may visit Buildings S, T, and W in that order.

23. A philosopher makes the following statements: "I think, therefore I am. If I am not, then I think not. If I think, then life means nothing."

Applying the preceding argument, if life does not mean nothing, then what more can the philosopher conclude?

(A) I am.

(B) I think.

(C) I do not think.

(D) I think and I am.

(E) I think not and I am.

24. New electric heating elements that use the patented "coiled element system" save energy by requiring less electricity. Therefore, if homeowners use only heating elements with the "coiled element system," their electric bills will decrease.

Which of the following represents a necessary assumption that is part of the preceding argument?

(A) Homeowners are always concerned with lowering their utility bills.

(B) By lowering electricity use, homeowners can help decrease pollution levels in their communities.

(C) Heating units with the "coiled element system" are less expensive than more standard heating units.

(D) Heating units with the "coiled element system" are as effective in providing heat as standard heating units.

(E) Heating units with the "coiled element system" have been shown to create less low-level radiation in the home, and people using them have fewer medical problems.

25. A manufacturer of filmmaking supplies and equipment advertises that Alfred Hitchcock, one of the world's greatest directors, routinely obtained his filmmaking supplies from their suppliers. As a result, the manufacturer suggests, anyone buying their supplies would become an equally great film director.

Which of the following statements, if true, would most weaken the claims made by the manufacturer?

(A) Hitchcock, at the time that he was making his films, was provided extensive funding from large film production companies that allowed him to use the best materials then available.

(B) Most of the customers of this manufacturer are amateur photographers who are not professionally trained and who do not realize the value of using professional-quality film supplies.

(C) The supplies made by this manufacturer are more expensive than similar supplies from other manufacturers.

(D) A filmmaking professor at the local community college supplies all of his students with materials from this manufacturer.

(E) Even when using supplies from this manufacturer, many amateur filmmakers create films that movie critics call inferior and meaningless.

ANSWERS AND EXPLANATIONS

PRACTICE TEST 1—ANSWERS

Answers 1–5

DISCUSSION—This is a ranking problem, which can be identified because the number of people matches the number of floors involved and there is the requirement that no two people can leave the elevator at the same place. Your task for this problem is to rank the people in the order that they leave the elevator.

1. The correct answer is (D). For this first question, test each of the five answer selections against the rules for conflicts. Answer (A) is incorrect because, if Helen exited on Level 3, Graham would also have to get out on Level 3; because Graham is getting out on Level 1, then Helen cannot get out on Level 3. Answer (B) is incorrect because Graham must get out before Johnny. Answer (C) is incorrect because Irving must get out on either the first or sixth floor. Answer (D) is the correct answer because all rules are satisfied. Answer (E) is incorrect because Graham must get out before Johnny.

2. The correct answer is (B). If Graham exits on Level 4, then Graham is not exiting on Level 3. Therefore, because of the second rule, Helen cannot exit on Level 3. Irving must exit on either Level 1 or 6 and so cannot exit on Level 3. Because Graham must exit before Johnny, then Johnny must exit on either Level 5 or 6. Only Kevin and Louise could exit on Level 3. Therefore, answer (B) is the correct answer.

3. The correct answer is (D). If Graham and Irving exit together, then Graham must exit on either Level 1 or Level 6 because of the rule requiring Irving to exit on these levels. Graham cannot exit on Level 6 because Graham must exit before Johnny, and if Graham exited on Level 6 then Johnny would have nowhere to go. Therefore, Graham must exit on Level 1, so answer (D) is correct. The other answers could be true but are not required to be true.

4. The correct answer is (D). If nobody gets out on Levels 1 or 2, Irving must get out on Level 6. No other information is readily available from the rules, so the best approach is to check the possibility of each answer. Answer (A) is incorrect because Irving must get out on Level 6. Answer (B) is incorrect because if Helen gets out on Level 3, Graham must also get out on Level 3. Answer (C) is incorrect because Irving must exit on Level 6, so Graham and Johnny cannot both get out on Level 6. Answer (D) is correct because nothing prevents Kevin from getting out on Level 5. Answer (E) is incorrect because Irving must get out on Level 6.

5. The correct answer is (C). The added fact that Irving gets out alone adds nothing to the given information that Irving exits on either Level 1 or 6. However, the added fact that Helen gets out alone means that Helen cannot exit on Level 3. As addressed above, if Helen were to exit on Level 3, then Graham would also have to exit on Level 3; since Helen is exiting alone, then Level 3 is not an option. Therefore, answer (C) is the correct answer for a statement that must be true. All other answers might be true or might be false but are not required to be true.

6. The correct answer is (B). The question stem for this problem tells you that this is an "additional fact" question. This becomes obvious as soon as you see the structure, "Which of the following, if true . . . ?" To solve this type of question, you should first identify the primary relevant topics or issues of the introductory argument. For this problem, the argument introduces the two different schools, the difference in the percentages going to college, and the conclusion that the percentages are the result of better teaching ("a better education"). Any answer with extraneous information must be incorrect. Answer (B) is correct because it indicates that another factor, the entry scores of its applicants, may be responsible for the success of the students. The other statements all could be true, but they are not as directly related to the argument as the statement in answer (B).

7. The correct answer is (C). This author assumes that a low percentage of voters under 25 years old in comparison to the entire population of voters corresponds to a lack of interest among younger voters. Answer (C) contradicts this assumption by showing that the entire voting population of the state has a small percentage of voters younger than 25 years old, so the 9 percent who turn out to vote actually represent a large percentage of that group of voters. Answer (A) provides information that might be relevant to the argument but is insufficient to attack the conclusion because it does not include information about the actual number of young voters. Answers (B) and (D) provide information that is completely irrelevant to the argument. Answer (E), like (A), provides information that addresses only half the argument.

8. The correct answer is (A). This is a question that asks you to analyze the structure of the initial argument and then find the answer that parallels the original structure. Do not get tricked into selecting an answer just because it addresses the same general subject. For example, although answer (C) also deals with education and college acceptance, answer (C) is not the best answer. First, try to summarize the initial argument in very general terms. For this argument, the general summary would be 1. Data shows a certain connection ("test scores = graduation likelihood"), 2. a certain group shows a measure of success ("New England girls graduating"), and 3. conclude that the group (New England girls) shows the initial factors (high test scores). Only answer (A) comes close to matching this general structure by discussing the connection between music programs and success, then identifying a certain group ("from New Orleans"), and then connecting the two in the conclusion. The other answers do not follow this pattern. NOTE: The argument is not necessarily a logically sound argument. You are being tested not on the validity of the argument but only on recognizing its structure.

Answers 9–14

DISCUSSION—This is a ranking problem. Your task is to arrange, or rank, the people according to the order that they leave the train. This is similar to placing them in seats or other position markers, where there is a "one-to-one" match. The "one-to-one" match is created by the rule that the people "all get off at different stops." When you create an initial diagram, you can see the following:

1	2	3	4	5	6	7
		Willy				

You also know the relative orders of four people: S > U > T and V (the marking ">" means "gets off before" for this problem). These initial rules are relatively short, so there is nothing more to diagram at the beginning. You should also note, however, that the "group" of S > U > T, V accounts for four people; Willy is already accounted for, so the two remaining people, Xania and Yolanda, are free to be "placed" anywhere.

9. The correct answer is (C). Check each of the lists of answers against your initial diagram and the initial rules to see which answer violates any of the rules. Answer (A) is incorrect because Violet is not after Unger. Answer (B) is incorrect because Willy is not third. Answer (C) is correct because all the rules are satisfied. Answers (D) and (E) are incorrect because Tom may not get off before Unger.

10. The correct answer is (C). This is just the opposite of the preceding question. Your task for this question is to find the one list of people that does NOT follow all of the rules. The one that violates the rules is answer (C), which violates the rule that Tom and Violet get off after Unger. All other answers are possible arrangements so are incorrect.

11. The correct answer is (B). The best way to answer this question is to analyze the initial rules and consider which people must get off before any others. The initial rules tell you that Steve gets off before someone and Unger gets off before someone. Willy is specifically placed third. Therefore, neither Steve, Unger, nor Willy may ever be last. The only one of these that is an answer is Unger, answer (B). This is the answer.

12. The correct answer is (D). The analysis for this question is basically the same as for the preceding question, with a different focus. Because Willy is third, he can never be first. Because of the initial "group" of four people, S > U > T, V, it is easy to see that neither Unger, Tom, nor Violet

may ever be first. There is not enough information to decide whether Steve, Xania, or Yolanda is first, but they COULD be first. The correct answer is answer (D), the answer that includes Tom, Unger, Violet, and Willy.

13. The correct answer is (D). You already know that Willy is third, so if Willy gets off before Unger, then Unger must be either fourth, fifth, sixth, or seventh. Because two people, Tom and Violet, get off after Unger, then Unger cannot be sixth or seventh, so Unger must be either fourth or fifth. The final four positions, fourth, fifth, sixth, and seventh, must be taken, in some order, by Unger, Xania, Tom, and Violet. With these four people accounted for and Willy getting off third, the two remaining people, Steve and Yolanda, must be first and second, though not necessarily in that order. A diagram of this analysis is as follows:

1	2	3	4	5	6	7
Steve or Yolanda	Steve or Yolanda	Willy	Unger, Tom, Violet, Xania (not necessarily in order, but in these four positions)			

Now check the answers against this analysis and diagram. Answer (D) is the only statement that "must be true." All the remaining statements can be seen in the diagram as possibilities, but they are not statements that "must be true."

14. The correct answer is (A). Focus on the limitations on the placement of Steve since the question tells you that Steve cannot be first. Based on the initial rules, you know that Steve cannot be third, and Steve also cannot be one of the last three people since Steve must get off before Unger, Tom, and Violet. Therefore, Steve can only be second or fourth.

1	2	3	4	5	6	7
	Steve ?	Willy	Steve ?			

Also focus on where in the diagram other people can or cannot be placed. Because Steve must get off before Unger, Violet, and Tom, it is clear that neither Unger, Violet, nor Tom may be first or second. As a result, answer (A) must be false, since Unger's leaving before Willy would make Unger either first or second. This is a false statement, so the answer must be answer (A). The others are all statements that either could or must be true.

Answers 15–18

DISCUSSION—This is another ranking problem, which can be identified because the initial rules are giving you information about the finishing order of the contestants, and your task is to rank their finishing order.

15. The correct answer is (A). For this first question, Answer (A) is the only one that complies with all of the rules about the finishing order. Answer (B) is incorrect because Elmer is not in third. Answers (C) and (E) are incorrect because Alan may not finish first or last. Answer (D) is incorrect because Betty must finish before Charles and David.

16. The correct answer is (C). The one answer that is incorrect is answer (C) because Betty must finish before both Charles and David. All other answers present possible finishing orders.

17. The correct answer is (B). Alan specifically cannot finish first or last. Betty may finish first. Charles and David may not finish first because they must finish behind Betty. Elmer may not finish first because he must finish third. Faith may finish in any position. Therefore, either Betty or Faith could finish first, so the correct answer is (B).

18. The correct answer is (E). Based on the previous question, only Betty or Faith may finish first, so the only possible answers to this question are either answer (A) or (E). Betty may not finish last because she must finish ahead of Charles and David. Therefore, the answer is (E).

Answers 19–22

DISCUSSION—This is one of the hybrid problems that doesn't really fit neatly into one of the primary five categories. In a way, this is like a distribution problem since you have to place the people into different categories, but the rules are somewhat different. You need to pay close attention to the two different categories of employees (accountants and managers) and focus on how many of each are included in the selections.

19. The correct answer is (B). Answer (A) is incorrect because Frank must be chosen for Committee A. Answer (B) is the correct answer. Answer (C) is incorrect because placing Holly on Committee B would require Gina also to be on Committee B. Answer (D) is incorrect because Committee A is given more juniors than seniors. Answer (E) is incorrect because Committee B is given more seniors than juniors.

Peterson's Logic & Reading Review

20. The correct answer is (D). If Holly is chosen for Committee B, then Gina must also be on Committee B. Because Holly and Gina are both seniors and Committee B may not have more seniors than juniors, then the remaining two slots on Committee B must go to juniors. Answer (D) is correct because it prevents Ed, a senior, from taking a position on Committee B. The other statements could be either true or false.

21. The correct answer is (E). To prepare for this question, it is important to note that with eight committee slots and ten students, exactly two students will not be chosen. Because of the last rule about the committees, Paula and Ilsa may not both serve on committees at the same time. Therefore, either one or both of them must not be chosen. If Ed is one of the students who is not selected, then the other unselected student must be either Paula or Ilsa. As a result, everyone else except Paula and Ilsa MUST be chosen. Therefore, the answer is (E).

22. The correct answer is (C). This question relies on the exact same reasoning as question 21 above. If Holly is chosen for Committee B, then Gina must also be on Committee B. This places two seniors on Committee B already, so no more seniors may be selected for Committee B. Answer (C), therefore, is the correct answer, since Ed cannot serve on Committee B.

23. The correct answer is (E). The premise of this argument is presented as an if-then syllogism. The trick is that the sentence is inverted. It is easier to understand if you invert the sentence to read, "If you don't use Blind-O Window Cleaner, then honk." With an if-then argument, a valid conclusion may be reached if you are told that the "if" clause is true or that the "then" clause is false. Therefore, knowing that a driver does not use Blind-O Window Cleaner can result in a conclusion that the driver will not honk. Conversely, knowing that a driver is not honking can result in a conclusion that the driver does use Blind-O Window Cleaner. Hearing a driver honk is not sufficient to draw any conclusion, since that driver could be honking merely in relation to the traffic or for some reason unrelated to Blind-O Window Cleaner. Therefore, answer (A) is incorrect. Answer (B) is incorrect because it gets the argument backwards, since not honking would indicate using Blind-O Window Cleaner. Answer (C) is incorrect because it is logical to conclude, based on the message on the billboard, that not honking implies use of Blind-O Window Cleaner. Answer (D) is incorrect because knowing that a driver uses Blind-O Window Cleaner does not necessarily imply that he or she will or will not honk.

24. The correct answer is (D). Tom appears to believe that the problems that occurred to his 1994 car will occur again to any other car from the same manufacturer. This is a restatement of answer (D), the correct answer. Answer (A) is incorrect because nothing in the problem provides general evidence about the functioning of all electrical systems. Answers (B) and (C) are incorrect for a similar reason, that they overgeneralize the situation. Finally, nothing in the problem provides any evidence that could support answer (E).

25. The correct answer is (C). This problem presents Rep. Brown and Rep. Smith as nearly identical. If the result that happens to one, i.e., the recall, should happen to the other, this suggests that the outside forces—the voters— are also the same. Therefore, answer (C) should be the correct answer to explain why the two representatives should be treated the same way. The other answers all present information that is irrelevant to the argument.

PRACTICE TEST 2—ANSWERS

Answers 1–5

DISCUSSION—This is a ranking problem, since you have to rank the six newspapers according to subscription levels. The rules specify that "no two newspapers ever have the same number of customers," so you are assured of a "one-to-one" match, which is one of the key elements of a ranking problem. Your best way to succeed is to diagram the rules as much as possible.

The first rule tells you that *Tattler* has more subscribers than any other newspaper, so your diagram will begin like this:

Least					Most
					Tattler

The second rule lets you only add the note that I > G, but you cannot yet place this information into the diagram.

The third rule tells you that *Newsmag* cannot ever be fifth or sixth since it must be greater than at least two others. Therefore, *Newsmag* must be in either 2, 3, or 4:

Least					Most
		News-mag ?	*News-mag ?*	*News-mag ?*	*Tattler*

The final rule is not one that can be diagrammed, but it must be remembered for use when it becomes relevant. If I > S, then D > S. However, if I is not greater than S, then the second half of the rule is irrelevant.

Now you are ready to consider the questions.

1. The correct answer is (D). The best approach for a question like this is to check each answer to see if it violates any of the rules. Answers (A) and (C) are incorrect because *Newsmag* must be greater than at least two others. Answer (B) is incorrect because *Imprint* must be greater than *Globe*. Answer (E) is incorrect because *Imprint* is greater than *Spectator*, but *Dialer* is not also greater than *Spectator*, as required by the final rule.

2. The correct answer is (E). When you have a question like this with the "Roman numeral choices," first consider each of them individually like single "true/false" questions and then match those responses to the five answers. Based on the diagram, the only information that is clear is that neither *Tattler* nor *Newsmag* could ever have the lowest subscription. Other than that, any other paper is possible. Therefore, the possible answers are I, II, and IV, so the answer is (E).

3. The correct answer is (C). The only initial rule relating to *Spectator* and *Dialer* is the fourth rule, which says that "Whenever *Imprint* gets more subscribers than *Spectator*, then *Dialer* will also have more subscriptions than *Spectator*." If, as this question now adds, *Spectator* is greater than *Dialer*, then it would be logically impossible for *Imprint* to have more than *Spectator*. (If *Imprint* were to have more than *Spectator*, then *Dialer* would also have to have more than *Spectator*, and you would be caught with an impossibility.) Therefore, answer (C) is the statement that must be true, although it is stated in the negative (if *Imprint* cannot have more than *Spectator*). This is the same as saying that *Spectator* must have more than *Imprint*, which is answer (C).

4. The correct answer is (D). The best step when you are given a specific bit of information as in this question is to add that information to your diagram and then see what other conclusions you can draw:

Least					Most
		Globe	*News-mag ?*	*News-mag ?*	*Tattler*

Because of the rule that *Imprint* must have more than the *Globe*, then *Imprint* must be either second or third, with *Newsmag* taking the spot not taken by *Imprint*:

Least					Most
		Globe	*Imprint* or *News-mag*	*Imprint* or *News-mag*	*Tattler*

Now the final two spaces must be taken by *Dialer* and *Spectator*. In either position, *Imprint* will have more subscriptions than *Spectator*, so *Dialer* must also have more subscriptions than *Spectator*. Therefore, *Spectator* must be last, and *Dialer* second to last:

Least					Most
Specta-tor	*Dialer*	*Globe*	*Imprint* or *News-mag*	*Imprint* or *News-mag*	*Tattler*

Now just check the answers for a statement that matches this diagram. It is evident that answers (A), (B), (C), and (E) are all statements that must be true. The only one that could be false is answer (D), which could either be true or false, depending on the placement of *Imprint* and *Newsmag* as second or third. Therefore, the answer is (D).

5. The correct answer is (D). As with the preceding question, the best approach is to add the new information, that there are only two spaces lower than *Imprint*, into a diagram:

Least					Most
		Imprint	*News-mag ?*	*News-mag ?*	*Tattler*

Now, because *Imprint* must have more than *Globe*, you can mark that *Globe* must be in one of the last two spaces:

Least					Most
Globe ?	*Globe ?*	*Imprint*	*News-mag ?*	*News-mag ?*	*Tattler*

You don't have as much detail completed as with the preceding question, but at this point there is nothing more that can be concluded. Since the question asks you to find the one statement that could NOT be true, you are looking for a statement that must be false. From the diagram, answers (A) and (B) clearly could be true, and so are incorrect. Answer (C) is not evident from the diagram, either true or false. For that reason, it is smart test-taking strategy to skip it for now, and go on to see if you find another answer that clearly must be false. Answer (D), in fact, shows that it must be false, since the diagram shows that either of the two possible positions for *Globe* are both lower than either of the two possible positions for *Newsmag*. Therefore, answer (D) must be false and is therefore the correct answer. Answer (E) may or may not be true.

6. The correct answer is (C). This passage presents the argument that crime rates have been lowest when inflation has been highest and that raising inflation again will lower crime rates. Thus, selection I is a valid assumption. In the final sentence of the passage, the statement that the Federal Reserve needs to take action assumes that the Federal Reserve has the power to do something about this issue. Therefore, selection III is an invalid assumption. Selection II goes beyond the scope of the passage, which says nothing about the causes of inflation or its effects on society. Therefore, the correct answer is (C).

7. The correct answer is (B). Answer (B) would weaken the argument by illustrating that crime rates can remain high when inflation is also high, thus contradicting a part of the argument's assumption. Answer (A) is close, suggesting that the Federal Reserve cannot take action as recommended, but answer (A) is not as strong an answer as (B); it is still possible that the Federal Reserve may act and the President may approve of its actions. Answers (C) and (E) both focus on crime rates in particular parts of the country, but neither addresses the nationwide aspect of the problem or the connection to inflation. Answer (D) is incorrect because the relative rates of inflation of the two time periods is irrelevant; nothing in the argument mentions anything about the 1980s.

8. The correct answer is (D). This question asks for a statement to strengthen the conclusion that Megan's Law will decrease repeat sexual offenses. Answer (D) shows that community members will take actions to protect their children as a result of the law, resulting in less opportunity for repeat offenses to occur. Answer (A) addresses initial convictions but not repeat offenses. Answer (B) addresses what residents "prefer" but does not address any direct action they might take to reduce repeat offenses. Answer (C) appears to be a similar situation, but without more information making a connection between drunk driving incidents and sexual offenses, it is irrelevant. Answer (E) is entirely irrelevant.

Answers 9–14

DISCUSSION—This is a distribution problem since you do not have a "one-to-one" match, but you are essentially "placing" items in their positions. The general strategies of a ranking problem apply, but you have the added element of having two sides of the street to deal with. (If these were simply 10 stores in a straight row, it would probably be a ranking problem.)

The first step is to determine the "structure" of the diagram. You are told that there are five stores on one side of the street and five stores on the other, so the initial diagram looks like this:

North					
South					

You are told that the stores are numbered consecutively, as follows:

North	1	2	3	4	5
South	6	7	8	9	10

Now try to place the information from the rules into the diagram. The most "diagrammable" rule is the last one, that Frank's Auto is in Building. 7:

North	1	2	3	4	5
South	6	7 Frank	8	9	10

Now the second rule, that Cat Supplies Plus and Everything's Roses may not be adjacent to Frank's Auto can be marked in:

North	1	2	3	4	5
South	6 NOT C/E	7 Frank	8 NOT C/E	9	10

If Bell Bottom Jeans and Danny's Hobbies must be at opposite ends of the same street, then they must be in either 1 and 5 or 6 and 10. Because of the rule that Danny's Hobbies and Everything's Roses must both be in odd-numbered buildings, you can tell that the B and D combination must be in 1 and 5:

North	1 B/D	2	3	4	5 B/D
South	6 NOT C/E	7 Frank	8 NOT C/E	9	10

Because E must be in an odd-numbered building, it must be in either 3 or 9, the only odd-numbered buildings remaining:

North	1 B/D	2	3 E??	4	5 B/D
South	6 NOT C/E	7 Frank	8 NOT C/E	9 E??	10

Now, still before beginning the questions, it is useful to take stock of all the information you know and analyze the conclusions you can draw.

Building 1 must contain either B or D.

Building 2 has no specific information apparent, but you can determine some information about "negative" information. Building 2 CANNOT contain B, D, E, or F. It may or may not contain A, C, or G (it might just be left empty).

Building 3 may contain E. It CANNOT contain B, D, or F, so other possibilities are A, C, E, or G, or it could be empty.

Building 4 has no specific information, but it is clear that it CANNOT contain B, D, E, or F, so it might contain A, C, or G.

Building 5 must contain either B or D (whichever is not in Building 1).

Building 6 has no specific information about which stores it MAY contain, but you know a lot about what it CANNOT contain. Building 6 CANNOT contain B (which is in either 1 or 5), C (which cannot be next to F), D (which is in either 1 or 5), E (which must be in an odd numbered building), or F (which is in 7). Therefore, Building 6 may contain only A or G or be empty.

Building 7 must contain Frank's Auto.

Building 8 has exactly the same limitations as Building 6, so its options are A, G, or empty.

Building 9 could contain E. It CANNOT contain B, D, or F, so its options are A, C, E, G, or empty.

Building 10 CANNOT contain B, D, E, or F, so the options are A, C, G, or empty.

You are now ready to consider the questions.

9. The correct answer is (D). For this question, just check each of the answers against the rules to see which answers violate any of the rules. Answers (A), (B), and (E) are all incorrect because Building 1 may only contain B or D. Answer (C) is incorrect because ABC Learning and Cat Supplies Plus cannot be on the same side of the street. Therefore, the answer must be (D).

10. The correct answer is (C). This analysis is similar to the analysis for the first question, but you must focus on the requirements for the other side of the street. Answers (A) and (E) are incorrect because ABC Learning and Cat Supplies Plus cannot be on the same side of the street. Answers (B) and (D) are both incorrect because Bell Bottom Jeans and Danny's Hobbies must be on the north side of the street, and therefore neither one can be on the south side. Therefore, the answer must be answer (C).

11. The correct answer is (E). Consider the initial analysis for Building 6 and Building 8. The only options for both buildings were A, G, or empty. If "empty" is removed as an option, then it becomes evident that A must be in one of these two building, and G must be in the other.

North	1 B/D	2	3	4	5 B/D
South	6 A or G	7 Frank	8 A or G	9	10

Because ABC Learning is on the south side of the street, then Cat Supplies Plus must be on the north side, in either 2, 3, or 4. Recalling the original analysis, the only options for Building 10 were A, C, G, or empty. Since A, C, and G have all been accounted for, it is therefore clear that Building 10 must be left vacant.

North	1 B/D	2 C??	3 C? E?	4 C?	5 B/D
South	6 A or G	7 Frank	8 A or G	9 E?	10 empty

Compare this diagram to the answers, and it is clear that the answer must be E. All the other statements either must be false or could be made false.

12. The correct answer is (A). Because Frank's Auto is known to be on the south side of the street, this question requires that Everything's Roses must be on the north side. Since Everything's Roses must be in an odd-numbered store, the only place it can go is Building 3. Immediately, you see that answer (A) must be false and is the answer. No further analysis is necessary.

13. The correct answer is (B). Again, because Frank's Auto is locked into Building 7 on the south side, this question now places ABC Learning on the north side of the street, into Building 2, 3, or 4. The options for Buildings 6 and 8 are now limited to either "Gotta Dance" Studio or empty. Finally, because ABC Learning is on the north side of the street, Cat Supplies Plus must be on the south side. The only places for it are either Building 9 or 10. The diagram now looks like this:

North	1 B/D	2 A?	3 A? E?	4 A?	5 B/D
South	6 G/empty	7 Frank	8 G/empty	9 C? E?	10 C?

Because the question asks for the statement that "could be false," any statement that must be true is incorrect. Answer (A) must be true and is therefore incorrect because the diagram shows that Cat Supplies Plus must be either Building 9 or 10, both on the south side of the street. Answer (B) is the answer, since Everything's Roses might be in Building 9 or it might be in Building 3. Answer (C) is true, so it is incorrect. Answer (D) could be true, so it is incorrect. Answer (E) must be true since A is in either 2, 3, or 4 and C is in 9 or 10.

14. The correct answer is (E). Because the question asks you to test which situations are impossible, if you can find any possible arrangement that makes the situation work, then it is incorrect. For the first selection, that all stores on the north side are occupied, it is possible to arrange the stores as follows:

North	1 B	2 C	3 E	4 G	5 D
South	6 A	7 Frank	8 empty	9 empty	10 empty

Remember that this is not necessarily the only arrangement of the stores, but you are only asked for any possible arrangement that has the north side fully occupied. Because it is possible, then selection I cannot be included in the answer of impossible situations. Therefore, the correct answer must be either answers (B), (C), or (E).

Now test situation II. The only options for occupying Buildings 6 and 8 are ABC Learning and "Gotta Dance" Studio, so one of them would have to go in one building and one in the other. Because these two stores are taken, the only one remaining to occupy Building 10 is Cat Supplies Plus (recall the initial analysis that the only options for Building 10 are A, C, G, or empty). However, this creates an impossibility, since A and C cannot be on the same side of the street. Therefore, situation II is impossible, so the correct answer must be either answers (B), (D), or (E). Because (D) has already been eliminated, the options are (B) or (E).

Now test situation III. Recognize that Buildings 1, 5, and 7 are already occupied by, B, D, and F. Therefore, there are only four store names left to be placed, but there are five even-numbered buildings. Therefore, it would be impossible to have all even-numbered stores occupied, so situation III must be included in the answer.

The correct answer is (E), which includes both II and III.

Answers 15–18

DISCUSSION—This is a hybrid type of problem, which does not fit into any of the five primary categories. When faced with a problem type that is otherwise unidentifiable, your best method of success is to read the initial set of rules very carefully and pay close attention to the details.

15. The correct answer is (D). Counting the languages spoken by the individual people reveals that A, C, D, and E speak Spanish. No other language has four people.

16. The correct answer is (E). The only two people listed who share a common language are B and F, who could speak to each other in Swedish. None of the other pairs of people have a common language.

17. The correct answer is (B). Both A and D could talk to B in English and then translate to C in Spanish. E and B have nothing in common, so E could not translate. F and C have no language in common, so F could not translate. Therefore, the answer is (B).

18. The correct answer is (C). The only person who can talk directly to F is B, in Swedish, so there must be at least this one translator. However, B and C cannot talk directly to each other, so another translator is needed. Based on the previous question, B and C need only one translator, either A or D, so the fewest number of translators necessary between C and F is two. Therefore, the answer is (C).

Peterson's: www.petersons.com

Answers 19–22

DISCUSSION—This is a mapping problem, which should be easy to identify by the several references to directions, such as north, south, east, and west. Whenever you see initial rules with these references, you almost always have a mapping problem. This mapping problem is slightly different from most others because there is not a central "point" that divides the area into four quadrants. Instead, you have only a single dividing line, cutting the playing field into two halves. Otherwise, the strategy is the same as for a mapping problem.

19. The correct answer is (D). The first rule requires that 1, 2, and 3 belong to Team A. Therefore, answer (B) is incorrect. Outposts 4 and 5 belong to Team B, so answers (A) and (C) are incorrect. Answer (E) is incorrect because both Outpost 9 and Outpost 10 cannot belong to the same team, or that team would have six outposts. Therefore, answer (D) is correct.

20. The correct answer is (B). Team B must have Outposts 4, 5, and 6, so answer (A) is incorrect. Because Outpost 7 is the farthest west, it must belong to Team A, so answers (C) and (E) are incorrect. Answer (D) is incorrect because Outposts 8 and 9 may not belong to the same team. Therefore, answer (B) is correct.

21. The correct answer is (E). Outpost 8 has not previously been assigned to either team. However, because Outpost 1 is farther north than any other, then Outpost 8 may not belong to the same team as Outpost 1. Therefore, Outpost 8 must belong to Team B, so answer (D) is incorrect. Because Outpost 8 and Outpost 9 cannot belong to the same team, Outpost 9 must belong to Team A. Therefore, answer (E) is correct. Answers (A) and (B) could be true but could also be false since Outposts 8, 2, and 3 do not belong to the same team. Answer (C) could be either true or false since there are no limits on the placement of Outposts 8 and 5 in the east-west directions.

22. The correct answer is (D). Answer (A) is incorrect because it has already been shown that Outposts 8 and 9 cannot belong to the same team, regardless of the placement of Outpost 7. Answer (B) is incorrect because if Outpost 2 is north of Outpost 7, then Outpost 5, which is due east of Outpost 2, must also be north of Outpost 7. In addition, Outpost 1 must be north of all other outposts. Therefore, if Outposts 2 and 8 are north of Outpost 7, then a total of four outposts will be north of Outpost 7. Similarly, answer (C) is incorrect because placing Outposts 4 and 5 north of

Outpost 7 would require a total of four outposts (4, 5, 2, and 1) to be north of Outpost 7. Answer (D) could be true, and is therefore the correct answer, because Outpost 8 could be placed anywhere and could therefore be south of Outposts 1 and 5 (and 2). Answer (E) is incorrect because Outpost 7 is on the same side of the border as Outpost 1, and Outpost 1 must be the farthest north.

23. The correct answer is (B). The stated premises lead to the conclusion that someone in desperation may turn to unethical or illegal behavior. Answer (B) illustrates someone in a desperate situation turning to illegal behavior. Answer (A) goes beyond the scope of the argument by making unsupported judgment decisions about bankruptcy. Answer (C) is unsupported because nothing in the argument addresses the federal budget. Answers (D) and (E) may be correct statements, but they are not directly connected to the passage and are therefore incorrect answers.

24. The correct answer is (E). The passage assumes that neanderthals began at least 1 million years ago because of the statement that *Homo erectus* survived until about 1 million years ago. The assumption, therefore, is that there must have been some overlap between the two species. Answers (A), (C), and (D) may all be accurate scientific statements, but they are incorrect answers here because nothing in this passage says that current humans are in any way related to the other two species. Answer (B) is incorrect because the passage does not depend on the method of determining the dates; the dates that are provided in the premises are accepted as true.

25. The correct answer is (A). This passage concludes that a cover letter is instrumental in obtaining a job in sales. Answer (A) directly contradicts this by showing that the cover letters often are not read at all. Answer (B) is incorrect because the passage is not concerned with the merits of a job in sales but only with the methods of getting one. Answers (C) and (D) are incorrect because the passage is concerned with those jobs for which a resume is required; these statements are irrelevant. Answer (E) is incorrect because it says nothing about the cover letter.

PRACTICE TEST 3—ANSWERS

Answers 1–5

DISCUSSION—This is a connection problem. You can identify this because of the initial rules that provide many locations, with many rules informing you of connections between them. The best diagram for this kind of problem is to begin with the first rule and then draw a "map" of connections as the rules present them. Then simply use the diagram to answer the questions. The diagram for these initial rules would look like this:

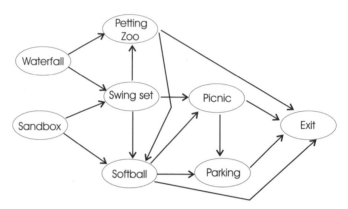

With your completed diagram, you are ready to work on the questions.

1. The correct answer is (D). The best approach for this kind of question, which asks for a statement that "must be true," is to test each selection to see if it could possibly be false. If any statement could be false, then it will be incorrect. Answer (A) is incorrect because there is no pathway from the Waterfall to the Sandbox. Answer (B) is incorrect because it is possible for a visitor to visit the Picnic Area after entering at the Waterfall (example: Waterfall, Swingset, Picnic Area). Answer (C) is incorrect because it is possible for a visitor NOT to visit either the Swingset or the Softball Field. Answer (D) must be true because the visitor will first see the Waterfall but cannot then go directly to the Exit and so must visit at least one other area. Answer (E) is incorrect because it is possible for a visitor to visit more than five areas (example: Waterfall, Swingset, Petting Zoo, Softball Field, Picnic Area, Parking Lot).

Peterson's Logic & Reading Review

2. The correct answer is (D). There are seven areas in the park. It is impossible for someone who enters at the Sandbox to see the Waterfall. The same visitor MAY visit all remaining areas (Sandbox, Swingset, Petting Zoo, Softball Field, Picnic Area, Parking Lot). Therefore, the maximum number of different areas is six.

3. The correct answer is (E). If the Picnic Area is the last area visited before the Exit, the visitor cannot go to the Parking Lot because from the Picnic Area, a visitor may only go to either the Parking Lot or the Exit. Therefore, answer (E) must be false. Any selection that could be true is incorrect. Answer (A) could be true, and is therefore incorrect, because it is possible to get to the Picnic Area from either entrance. Answer (B) could be true, and is therefore incorrect, because it is possible to get from the Petting Zoo to the Picnic Area. Answers (C) and (D), both regarding the Softball Field, could each be true, and are therefore incorrect, because it is possible but not necessary to visit the Softball Field on the way to the Picnic Area.

4. The correct answer is (C). From the Softball Field, the only possible remaining pathways are (1) to the Exit directly, (2) to the Picnic Area and then the Exit, (3) to the Parking Lot and then the Exit, or (4) to the Picnic Area, the Parking Lot, and then the Exit. Because of the last of these options, then answer (C) could be true and is therefore the correct answer. For the same reasons, (A) and (B) are incorrect. Answer (D) is incorrect because the maximum number of areas visited before the Softball Field is three (Waterfall, Swingset, Petting Zoo or Sandbox, Swingset, Petting Zoo). Answer (E) is incorrect because the visitor cannot visit the Picnic Area before the Softball Field.

5. The correct answer is (A). Test each answer against the map of pathways to find a flaw. Answer (A) is the only possible selection. Answer (B) is incorrect because a visitor cannot go from the Petting Zoo to the Swingset. Answer (C) is incorrect because a visitor cannot go from the Waterfall directly to the Softball Field. Answer (D) is incorrect because a visitor cannot go from the Picnic Area to the Softball Field. Answer (E) is incorrect because a visitor cannot go from the Parking Lot to the Petting Zoo.

6. The correct answer is (D). This is a conclusion question, in which you need to consider the details in the argument and use those facts to reach a conclusion. From the first sentence, if the sun rises before 6:00, then it can be concluded that Michael will not walk his dog before sunrise. This is answer (D).

7. The correct answer is (A). The question stem tells you directly that you are being asked to identify the assumption for this argument. To identify an assumption, you must read the initial facts of the argument, find the conclusion of the argument, and then figure out what the "connection" between them must be. That connection is the assumption. The conclusion in this argument assumes that an increase in Greek restaurants indicates an overall increase in people going to restaurants. Answer (A) indirectly restates this assumption by requiring that the number of other restaurants must not be declining to make room for the new Greek restaurants. Answer (B) is close to the correct answer, but it would allow the number of other restaurants to decline in order to make room for the Greek restaurants, so the total number of people attending restaurants may not be increasing. Answer (C) is incorrect because the issue is the number of people going out to eat, not the popularity of any particular kind of restaurant. Answer (D) raises a new issue, which might provide another fact suggesting an increase in the number of people eating out, but it is not directly enough related to this problem. Answer (E) is incorrect because the total number of people eating out may still be increasing, even if every restaurant is not filled to capacity.

8. The correct answer is (B). The "Which of the following, if true . . . ?" structure of this question shows you that this is an additional fact question. Your task is to find the answer that provides information that remains relevant to the initial argument and then answers the question. In this case, you are asked to find a statement that weakens the initial argument. This problem assumes that all sports figures will earn more than $1 million from merchandising and endorsements. By negating this assumption, answer (B) weakens the argument. Answers (A), (C), and (D) are all true statements, but they do not directly connect the Chief Justice's salary to sports figures' incomes. Answer (E) is incorrect because the relative levels of fame of different sports figures is not part of the problem.

Answers 9–14

DISCUSSION—This is a ranking problem. This can be seen from the initial rules that give you information about the finishing order of the contestants. There is a requirement that there are no ties, which lets you know that there is a "one-to-one" relationship between the finishing spaces and the people involved, one of the key elements of a ranking problem.

The best preparation for this kind of problem is to diagram as much as you can using the information given.

		Ed			(not Adam)
1	2	3	4	5	6

Ben/David or David/Ben must finish together, i.e., either first and second, fourth and fifth, or fifth and sixth.

9. The correct answer is (E). For a question like this one, asking you to choose a possible ranking, the best method is to check each answer against the rules provided until you find a conflict with the rules. Answer (A) is incorrect because Edgar is not third. Answer (B) is incorrect because Adam is not allowed to finish last. Answers (C) and (D) are incorrect because David and Ben must finish adjacent to each other. Answer (E) is the only answer that conforms to all the rules.

10. The correct answer is (A). This kind of question is approached the same way as the one above, but the correct answer is the one choice that does not conform to all the rules. Answer (A) is the correct answer because it does not have Edgar finishing third. All other answers are possible arrangements.

11. The correct answer is (C). When the question provides additional information, place that information into the diagram and see how much additional information you can learn. In this case, if Adam is fifth, the only possible placement for Ben and David to finish adjacent to each other is in the first and second positions. Therefore, answer (C) is the correct answer. Answer (A) is incorrect because Frank could be last but may not be first since either David or Ben must be first. Answer (B) is incorrect for the same reason. Answer (D) is incorrect because Ben could finish second. Answer (E) is incorrect because Edgar must finish third, from the initial rules.

12. The correct answer is (B). If Edgar, in third place, finishes before Ben, then Ben must be either fourth, fifth, or sixth. Because Ben and David must finish in adjacent positions, then David must be fifth if Ben is fourth, David may be fourth or sixth if Ben is fifth, and David must be fifth if Ben is sixth. From this analysis, it is clear that the fifth position must be taken by either Ben or David (and the other one may be in either fourth or sixth). Because fifth place must be taken by either Ben or David, then answer (B) must be false and is therefore the correct answer. Each of the other answers could be true, even though they may not be required to be true.

13. The correct answer is (D). The best approach to this question is to consider which runners CANNOT finish last, and then the answer must list all other runners. From the initial rules, Adam may not finish last. Edgar must finish third and so cannot be last. There are no other rules prohibiting any other runner from finishing last. Therefore, the correct answer must be (D), listing the remaining four runners.

14. The correct answer is (D). If David is first, then Ben must be second, since these two must finish together. Third place is taken by Edgar. Adam must be either fourth or fifth since he cannot be last. Carl and Frank may take any position from fourth to sixth. Answer (A) is incorrect because for Carl and Frank both to finish before Adam would place Adam into last position, which is not allowed. Answer (B) is incorrect because Ben finishes second only to David. Answer (C) is incorrect because Adam must finish after Ben. Answer (D) is the correct answer because Frank could finish fourth, with Adam fifth and Carl sixth. Answer (E) is incorrect because Edgar must finish before Carl.

Answers 15–18

DISCUSSION—This problem can be identified as a distribution problem as soon as you realize that there are "two rows" of people to be placed. This is not a simple ranking problem because the people are not all placed in a single straight row. You need to pay attention not only to where people are in relation to each other side by side but also to whether they are "in front" or "in back." The rules are mostly the same, but you have this additional factor to consider. The solution still begins with creating a diagram to mark out the initial rules, which will then help you with answering the questions.

15. The correct answer is (D). This question presents four correct seatings and one incorrect one. Answer (D) is the incorrect seating because it places Leroy directly in front of Marion. All the other answers present possible seating arrangements.

16. The correct answer is (B). Answer (B) is the one sentence that must be false. Suggesting that Peter and Ophelia sit next to Quint would place them in Seats 1 and 3 of the second row. However, Peter and Ophelia must both sit somewhere to the right of Kathy. If one of them is in Seat 1, then this rule is broken. Therefore, answer (B) must be false. All other statements could be true.

17. The correct answer is (E). If Ophelia and Peter sit next to each other in the front row, then Kathy must be in either Seat 1 or 2 of the front row so that they will remain on her right. This will leave one empty seat in the front row and three empty seats—Seats 1, 3, and 4—in the second row. Answer (E) is the statement that must be false because placing Marion and Leroy left of Quint would require them to be either directly next to each other or one directly in front of the other. All other answers are possible.

18. The correct answer is (C). If Kathy and Nate must both be in Seat 3s and because Kathy must be in the front row, then Kathy is in the front row Seat 3 and Nate is in the back row Seat 3. Because Peter and Ophelia must be somewhere to the right of Kathy, then they must both be in Seat 4, one in front of the other (either order). This leaves Leroy, Marion, and Robert, and the open seats are Row 1, Seats 1 and 2, and Row 2, Seat 1. Because Leroy and Marion may not be next to each other, they cannot both be in Row 1, and because they cannot be directly in front or back of each other, they cannot both be in Seat 1. Therefore, one of them must be in Row 2, Seat 1, and the other must be in Row 1, Seat 2. Finally, Robert must be in Row 1, Seat 1, because it is the only available seat. Therefore, the one statement that could be false is answer (C), since Leroy could be in either Row 2, Seat 1, or Row 1, Seat 2. All other statements must be true.

Answers 19–22

DISCUSSION—This is a hybrid question, which is unlike any of the five primary question types. This "secret code" requires you to pay attention to the rules, but the rules are not the kind that can be easily diagrammed. Instead, you must review the rules carefully at the beginning of the problem and then, for each question, make sure that you take account of all the rules involved.

19. The correct answer is (A). Answer (A) is the one choice that satisfies all the rules. Answer (B) is incorrect because 4 may not be the last number in a code word. Answer (C) is incorrect because 2 must be the last number, since 2 is the second number. Answer (D) is incorrect because 1 must be the first number. Answer (E) is incorrect because the word must have a 4 if it ends in 5.

20. The correct answer is (D). This question contains a negative "not." Therefore, four of the answers may make acceptable three-number code words and one does not. The first thing to notice is that every word must contain the number 1 and may only use the number 1 once. Therefore, answers (A), (D), and (E), with only two numbers, will start with 1 and repeat the other number twice. Answer (A) is incorrect because the word 122 would be acceptable. Answer (B), with three numbers given, would allow the answers 124 and 142; the first of these is not possible because a word may not end in 4, but the second, 142, is allowable, so B is incorrect. Answer (C) would allow the words 125 or 152. 125 is not allowed because, with 2 as the second number, it would have to end with 2; however, 152 is allowable, so (C) is incorrect. Answer (D) is the correct answer because the word 155 is not allowed, since a word ending in 5 would have to contain the number 4. Answer (E) is incorrect because the word 133 is allowable.

21. The correct answer is (B). With the three numbers 1, 2, and 3, where the number 1 must appear only in the first position, the possibilities are 122, 133, 123, and 132. The only word that is not allowable is 123, since having 2 in the second position would require a 2 at the end. Therefore, the answer is three words are possible.

22. The correct answer is (B). If a word ends in 5, then the word must contain a 4. The word will also have to start with 1 since all words must. However, the three-number word 145 would be allowable, so answer (A) is incorrect. Answer (B) is the answer, since, if 2 were the second number, then a 2 would also have to be the last number; if this were the case, then the word could not end in 5. As a result, 2 may not be the second number. Answers (C) and (E) could both be true, but they could also be false. Answer (D) must be false since 1 may only appear first.

23. The correct answer is (B). For a conclusions question, which is the category for this question type, your first object is to read the statements of the argument closely and limit your conclusion to the explicit statements that are provided for you. Be careful not to make connections that are not already stated in the argument. Nothing in the two sentences of the problem directly links Redford and Spielberg. Therefore, it is possible that the two could be linked, so answer (B) is correct. (Note that answer (B) does not say that ANY movies directed by Spielberg ARE starring Redford, just that they could.) Answers (A) and (E) are incorrect because there is no link between Spielberg and the Academy Awards. Answers (C) and (D) directly contradict the first sentence and so are incorrect.

24. The correct answer is (B). This argument directly connects the number of variations created based on a composer's original music to that composer's "greatness." This is answer (B). Answers (A) and (D) both stretch beyond the scope of the original argument. Answer (C) is incorrect because it adds the fact of a single additional composer, generally irrelevant to the argument. Finally, answer (E) is incorrect because Chopin's motive is not mentioned in the problem.

25. The correct answer is (E). Whenever you see a question stem that asks, as this one does, for you to select a statement that "must be true," the question is a conclusions question. Your task for this question is to focus carefully on the specific facts in the argument alone, and do not make any assumptions or even any "common sense" connections that are not explicitly stated. In this question, since no President had been impeached since 1865, then at no time since then has the government spent more than $2 billion on travel expenses. As a result of that conclusion, it can also be concluded that no budget since then has exceeded $8 trillion. Therefore, answer (E) is the correct answer. Answers (A), (B), and (D) all contradict these conclusions. Answer (C) may or may not be a true statement, but that does not make it a logical conclusion based on the information provided.

PRACTICE TEST 4—ANSWERS

Answers 1–5

DISCUSSION—This is a distribution problem, since the number of classrooms does not directly match the number of available room spaces. Your task is to distribute the classes into the appropriate rooms.

1. The correct answer is (D). The rules provided do not give enough introductory information to allow a complete diagram of the classroom spaces, so the best approach is to test each of the answers to see which one must be false. Answer (A) is incorrect because no two history classes may be on the same floor. Answer (B) is incorrect because Ancient Asia may not be on the first floor. Answer (C) is incorrect because Special Stocks must be paired with Confucius at Work and therefore cannot be paired with Unstable Markets. Answer (D) is the correct choice because there is not enough information to suggest that Babylon Times and Confucius at Work may not be on adjacent floors. Answer (E) is incorrect because placing the business classes on the even-numbered floors only would require Confucius at Work and Special Stocks to share one floor and Turnovers & Mergers and Unstable Markets to share the other floor. Only two other classes remain, with three vacant floors. Since no floor may remain vacant, this arrangement is impossible.

2. The correct answer is (E). For the same reason that answer (E) of the previous question is incorrect, Unstable Markets may not share a floor with any other classroom. If Unstable Markets shared a floor with any other classroom and considering that Confucius at Work and Special Stocks must share a floor, then only two other classes would remain to fill three vacant floors. (By this point you should recognize, for following questions, that Confucius at Work and Special Stocks are the only two classes that are allowed to share a floor.)

3. The correct answer is (B). If the business classes are on odd-numbered floors only, then Dental Associates and Special Stocks must be on the first floor, since that is the only odd-numbered floor with two classroom spaces. Therefore, Turnovers & Mergers and Unstable Markets will be on Floors 3 and 5, in either order, and Ancient Asia and Babylon Times will be on either Floor 2 or 4. Considering this information, answer (B) is the only possible answer. All other selections must be false.

4. The correct answer is (A). If Confucius at Work is on the first floor, then Special Stocks must also be on the first floor. Because the business classes may not be on adjacent floors and because the remaining Floors 2 through 5 will each have exactly one class, then the business classes will have to be on the odd-numbered floors and the remaining two history classes will have to be on the even-numbered floors. Therefore, answer (A), placing a business class on an even-numbered floor, must be false and is the correct answer. The other answers are all possibly true.

5. The correct answer is (A). From the analysis of the previous questions, it should be evident by now that the combination of Confucius at Work and Special Stocks must be on the first floor. No other location is possible. If this pair were placed on the second floor, then no business class could be on either the first or third floor, since two business classes may not be on adjacent floors. As a result, the remaining two business classes must either both be on the fourth floor or must be on levels four and five. They cannot both be on level four because that would leave three empty floors to be occupied by only the two remaining history classes. They cannot be on levels four and five because two business classes may not be on adjacent floors. Therefore, the Confucius at Work/Special Stocks combination may not be on the second floor. The same analysis would show why this pair cannot be on the fourth floor. Therefore, Confucius at Work and Special Stocks must be on the first floor, so neither one, obviously, may be on the second floor. Therefore, answers (D) and (E) are incorrect. Because no two business classes may be on adjacent floors, then the second floor may not have either Turnovers & Mergers or Unstable Markets. Therefore, answers (B) and (C) are incorrect.

6. The correct answer is (D). The conclusion assumes that stock brokers would have some added knowledge or insight that would give them more success at playing the game. Answer (D) negates this assumption by making all players equal, providing everyone with the complete rules and strategies. Answer (A) is incorrect because it would strengthen, not weaken, the conclusion. Answers (B) and (E) are irrelevant statements about the game, which do not address the issue of the stock brokers. Answer (C) is incorrect because, although it may be a true statement, it does not address the level of success of the stock brokers who do have time to play the game.

7. The correct answer is (A). If the iguanas have been on the Earth "continuously" for 5 million years and the dinosaurs have never existed at the same time as the iguanas, then it can be concluded that the dinosaurs disappeared before the iguanas appeared more than 5 million years ago. This is answer (A). Note that the first sentence of the problem only says that the dinosaurs became extinct "at least" 3 million years ago; 5 million years ago is still consistent with this statement, so answer (B) is incorrect. Answer (C) cannot be concluded because it goes beyond the scope of the problem. Answer (D) directly contradicts the last sentence of the problem, and answer (E) directly contradicts the second sentence.

8. The correct answer is (A). The conclusion assumes that the total number of inches of rainfall is the only fact that determines the amount of money needed for flood insurance or recovery. Answer (A) suggests that it may be the number of individual rainfalls, regardless of the amount of rain that falls each time, that indicates the amount of money required. Answers (B), (C), and (D) all address issues not directly related to this argument. Answer (E) is incorrect because it talks about the history of the area but does not make the connection between this year's rainfall and this year's costs.

Answers 9–14

DISCUSSION—This is a scheduling problem, which becomes evident when you see the key words that the teacher is "scheduling" teaching sessions, with one student per session, and those sessions are scheduled for mornings and afternoons during the week.

9. The correct answer is (E). Check each answer against the rules to see which cause conflicts. Answer (A) is incorrect because Albert and Billie must have their lesson on the same day and therefore cannot both appear in the morning. Answer (B) is incorrect because Chuckie can only appear in the afternoon. Answer (C) is incorrect because Felicia must be on Monday. Answer (D) is incorrect because George cannot have his lesson on Thursday. Answer (E) is correct because it satisfies all the rules.

10. The correct answer is (C). This question needs the same approach as the previous question. Answer (A) is incorrect because Felicia must have her lesson in the morning. Answer (B) is incorrect because Dolly must have her lesson in the morning. Answer (C) is the correct answer. Answer (D) is incorrect because Albert and Billie must appear on the same day. Answer (E) is incorrect because Dolly must appear in the morning.

11. The correct answer is (D). Answer (A) is incorrect because Albert and Billie must be scheduled for the same day, so Albert and Felicia cannot be on the same day. Answer (B) is incorrect for the same reason. Answer (C) is incorrect because George is not available on Thursdays. Answer (D) is the correct answer because Felicia must be Monday morning and Chuckie must be any afternoon. Answer (E) is incorrect because Felicia must be on Monday morning.

12. The correct answer is (B). The first couple, George and Felicia, could be together, both on Monday. The second couple, Albert and Chuckie, cannot be on the same day because Albert and Billie must be on the same day. The third couple, Felicia and Dolly, cannot be on the same day because Felicia must be Monday morning and Dolly must also be in the morning only. The fourth couple, Ellis and Chuckie, have no limitations and may be together. Therefore, the correct answer is selection (B), answers II and III.

Peterson's Logic & Reading Review

13. The correct answer is (C). If Albert's lesson is on Wednesday afternoon, then Billie must be on Wednesday morning. As a result, answer (C) must be false, since Billie and Chuckie cannot be on the same day. The other answers are all possible, though not necessarily true.

14. The correct answer is (D). If Albert is on Friday, then Billie must also be on Friday. Therefore, neither of them can be on Monday. So answers (A) and (C) are incorrect. Because Felicia must be Monday morning, the correct answer must include Felicia. However, because Dolly must also be in the morning, she cannot be on Monday, since Monday morning is already taken by Felicia. Therefore, the correct answer cannot include Dolly. As a result, answers (B) and (E) are incorrect and answer (D) must be the answer.

Answers 15–18

DISCUSSION—This is a mapping problem, as can be seen by the directional rules "north," "south," "east," and "west." The central station for the network is at the center of the grid for your diagram.

15. The correct answer is (C). From the set of initial rules, Station D may not be north of Station C, and Station C must be in Quadrant II. Therefore, Station D may not be in Quadrant I or IV. If Station C is the only station in Quadrant II, then Station D will have to be in Quadrant III. Therefore, the answer is (C). The other answers are all possibly true but are not necessarily true.

16. The correct answer is (D). If Quadrant I has three stations, and Quadrant IV must have at least two stations from the initial rules, then only three stations remain for Quadrants II and III together. Station C must be in Quadrant II. As a result, at most two stations remain for Quadrant III. Therefore, answer (A) is incorrect. Answer (B) is incorrect because Station E must be in the same quadrant as Station F, so this answer would place Stations C, E, and F into Quadrant II, leaving no stations for Quadrant III. Answers (C) and (E) are incorrect for the same reason, since they would require three stations to be in Quadrant III. Answer (D) is possibly true.

17. The correct answer is (E). If every quadrant must have exactly two stations, then E and F must be in a quadrant together. Therefore, answers (C) and (D) are incorrect for including Station E. All of the remaining stations could be in the same quadrant with Station D. Therefore, the correct answer is (E).

18. The correct answer is (B). If Quadrant I and Quadrant II each have only one station, then Station C is the only station in Quadrant II. Also, because no quadrant may have more than three stations, Quadrant III and Quadrant IV will each have three stations. Because Station D may not be north of Station C, Station D will have to be in Quadrant III, placed no farther north than Station C. Based on this analysis, answer (B) is the one statement that must be false. All the other statements either must be true or could be true.

Answers 19–22

DISCUSSION—This is a hybrid problem. You need to focus not only on the placement where each person will end up but also on the "category" that each person comes from. This adds an extra twist to the standard distribution problem type.

19. The correct answer is (B). Answer (A) is incorrect because Diane and Carl may not work for the same office. Answer (C) is incorrect because Heather and Florence must work for the same office. Answer (D) is incorrect because if Diane and Elvin work together, then that office must take four interns. Answer (E) is incorrect because The Senate Legal Office may not take four interns without taking Diane.

20. The correct answer is (C). If Diane works for The Senate Legal Office, then Carl and George must both work for The Supreme Court Library, since Carl and Diane may not work together and George must always work for The Supreme Court Library. Heather and Florence, who must work together, may not work for The Supreme Court Library, since that would give The Supreme Court Library four students without having Diane. As a result, The Senate Legal Office will have Diane, Heather, and Florence and The Supreme Court Library must have George and Carl. Elvin and Ivan will then be split, with either one working for The Senate Legal Office and the other one for The Supreme Court Library. This analysis requires that answer (C) is the only statement that must be true. The other statements either must be false or could be either true or false.

21. The correct answer is (E). If Heather works for The Supreme Court Library, then Florence must also work for The Supreme Court Library. George, as always, must also work for The Supreme Court Library. That leaves one more student to be hired by The Supreme Court Library, with the remaining three to work for The Senate Legal Office. Diane and Carl cannot both work for The Senate Legal Office because they are not allowed to work together. Diane and Elvin cannot both work for The Senate Legal Office because if they were put together, then The Senate Legal Office would have to have four students. The only way to separate Diane from both Carl and Elvin is to have Diane work for The Supreme Court Librar, and Carl, Elvin, and Ivan work for The Senate Legal Office. This analysis shows that answer (E) is the only statement that could be true.

22. The correct answer is (A). The best way to approach a question like this one is to test each answer to see if it is possible to make each answer be true; if so, then it is not a statement that must be false and it is therefore an incorrect answer. Answer (A) is the correct answer because there is no way to arrange Heather and Elvin so that they work for the same office. It is important to notice, first, that Heather must work together with Florence. Therefore, Heather, Elvin, and Florence would have to be placed as a group. If these three people work for The Senate Legal Office and if The Senate Legal Office is only hiring three people, then the remaining four students would all have to work for The Supreme Court Library. This is impossible since Diane and Carl may not work together. The second check is to see if Heather, Elvin, and Florence could work for The Supreme Court Library. Since George also must work for The Supreme Court Library, then the remaining three students must work for The Senate Legal Office, and Carl and Diane are again thrown together. Therefore, answer (A) must be false. The other four statements could be either true or false.

23. The correct answer is (C). This is a "nonsense" conclusion problem, forcing added concentration on the logical relationship of the information provided while ignoring "common sense," which is of no help. If there are any blue cars, as suggested by the first sentence, and no blue things have ever traveled to the bottom of the ocean, then it can be concluded that some cars—the blue ones—have never been to the bottom of the ocean. Therefore, (C) is the best answer. Answer (A) cannot be concluded because there is no information provided about what has traveled to the bottom of the ocean—just about what has NOT. Answers (B), (D), and (E) all go beyond the information provided and so cannot be concluded, no matter how reasonable they may or may not seem.

24. The correct answer is (A). This argument assumes that David would be able to defeat all his opponents as easily as he defeated Goliath. Therefore, if answer (A) were true, this argument would be more likely to be true. Answer (B) is incorrect because it weakens the argument and suggests that David would be defeated before he could use all his ammunition. Answers (C) and (D) are incorrect because nothing in the problem suggests that the relative sizes of David and Goliath had anything to do with the outcome of the fight. Answer (E) would support the argument, but it does not strengthen it as directly as answer (A) does.

25. The correct answer is (B). This is a hidden assumption question, which requires you to first identify the conclusion and then determine what additional information, beyond the facts that are explicitly stated in the argument, is necessary to make that conclusion a necessary truth. Based on the first sentence in this argument, the dog will bark and assume an alert position when she "hears" footsteps. The conclusion of the argument therefore depends on the dog's hearing, suggesting answer (B). Answer (A) is incorrect because the problem only focuses on the situation of intruders as they approach the house, not after they enter. Answers (C), (D), and (E) are all irrelevant because they introduce facts that are not part of the problem.

Peterson's Logic & Reading Review

PRACTICE TEST 5—ANSWERS

Answers 1–5

DISCUSSION—This is a scheduling problem. The clues to identifying this kind of problem are the references to days of the week and the fact that some items are placed "before" and "after" others. In this way, it is similar to a ranking problem, but you need to pay attention to the particular details about the timing.

1. The correct answer is (D). The key to this question is not only the list of shows that are provided for the 8:00 slot but also the list of shows remaining for the 9:00 slot. Answer (A) is incorrect because Tuesday, which starts with a drama, must have a variety show at 9:00 because a comedy may not follow a drama. This is impermissible because two variety shows may not be scheduled on consecutive nights. Answers (B), (C), and (E) are all incorrect for the same reason. Answer (D) is the only permissible schedule.

2. The correct answer is (B). It should be clear that, since variety shows may not be scheduled on consecutive nights and no show may be scheduled twice on the same night, the three variety shows must be scheduled on Monday, Wednesday, and Friday. Therefore, Tuesday and Thursday may only have comedies and dramas. Since a comedy may not follow a drama on any given night, then Tuesday and Thursday must both have a comedy at 8:00 and a drama at 9:00. Based on this analysis, answers (A), (C), (D), and (E) must all be false. Answer (B) is the only statement that could be true.

3. The correct answer is (A). Based on the analysis of the previous question, Tuesday and Thursday must both have a comedy at 8:00 and a drama at 9:00. (The additional information given for this question stem, that a drama is scheduled for 9:00 on Tuesday, is actually superfluous, because that must be the case.) Therefore, answer (A) must be true and is the correct answer. The other four statements either must be false or may be either true or false.

4. The correct answer is (D). Recall from previous questions that the variety shows must be on Monday, Wednesday, and Friday. Also recall that Tuesday and Thursday must both have the comedy-drama combination. Therefore, all three comedies are used up on Tuesday, Wednesday, and Thursday, so Monday and Friday must have dramas and varieties. Because a drama may not follow a variety, then Monday and Friday must both start with a drama and end with a variety. Therefore, the entire week is scheduled, except that Wednesday could have either the comedy or the variety scheduled first. The 8:00 schedule for the week must be D-C-(C or V)-C-D. The 9:00 schedule must be V-D-(V or C)-D-V. As a result, answer (A) could be true, answer (B) must be true, answer (C) must be true, and answer (E) must be true. Only answer (D) must be false.

5. The correct answer is (C). The only type of show that could be scheduled at 8:00 on Wednesday and Thursday is a comedy. It could not be a variety because two variety shows may not be scheduled on consecutive nights. It could not be a drama because whenever a drama is scheduled for 8:00, the 9:00 show must be a variety. This would then require the three variety shows to be scheduled consecutively on Tuesday through Thursday at 9:00, which is also impermissible. Therefore, the comedies are all at 8:00 on Tuesday through Thursday. The 9:00 shows for Tuesday through Thursday must be drama, variety, and drama, in that order. That leaves two varieties and two dramas to fill the four slots on Monday and Friday. Since each night must have one of each type of show, then each night must have one drama and one variety. Finally, because a drama may not follow a variety on any one night, then both Monday and Friday must start with a drama and end with a variety. Therefore, Monday and Friday must have the same schedule, and answer (C) is the answer. All four remaining answers must be false.

6. The correct answer is (C). The question stem clearly tells you that your task is to identify the assumption in the argument, so you can identify this as a hidden assumption question. The assumption in this argument can be seen because the problem links the buried artifacts to a belief in religion. This "link," or connection, is the assumption. Answer (C) states this link by suggesting that burying people with tools and utensils shows a belief in religion and therefore an advanced society. The other statements could all be true, but they do not make the required connection between the buried artifacts and the belief in religion.

7. The correct answer is (D). If the PTA selects a senior as the Student Representative, then the second sentence of the argument says they will give more money to the high school. If they do not give more money to the high school (for whatever reasons), then it can be concluded that the PTA did not select a senior as the Student Representative, so answer (D) is the best answer. Answers (A) and (B) make "judgment" decisions about what the PTA should or should not do, which goes beyond the scope of the problem. Answer (C) is incorrect because nothing in the problem mentions anything about the current Student Representative. Answer (E) is close to the correct answer but is incorrect because the PTA could give more money to the school even if the Student Representative is a senior or a junior.

8. The correct answer is (C). Based on the statements provided, one would expect the stock prices of Acme Company to rise after the announcement. If the price decreases, then something about this particular merger must be causing a change in the opinion of investors. Answer (C) is the selection that repeats this conclusion, which is what you look for when a hidden assumption question asks you to "strengthen the argument." Answer (A) addresses only "average" investors, but nothing in the argument limits it to "average" investors. Answer (B) is irrelevant or at best would contradict the argument by suggesting that the price should increase because of lower supply. Answer (D) is incorrect because nothing in the argument suggests any reliance on the negotiations involved in creating the merger. Answer (E) is incorrect because there is nothing in the argument suggesting that prime lending rates have any effect on stock prices.

Answers 9–14

DISCUSSION—This is a ranking problem. You can identify this as a ranking problem because each travel package must include all eight cities, and your task is simply to rank or order the cities according to the rules.

9. The correct answer is (D). Answer (D) is the one that satisfies all of the rules. Answers (A) and (E) are incorrect because they do not have Quincy fourth. Answer (B) is incorrect because Montreal and New York are not visited together. Answer (C) is incorrect because Kingman is before Ottawa but no other city is visited between the two.

10. The correct answer is (C). If New York must be first, then Montreal must be second on the list. For that reason, every other city will be visited after New York and Montreal, so answer (C) is the correct answer. The other answers all COULD be true, but they are not necessarily true.

11. The correct answer is (E). If Kingman is second on the list and Quincy must always be fourth, then the only spaces in the tour for the combination of Montreal and New York to be visited together are fifth/sixth, sixth/seventh, or seventh/eighth. In any of these possibilities, both Montreal and New York will be visited after Quincy. Therefore, answer (E) must be false and is the correct answer. All of the other answers could be true or could be false, but there is not sufficient information to prove any of them false.

12. The correct answer is (A). If Jacksonville is seventh, then it would prevent the combination of Montreal/New York from being at the end of the tour. Lexington cannot be last because the rules prevent it from being either first or last. Quincy cannot be last because it must always be fourth. Jacksonville may not be last because it is being placed seventh. As a result, the only remaining cities are Kingman, Ottawa, and Philadelphia. Therefore, the correct answer must be (A).

13. The correct answer is (A). If Kingman is seventh, then, for the same reasons addressed above, neither Lexington, Montreal, New York, nor Quincy may be visited eighth. Therefore, answers (B), (C), and (D) are all incorrect. Answer (E) is incorrect because Ottawa may not be visited immediately after Kingman. Therefore, Jacksonville is the only selection that may be visited last. (Note that Philadelphia could also be last, but it is not one of the answers.)

14. The correct answer is (C). If Quincy is immediately after Ottawa, then Ottawa would have to be third (because Quincy is always fourth). Considering the rules provided, it seems reasonable to expect that the correct answer will probably have something to do with the two-space combination of Montreal and New York and use the first two spaces on the tour. Answers (C) and (E) are the only answers that address the first two spaces on the tour. Answer (C) must be false because, if Montreal is one of the first two cities visited, then New York would have to be the other one. Answer (E) is incorrect because Philadelphia and Lexington could be the first two cities on the tour. The other answers, (A), (B), and (D), could all be true, with insufficient information to prove them false.

Answers 15–18

DISCUSSION—This is a mapping problem, easily identifiable by the central administrative office and the directional references for the outlet stores placed around it.

15. The correct answer is (C). Answer (A) is incorrect because the only limitation on OS 2 is that it must be due south of OS 1. It is possible for OS 1, which is only required to be somewhere north of the Administrative Office, to be far enough north and west of the Administrative Office so that OS 2 may be south of OS 1 and still be northwest of the Administrative Office. Answer (B) is incorrect because there are no limitations at all on the placement of OS 3, so it may be northwest of the Administrative Office. Answer (C) is the correct answer. Because OS 4 must be southeast of the Administrative Office and OS 5 must be due east of OS 4, then OS 5 must also be southeast of the Administrative Office. Answers (D) and (E) are incorrect because the only limitation on OS 6 and OS 7 is that they must be somewhere west of the Administrative Office; they may, of course, be northwest.

16. The correct answer is (E). Answer (E) is correct because OS 1 must be somewhere north of the Administrative Office, and this question requires OS 6 to be southwest of the Administrative Office. Therefore, OS 1 will be somewhere north of OS 6. The other answers could all be true but could also be false and are therefore incorrect. Answers (A) and (D) are incorrect because there is no connection between OS 6 and OS 7, so OS 7 must only be somewhere west of the Administrative Office. Answer (B) is incorrect because OS 2, which must be due south of OS 1, could be so far south of OS 1 that it is also south of OS 6. Answer (C) is incorrect because OS 4, which must be southeast of the Administrative Office, could be less south than OS 6.

17. The correct answer is (B). If OS 4 is due east of OS 2 and OS 5 is already due east of OS 4, then OS 5 must also be due east of OS 2. Because OS 2 is due south of OS 1, then both OS 4 and OS 5 are somewhere southeast of OS 1. Therefore, answer (B) must be false. The other selections are all possibly true.

18. The correct answer is (D). OS 4 and OS 5 must be east of the Administrative Office because OS 4 is southeast of the Administrative Office and OS 5 is due east of OS 4. Therefore, only one other store may be built east of the Administrative Office. Because OS 1 and OS 2 must be directly in a north-south line with each other but may be in any position east or west of the Administrative Office, then if one of them is east of the Administrative Office, they both would have to be east of the Administrative Office. Since only one more store may be east of the Administrative Office, then neither OS 1 nor OS 2 may be east of the Administrative Office. OS 6 and OS 7 are both required to be west of the Administrative Office. Therefore, OS 3, the only remaining store, must be east of the Administrative Office. Considering this analysis, answer (D) is the only statement that may be false, since there is no limitation on the relative placements of OS 6 and OS 7.

Answers 19–22

DISCUSSION—This is a connection problem, which can be identified by the initial rules with the several buildings and the walkways connecting them. The best method for solving a connection problem, once it is identified as such, is to read through the rules individually, creating a "map" of the connections.

19. The correct answer is (C). Because of the arrangement of the walkways, the only way to or from Building U is the walkway to Building S, and the only way to or from Building V is the walkway to Building W. As a result, visiting either Building U or Building V will end the travels. With this in mind, the maximum number of buildings is 7 (example: RSXYZWV, RTXYZWV, or RWZYXSU).

20. The correct answer is (E). There are three possible paths that provide the shortest route from Building R to Building Y: RSXY, RTXY, and RWZY. Recognizing these three possibilities shows that answer (E) is the only statement that must be true. Answer (A) could be true and could also be false. The other three answer must all be false.

21. The correct answer is (C). In order to visit both Buildings U and V, a visitor will have to visit either Building S or Building W more than once. Therefore, answer (C) is the one statement that must be false. The other statements could all be true. Answer (A) could be true with the pathway RSUSXYZWV. Answers (B) and (D) could both be true with the pathway RWVWZXSU. Answer (E) could be true since this question allows the visitor to visit any building as often as necessary; therefore, it is possible to visit all nine buildings.

22. The correct answer is (A). With a new walkway connecting Buildings V and Z, a visitor may now visit all nine buildings without going to any building twice: RTWVZYXSU. The other statements must all be false.

23. The correct answer is (C). This is a conclusion argument, which can be seen from the direct wording of the question stem, asking you to identify what other conclusion the philosopher can make. For a conclusion question like this one, you must read the specific facts contained in the initial argument very closely before testing the answers. In selecting an answer, be sure to choose the answer that is based only on explicit statements in the argument and not on any other inferences you might make. The conclusion of this argument can be reached by considering only the last sentence. The added information says that life does NOT mean nothing, thereby contradicting the conclusion of the last sentence of the argument. By contradicting the conclusion of an if-then argument, one can conclude the opposite of the premise of the sentence, i.e., that "I do not think." Recognizing this, the only correct answers could be (C) or (E). (E) is incorrect because the argument states that if the speaker does not think, then ". . . I am not." Therefore, the only correct answer is (C).

24. The correct answer is (D). This is a hidden assumption question, which is evident in the question stem that asks you to find the "necessary assumption" in the argument. This argument assumes that homeowners can receive as much effective heat by using the same amount of "coiled element system" heaters as they can with standard heating units. If, on the other hand, the heating units were half as effective and required homeowners to use twice as many heating units, then electric costs may not actually decrease. Answer (D) repeats this necessary assumption. Answer (A) seems to be an obvious truth, but it addresses a homeowner's motivation rather than the actual effect of using the new heating units. Answers (B) and (E) address other effects of using the special heating units but say nothing about electric bills. Answer (C) addresses lowering the cost of purchasing the heating units but not of using them.

25. The correct answer is (E). This argument depends on the hidden assumption that the quality of a filmmaker's materials and equipment leads directly to the quality of the finished product and that no other factors are involved. Answer (E) shows that even with the best materials, some filmmakers do not create excellent movies. Answer (A) is incorrect in that it does not recognize the individual quality of the filmmaker. Answer (B) does not address the quality of the finished product and so is insufficient. Answer (C) is irrelevant because nothing in the argument suggests that the cost of the materials is a factor. Answer (D) is insufficient without the additional information about the finished films produced by the students involved.

Part IV

READING COMPREHENSION

Reading comprehension is one of the key skills necessary for success. Whether you read instructions for assembling furniture, the terms of a contract, or a chapter in a textbook, you must be able to understand what you read. An assessment of reading comprehension is a good predictor of performance in graduate-level courses. Taking national tests is one way to determine a student's ability to read passages and grasp major ideas, skills that are especially crucial in graduate classes.

Traditionally, course work at the graduate level depends heavily on lengthy reading assignments. Students, then, are required to read and comprehend a great deal of material on their own in addition to synthesizing information gleaned from class lectures. Reading comprehension is one of the core skills. It requires the ability to vary one's reading rate, to determine unfamiliar vocabulary by using context clues, to make valid inferences, and to identify and understand main ideas.

The reading comprehension portion on standardized tests is often the part of the test that students dislike or even fear the most. Citing such reasons as boring content, students contend that it is difficult to maintain a strong focus on the ideas in the passage. Admittedly, the material can sometimes seem to be tedious or uninteresting, but the reader must nevertheless sustain steady attention to details. One question that arises is how the reader should approach these reading comprehension passages and questions.

As you read a passage, focus your attention on the ideas presented and ask yourself often, "What does this mean? What is the writer saying here? Why is this important? How is this information related to previous details? What can possibly come next?" Mark details that you believe to be important. Some important reading comprehension skills include the ability to recognize a sequence of events, to recognize cause-effect relationships, and to see connections among details

To complete the reading comprehension portion of standardized tests, you should read as carefully as possible without sacrificing content to time. As you read a passage, mark details that seem to be important. You can make any kind of marks in the test booklet; just don't make stray marks on the answer sheet. Underline key phrases; circle important details; make small notes in the margin. Read at a steady pace, being careful to note important information and to assimilate key ideas, but not too slowly. You want to read the passage only once. Rereading it can be a waste of precious time.

KEY READING SKILLS

The following are eight of the important reading skills that are necessary to do well on any Reading Comprehension question. In the next chapter, we will go into greater detail, with sample questions and fully explained answers. Consider this a warm-up.

1. DRAW INFERENCES

An inference is a logical conclusion or deduction a reader makes as a result of examining a passage. Often, reading comprehension questions focus on this skill because it requires the reader to draw his or her own conclusions rather than locate the specific answer in a passage. In other words, they test your ability to make a valid inference and a sound conclusion. The careful reader has to select an accurate response to a question involving inference without being deceived by "distracter" responses. Consider yourself as a kind of detective as you build your skills in this area. Pay attention to details but realize that you cannot merely scan the passage to find the correct answers to questions.

2. DETERMINE PRIMARY PURPOSE

One of the primary skills in reading comprehension is having the ability to determine the primary purpose of a passage. This skill is often tested by questions that ask the reader to determine what the author's purpose or reason for writing the passage is. What does the author seek to accomplish? Is the author trying to persuade the reader? to inform the reader? to entertain the reader?

3. FIND THE MAIN IDEA

Developing proficiency in this area depends on being able to recognize key words in a sentence, main ideas in a paragraph, and main ideas in a passage. Key words are important or essential words that determine the meaning of a sentence. Often, these words are nouns and verbs. Once you have selected key words in sentences, you can practice determining the main idea in a paragraph. Sometimes this idea appears in the paragraph's topic sentence; often, however, this main idea is implicit. The other sentences provide support or evidence for this idea.

4. IDENTIFY AUTHOR'S ATTITUDE

The author's attitude toward the topic is sometimes referred to as *tone*. At a minimum, the reader must be able to decide whether the author approves or disapproves of the topic of the passage. Look closely at the word choices to determine the author's attitude. Consider as well what kind of information appears in the passage. Is it positive or negative?

5. IDENTIFY EVIDENCE

Careful reading of the passage should uncover the evidence or supporting details the author uses to develop his or her views. Ordinarily, such information appears in concrete, specific details. Whether you agree or disagree with the information—which is irrelevant to the question and the test as a whole—you must be able to locate evidence and determine its validity.

6. HANDLE NEW INFORMATION

For this skill, the reader must be able to assimilate new information and apply it to the material already provided in the passage. Often, the question requires the reader to decide how this new information can be applied to the details in the passage. The author may imply or suggest ideas or information. Be sure that you read all of the possible answers before you select one.

7. SYNTHESIZE DETAILS OR CONCEPTS

The ability to collect information and combine the details to arrive at a new conclusion is essential in higher thinking. Therefore, the passage may also offer possible applications of the author's ideas to other situations similar to those described in the passage. Even if you are unfamiliar with the material in the passage, don't panic. The questions are to be answered on the basis of the information provided in the passage. You are not expected to have any outside knowledge of a particular topic.

8. DERIVE IMPLICATIONS

This skill is absolutely invaluable for success on these standardized tests. Your ability to read and draw logical conclusions based on the information provided truly indicates higher thinking skills. To succeed on these graduate tests, you must clearly demonstrate sophisticated thinking. Watch for such terms as the following in this kind of question: hints, suggestions, insinuation, mood, significance.

WHERE DO READING COMPREHENSION QUESTIONS APPEAR?

All four of the tests we have discussed in this book—GRE, GMAT, LSAT, and MCAT—contain some type of reading questions.

On the GRE, the reading passages are part of the Verbal Ability sections. The GRE Computer Adaptive Test (CAT) has 30 questions on the Verbal Ability portion, and you will encounter at least one reading passage.

The GMAT is also administered as a CAT, and there are a total of 41 questions in the Verbal section. You will receive at least one reading passage.

The Verbal Reasoning portion of the MCAT presents nine passages, with a total of 65 questions. However, in both the Biological and Physical Sciences sections of this exam, you are required to read and interpret passages. The difference here is that you are expected to have a knowledge of the basic sciences, but having the ability to read and interpret these passages will definitely be beneficial.

Finally, the LSAT has a Reading comprehension section, consisting of four passages, with a total of 28 questions.

READING COMPREHENSION SKILLS REVIEW

To improve your overall reading comprehension skills, you may find it helpful to review important components of those skills. Keep in mind, you need to maximize your speed and retention without sacrificing comprehension. A number of important strategies can help you accomplish your objectives.

1. SPEED OF READING

People often assume that the faster you read, the better. That approach is not valid if you don't understand or retain what you read. The speed you're looking for is the rate at which you can most comfortably read, comprehend, and retain information. You also must be able to vary the speed at which you read, depending on the subject matter and your purpose. You read the newspaper or a magazine, for instance, at a speed different from the speed at which you read an assignment in your textbook. Learning how to vary your speed according to purpose and subject matter is a skill that you can develop with practice. Preparing for the reading comprehension sections on standardized tests is a good idea; it can help you become familiar with the speed at which you retain the most. It's also helpful to have an arsenal of strategies as you practice your reading skills.

2. SQ3R

An important part of improving your reading skills is finding a dependable method or approach. The SQ3R method is one that many students have found to be beneficial. This approach gives you a logical way to boost your reading comprehension and maximize the time you have. The SQ3R study technique, developed in 1941 by Francis Robinson, can improve your reading comprehension in virtually all areas. Here are its components:

S = Survey	This first step, survey or preview, requires you to do a quick overview of what you're reading. Check the title of the passage (if there is one), read the first paragraph or introduction, and read the first sentence of each of the other paragraphs. Read the last paragraph or the conclusion. This approach gives you a glimpse of the material as well as an estimation of the time you'll need to complete the task.
Q = Question	Knowing the questions before you read a passage can give you a better sense of purpose as you read. You can quickly scan the questions that follow the selection to be a more actively involved reader. It's not necessary at this point to preview the choices of answers.
R = Read	This stage is definitely an important one. Don't rush! Completing the first two steps in this method should give you a clear sense of purpose. Read at a steady pace.
R = Recite	Although you cannot recite aloud the important ideas as you take a standardized test, you should make every effort to repeat them mentally. Studies have shown that reciting can increase your retention rate from 20 percent to 80 percent. As you read, try to summarize the main idea in each paragraph.
R = Review	Although this step is more effective for remembering information over a long period of time, you can review the details mentally, thus reassuring yourself that you have read and understood the material.

3. USEFUL READING TECHNIQUES

As you read your test questions silently, keep these points in mind. Vocalization or moving your lips while you read can slow your reading rate. It takes too much time to say the words with your lips. To break this habit, try practicing reading with a pencil held between your teeth or chewing gum while you read. Subvocalizing is a similar, problematic reading habit, except here the reader isn't forming words with his or her lips; the reader forms words in his or her larynx. Practice reading rapidly under timed conditions to eliminate this habit. Pointing is also a problem that can slow a reader's progress. Keep your hands in your lap to break yet another habit that interferes with the development of your reading skills.

The movement of your eyes across the page is another important component in the way you read. Instead of reading in a straight line across the page and looking at each word separately, your eyes should move in arcs across the page in a sort of "bouncing" pattern. Your brain "sees" the words, but you are unaware of these arcs and fixations. Fast readers take in 2.5 to 3 words per fixation. Practicing speed and comprehension drills also can be beneficial in saving you time and helping you become a better reader. Try this paragraph by reading it more rapidly than your normal speed, focusing on key words in each line:

> *Prereading a passage on a standardized test can add a sense of purpose to the reading. You can have a clear sense of what kinds of details are important. Often, reading the first and last sentences of the passage as well as the topic sentences in the body paragraphs can clarify the important points. Just taking a few minutes can be useful; however, you must preview rapidly. Even if you don't use the other steps in the SQ3R approach, previewing (or surveying) can help.*

Skimming and scanning are two other reading methods that can be profitable. Both of these skills can help you become a better reader. In scanning, you glance at material, usually looking from the top to the bottom of the page, until you locate a particular piece of information. For instance, when you look up a number in a telephone book, you scan the entries until you find the number. Skimming, on the other hand, gives you an overview of the major points of a passage. You look over material quickly, just seeking main ideas. Of these two skills, skimming is probably more useful when you take a standardized reading comprehension test. In only a very few instances can you scan a passage to find a specific detail as the answer to a question. Most questions, on the other hand, require inferences or conclusions that the reader must formulate after having read and understood the passage. The restrictions of time may be an important factor in deciding whether you can rely on skimming; a more deliberate pace is usually more suitable. In some instances, however, you'll need to read at a fast rate to finish the test.

4. IMPORTANCE OF READING COMPREHENSION SKILLS

The skills that are important to your success on any standardized test are the same skills that can be essential to your academic success in whatever field you choose. You need to be able to read and understand difficult material. Not only do you have to be able to read the passages themselves, but you also must decipher and answer the questions that follow each passage. Your scores on reading comprehension tests do offer some prediction of success. If you can perform well on any of these graduate standardized tests, you should be able to handle graduate-level course material.

Preparing for the reading comprehension portion of standardized tests is a wise course of action. Practicing as much as possible can only help you.

Part V

READING SKILLS REVIEW

DRAWING AN INFERENCE

Drawing an inference requires you to read carefully, examine information, and decide upon a logical conclusion. You are asked to make an assumption, form a hypothesis, or make a judgment. With this type of question, you will not find an explicit answer in the passage. Read the following passage, keeping in mind that you will *draw an inference*.

Line After more than two centuries of experience, control of the Missouri-Mississippi River has been reduced to four methods. First, we have levees, the oldest of all. Second comes the enlargement of the discharge capacity by straightening, widen-
5 ing, and deepening of natural channels. Third in importance are the spillways, which guide excess water into auxiliary channels or allow it to flood fairly small areas. Fourth, we have reservoirs to store up excess water, which may be released when natural channels are again able to carry it. Of these four methods, the
10 construction of levees is still the surest because flood elevations are well known. Reservoirs are good but limited in usefulness because their benefits decrease with distance from the communities that are to be protected.

Despite the height that the river water once reached at St.
15 Louis and despite the people left homeless and the damage to property and crops, the engineers have reason to survey their efforts at flood control with satisfaction. But, as has been frequently suggested, it is about time that a Missouri River Authority is created to deal with the problems of flood control,
20 navigation, and power development.

Question:

1. One may infer from reading this selection that:

   (A) People are moving away from the area of the rivers in order to save their property and themselves.
   (B) Life in the area of the rivers is difficult and dangerous, but living conditions are good.
   (C) The government and its agencies are conducting ongoing efforts to control the rivers and improve measures already in place.
   (D) The building of spillways, levees, and reservoirs is very expensive.
   (E) All of the above.

   The correct answer is (C). In the second paragraph, the statement is made that ". . . the engineers have reason to survey their efforts at flood control with satisfaction." Later in the same paragraph, an authority is suggested to deal with the river control. Answer (A) is incorrect; there is no mention of people moving. Answer (B) is incorrect; there is no mention of the quality of living conditions. Answer (D) is incorrect; the expense involved in control is not mentioned. Answer (E) is incorrect because answers (A), (B), and (D) have been shown to be incorrect.

Question:

1. The inference is made that when using material already available to control the rivers, engineers have developed methods that will utilize that material to:

   (A) designate locations that need control.
   (B) predict floods and warn the people.
   (C) prepare a history of the rivers.
   (D) construct the most viable means of control.
   (E) develop patterns of flooding.

   The correct answer is (D). The statement is made that constructing levees is the best control because the height of floods is well known along the river. This indicates that data have been gathered and utilized. Answer (A) is incorrect; this selection mentions only that flood control is needed. Answer (B) is incorrect. There is no evidence of this in the selection. Answer (C) is incorrect; there is no evidence that a history is in preparation. Answer (E) is incorrect. While probably true, this article does not indicate this.

Here is another passage to practice making inferences:

Line I once made the statement in a room full of college students that the most important thing a young person could acquire in college might be a sense of his or her own limitations. I realized it was not a very fashionable thing to say. Popular books of
5   do-it-yourself therapy stress the glorious potential of every human being and urge us to accept ourselves, finally, as being only a little lower than angels. I heartily approve any celebration of human potential, but I believe that we must acknowledge our potential for limitless evil as well. We must understand what we
10   can do in the way of evil before we can pretend to be good. This is the beginning of morality, the psychological or spiritual or, in a religious tradition, the mythical basis that makes morality possible. One of the most moral (in this sense) books of the past century is Joseph Conrad's *Heart of Darkness*, because Conrad
15   faces the problem of evil in man. He tells us that a man must recognize in himself the ability to gut the head of his enemy on a stick and dance around a fire with it, and only when he recognizes that can he even begin to deal with any moral questions at all. Students who have been nourished on pop
20   psychology and told "I'm OK; you're OK" have some trouble dealing with Conrad, and some of them regard him as perverse.

Question:

1. With which of the following statements would the author be most likely to agree?

    (A) As time goes on, man and civilization progress at equal rates.
    (B) Man is only slightly lower than the angels.
    (C) Man is born instinctively good and resistant to evil.
    (D) Joseph Conrad refused to face the problem of evil in man.
    (E) We must recognize man's propensity for evil, as well as his leanings toward good.

    The correct answer is (E). The author states directly that man "must understand what we can do in the way of evil before we can even pretend to be good." Answer (A) is incorrect; this is actually contrary to what the author feels, indicated by his examples mentioned in the second paragraph. Answer (B) is incorrect; this is a Shakespearean judgment that the author does not appear to accept as being necessarily true. Answer (C) is incorrect; the author feels that man actually has as much propensity toward evil as toward good. Answer (D) is incorrect; this is also contrary to what the author specifically states.

DETERMINING PRIMARY PURPOSE

To determine the primary purpose of a passage, you must make some decision or judgment about information in the selection. What does the author hope to accomplish? Read this brief passage and keep in mind that you are reading to *determine the primary purpose* of the selection.

Line   In the South American rain forest reside some of the greatest
        acrobats on Earth: monkeys. Yet agile as they are, the monkeys
        of the Old World cannot hang by their tails. It is only the
        monkeys of America that possess this skill. They are called
5   "ceboids," and their unique group includes marmosets, owl
        monkeys, sakis, spider monkeys, and howlers. Among these, the
        star gymnast is the skinny, intelligent spider monkey. Hanging
        head down like a trapeze artist from the loop of a liana, he may
        suddenly give a short swing, launch himself into space, and,
10   soaring outward and downward across a 50-foot void, lightly
        catch a bough on which he spies a shining berry. No owl
        monkey can match his leap, for their arms are shorter, their tails
        untalented. The marmosets, smallest of the tribe, are tough,
        noisy hoodlums that travel in gangs and are also capable of leaps
15   into space, but their landings are rough: smack against a tree
        trunk with arms and legs spread wide.

Question:

1. Which of these statements does the author clearly state?

    (A) The monkeys of South America are an exceedingly gregarious group and exhibit great affection for one another.
    (B) The monkeys of the Old World reveal an unusually high order of intelligence.
    (C) The monkeys of South America have the ability to hang by their tails.
    (D) Monkeys in general are very hostile toward other species of animals.
    (E) South American monkeys reveal an amazing ability to adapt to captivity and therefore make splendid house pets.

    This question requires you to recognize that the author's primary purpose is to point out special talents found in American monkeys. The correct answer is (C); this correct answer is drawn from sentences 2 and 3, in which the author says specifically that the monkeys of the Old World cannot hang by their tails; only the monkeys of America can. Thus, while the statement was not technically made in one sentence, you find the direct facts in the two sentences mentioned. Answer (A) is incorrect; there is nothing in the paragraph to bear out this conclusion. Answer (B) is incorrect; the only mention of intelligence is in regard to the spider monkey, one of the South American breeds. Answer (D) is incorrect; while the statement may or may not be true in general, there is no indication of this fact in the paragraph. Answer (E) is incorrect; again, there is nothing stated to substantiate this inference.

Question:

1. The "star gymnast" is especially talented because he can:

   (A) make huge leaps and casually catch a limb with his tail or arms.
   (B) perform stunts while swinging through the branches.
   (C) do triple somersaults in the air.
   (D) fly through the air like a spider to its web.
   (E) make a trapeze out of a liana.

This question also requires you to decide the main reason for the author's admiration for the spider monkey. The correct answer is (A); sentence 6 offers the details to support this answer. Answer (B) is incorrect because there is no mention of "stunts" per se. Answer (C) is incorrect because the selection contains no references to somersaults. Answer (D) is incorrect; even though the breed is a spider monkey, the analogy is not based on a web. The spider monkey's arms and legs resemble the legs of a spider. Answer (E) is incorrect; there is no mention of a monkey's being able to create anything out of a liana, which is a vine.

FINDING THE MAIN IDEA

Another common kind of question tests your ability to find the main idea in a passage. These questions test your ability to read for the theme or main idea that is the subject of the selection. Read this brief passage and keep in mind that you are reading to *find the main idea* of the selection.

Line Teachers and librarians need to be aware of the emotional, intellectual, and physical changes that young adults experience, and they need to give serious thought to how they can best accommodate such changes. Growing bodies need movement

5 and exercise, but not just in ways that emphasize competition. Because they are adjusting to their new bodies and a whole host of new intellectual and emotional challenges, teenagers are especially self-conscious and need the reassurance that comes from achieving success and knowing that their accomplishments

10 are admired by others. However, the typical teenage lifestyle is already filled with so much competition that it would be wise to plan activities in which there are more winners than losers, such as publishing newsletters with many student-written book reviews, displaying student artwork, and sponsoring science

15 fiction, fantasy, or other special interest book discussion clubs. A variety of small clubs can provide multiple opportunities for leadership as well as for practice in successful group dynamics. Making friends is extremely important to teenagers, and many shy students need the security of some kind of organization,

20 with a supportive adult barely visible in the background.

In these activities, it is important to remember that young teens have short attention spans. A variety of activities should be organized so that participants can remain active as long as they want and then go on to something else without feeling guilty

25 and without letting the other participants down. This does not mean that adults must accept irresponsibility. On the contrary, they can help students acquire a sense of commitment by planning for roles that are within their capabilities and their attention spans and by having clearly stated rules. Teenagers

30 need limitations, but they also need the opportunity to help establish what these limitations and expectations will be.

Question:

1. The main idea of this article is the:

   (A) need for having clubs for students that will help them to compete.
   (B) reality that student activities can help to provide a nonthreatening environment for youth.
   (C) environment for learning is set by furnishings.
   (D) implication that teachers and librarians should be aware of ways to assist young adults in coping with life's changes.
   (E) students have great needs that are not being met.

To find the main idea in a selection, you can often look at the topic sentence of the opening paragraph and then skim the topic sentences in subsequent paragraphs. In this passage, the main idea actually appears in the very first sentence. The correct answer is (D). Answer (A) is incorrect; while discussed in the passage, it is not the entire *concept* of the selection. Answer (B) is incorrect; there is no mention of a nonthreatening environment. Answer (C) is incorrect; there is a point that furnishings may be unpleasant when designed for children but used by adolescents; however, this is not the main idea of the selection. Answer (E) is incorrect; while this may be a true statement, it is not the main idea of the selection.

Here is another passage. Read to determine the *main idea*.

Line   In the mid-1960s, not only was a great deal of good work being done on Southern literature, but the work was also being accepted as legitimate scholarship by the profession of literary critics. No longer was one an exotic if writing about literature in
5   the South. The academic study of Southern literature had become a celebration of regional patriotism and local color.
       During the next two decades, there evolved an expertise in critiquing the Southern writer that involved being able to see beyond the simplicity of language and the scope of the area into the
10   deep and passionate emotions that are typical in the South. That means that the leading writers on the scene led the profession into the great days of the Southern Renascence, or Renaissance, which lasted for about ten years. These writers were in their 50s, 60s, and 70s and there seemed to be no one of significance coming
15   along to take their places. What had once set the South and its literature apart from the rest of the country, both for the good and the not so good, was now on the verge of extinction. Literary imagination was fast losing vitality. The novel appeared to be a

20 dead art form, and a new form, the nonfiction novel, was being groomed to take its place.

This has not become the case, however. In fact, during the past decade, there occurred a veritable explosion of important and interesting young writers—Southern novelists—ranging in age from 40 to 30 and even to 20. Their books were read and 25 reviewed not only everywhere in America but abroad as well. And, to the surprise of all, the so-called nonfiction novel, not the novel, was about to die.

Not enough time has passed to estimate how long this "Renaissance of the Renaissance" will last; however, with the 30 important writing coming out of the South in the 1990s, the reasoning is that the promise is as real today as it was back in those early years.

Question:

1. Which of the following best summarizes the main point of the passage?

(A) Recent studies indicate a turning away from writing done in the South.

(B) The existence of the novel is important to writing that is real.

(C) Southern writing is alive, well, and growing in importance on a global scale.

(D) The writing by Southerners is all by older authors.

(E) Southern writing and Northern writing are different.

The correct answer is (C). The point is made that writings are read "not only everywhere in America but abroad as well." Answer (A) is incorrect; the opposite is presented in the passage. Answer (B) is incorrect. The impending demise of the nonfiction novel is predicted. Answer (D) is incorrect. The author points out the writers range in age from 20 and older, unlike in the 1970s and 1980s, when writers tended to be older. Answer (E) is incorrect. There is no mention of Northern writing.

IDENTIFYING THE AUTHOR'S ATTITUDE

> To identify the author's attitude toward the subject of the selection, you must read carefully. Look for expressions such as *favorable, approve, unfair, biased,* or *resentful.* Quite often, this is simply the author's purpose for writing. Read this selection to determine the author's attitude or tone.

Line   There are a few books that go with midnight, solitude, and a
candle. It is much easier to say what does not please us at that
time than what is exactly right. The book must be, at last,
something benedictory by a sinning fellow human being.

5   Cleverness would be repellent at such an hour. Cleverness,
anyhow, is the level of mediocrity today: we are all too infernally clever. The first witty perverse paradox blows out the
candle. Only the sick mind craves cleverness, as a morbid body
turns to drink. The late candle throws its beam a great distance,

10   and its rays make transparent much that seemed massy and
important. The mind at rest beside that light, when the house is
asleep and the consequential affairs of the urgent world have
diminished to their right proportions because we see them
distantly from another and a more tranquil place in the heavens,

15   where duty, honor, witty arguments, controversial logic, or great
questions appear such as will leave hardly a trace of fossil in the
indurated mud which will cover them—the mind then smiles at
cleverness. For though at that hour the body may be dog-tired,
the mind is white and lucid, like that of a man from whom fever

20   has abated. It is bare of illusions. It has a sharp focus, small and
starlike, as a clear and lonely flame left burning by the altar of a
shrine from which all have gone but one. A book which
approaches that light in the privacy of that place must come, as
it were, with open and honest pages.

Peterson's Logic & Reading Review

Question:

1. Which of the following statements best approaches the author's attitude toward cleverness?

    (A) Cleverness is a human weapon against overwhelming odds.
    (B) There is something old, honest, and candid about being clever.
    (C) Cleverness has something deceptive and deceitful about it.
    (D) To be clever is to exhibit a high order of sophistication.
    (E) Most people these days prefer direct, honest judgment.

    Answer (C) is correct. This judgment of cleverness is borne out in several places: sentences 2 and 3 indicate that there is something "repellent" about cleverness when what man needs is something "benedictory." And the conclusion that a book must come with "open and honest pages" precludes a clever work. Answer (A) is incorrect. This is not indicated as the author's view. Answer (B) is incorrect. This is actually the opposite of what the author claims. Answer (D) is incorrect. Cleverness, to the contrary, is dubbed as indicative of mediocrity. Answer (E) is incorrect. This is what the author would wish, but it is not what is so.

Question:

1. The author's statement that "we are all too infernally clever" is to be accepted:

    (A) as his view of civilization in general.
    (B) as a sign that he is basically a misanthrope.
    (C) on a somewhat limited basis.
    (D) as a sign that he is a political and social conservative.
    (E) as indicating that he is out of step with his times.

    Answer (C) is correct. While a literal interpretation would regard this as a truly universal judgment, the generally subjective tone of the selection indicates that this statement is not meant as a profound philosophical conclusion. Answer (A) is incorrect. Since the author is limiting his discussion to reading, his judgments must be interpreted in that light. Answer (B) is incorrect. There is nothing to indicate that the author is one who hates mankind. Answer (D) is incorrect. This aspect of interpretation is not alluded to at all. Answer (E) is incorrect. While this might be valid in general, the interpretation we are asked to make involves principally midnight reading.

PART V

USING EVIDENCE

Some reading comprehension questions will direct you to locate specific evidence in the passage in order to answer accurately. As you read a passage, underline or circle details that you believe to be important. Read this brief passage and keep in mind that you are reading to *find specific evidence* that may help you answer questions about this selection.

Line   Komodo dragons, like most cold-blooded reptiles, sleep during the
night. As the sun rises and warms their blood, they become active,
awakening from their resting places among tree roots and rocks to
set out in search of food. Despite their great size, Komodo dragons
5   are quick moving and agile on the ground. They occasionally
climb trees, gripping them with their large, powerful claws. They
are also good swimmers, taking long, powerful strokes with their
tails. When the usually solitary Komodos meet, they establish a
clear hierarchy order based on size.

Question:

1. According to this article, Komodos are quite agile despite
their:

  (A) habitat's difficult terrain.
  (B) propensity to stay with their young.
  (C) large size.
  (D) enormous tails that are twice the size of their bodies.
  (E) powerful claws

    The correct answer is (C). The author states in the third
sentence: "Despite their great size, Komodo dragons are quick
moving and agile on the ground." Answer (A) is incorrect; the
terrain described is not described as *difficult*. Answer (B) is
incorrect; there is no mention of Komodo young in the passage.
Answer (D) is incorrect; rather than hindering the Komodos,
their tails are useful in swimming. Answer (E) is incorrect; the
Komodos claws aid their climbing and agility.

**Here is another passage for you to practice the skill of
using *evidence*:**

Line   The United States and other Western industrial countries may face
a period of joblessness in the 1980s, even if President Carter and
other nations' leaders succeed in their declared aim of expanding
business investment and ending the world recession.
5   This is the warning that an increasing number of economists, officials, and businesspeople are giving Western govern-

Peterson's Logic & Reading Review

ments as they prepare for the Bonn economic summit meeting, to be held this month. It reflects fears that any upturn in business spending, stimulated by the summit meeting, will
10   merely accelerate the present trend toward replacing human workers with sophisticated new machinery instead of creating additional jobs.

"The evidence that we have is suggesting increasingly that the employment-displacing effects of automation, anticipated for
15   the 1950s, are now beginning to arrive on a serious scale in the 1970s," concludes an unpublished report by the Organization for Economic Cooperation and Development, which monitors the economic progress of Western nations.

Question:

1. It is apparent that statements alluded to in this selection stem from thoughts expressed prior to:

  (A) a meeting of the Common Market nations.
  (B) a conference of the United Nations.
  (C) an international economic summit meeting.
  (D) a disarmament conference.
  (E) no particular meeting.

The correct answer is (C). The topic sentence of the second paragraph substantiates this statement: ". . . as they prepare for the Bonn economic summit meeting . . ." Here you are drawing evidence directly from the material presented. You have read carefully and can therefore go directly to the material questioned. Answers (A), (B), (D), and (E) are all incorrect. These answers are presented in an irrelevant manner to encourage you to read for detail. While they sound reasonable, there is no correlation at all to what you have read. You must use your ability to focus on what you are reading and thereby be able to differentiate the material presented from that which "sounds good."

Now read another passage to test your ability to find and use *evidence*.

Line   Black holes, when imagined, are unimaginable. But popular culture got used to them anyway. Black holes are the movie celebrities, the byword for all kinds of bad risks. They are overfamiliar and all but cliché. Luckily, astronomers are not
5   bored yet. In the last few years, they have found increasing evidence of black holes both in our galaxy and outside it. These

days, what's most unbelievable about black holes in that they
seem to be real.

For certain stars, black holes are the afterlife. Stars the size
10 of our Sun spend their lives burning fuel and radiating light,
balancing the radiation's push outward against gravity's pull
inward. As a star runs out of fuel, gravity begins to win. The star
condenses and shrinks smaller and smaller until gravity's pull is
again balanced, this time by the force that keeps electrons from
15 crowding too close together. The star, now called a white dwarf,
shines for a while, then gradually cools and dims.

In stars with masses more than eight times the Sun's,
gravity is correspondingly stronger. These stars die with a bang
in supernova explosions, which blow away much of the star's
20 mass. If what remains is less than three solar masses, gravity
jams the negatively charged electrons and the positively charged
protons together. The opposite charges neutralize each other,
and the remnant core, now composed entirely of neutrons, is
called a neutron star. It has shrunk to about 10 miles in diam-
25 eter. Matter this compact "beggars description," says Jeffrey
McClintock, an astronomer at the Harvard-Smithsonian Center
for Astrophysics in Massachusetts. If the Great Lakes were made
this compact, they would fit into a bathroom sink. " 'Compact' is
the word we like to use," McClintock adds, "because 'dense'
30 doesn't even cover it." Neutron stars shine when they're formed,
most brightly in X rays; they also have magnetic fields that can
send out crisp pulses of radio waves.

In stars with masses at least 40 times the Sun's, gravity is
strong enough to make the unthinkable happen. These stars also
35 die violently. If the remaining core is bigger than a neutron
star—that is, greater than three solar masses—it condenses to
nothingness, or near enough to make no difference. Physicists
call this point a singularity and tend not to talk about it because
they have no clue as to what happens to matter at these
40 densities. "It most likely goes unstable," says McClintock. "Does
it exist anymore? I don't know. It's basically out the window.
The elementary particles themselves are torn into fragments
whose nature is not known and cannot be guessed." Scientists
do know that matter at these densities loses all properties
45 except for mass, rotation, and charge. Says McClintock, "The
trees out there, those pearls, the computer—any property they
have, once in the black hole, they don't have anymore." The
physicists' phrase is "black holes have no hair." "That means
black holes don't have you-name-it, just-list-it," says McClintock.
50 "Nothing, nothing, nothing, nothing, nothing."

Question:

1. Which of the following statements is true, according to this selection?

   (A) The core of the black hole has a magnetic mass more than eight times the Sun's.

   (B) Neutron stars have more of a likelihood of sinking into the black hole than do supernova stars.

   (C) Stars larger than our Sun usually explode at their death, unlike stars that are smaller and less bright.

   (D) The density of the magnetic field determines the destiny of the star.

   (E) The compact density of the exploded star is easily explainable in terms that a layperson can understand.

Answer (C) is correct. The third paragraph of the article begins with a sentence that states this premise. Answer (A) is incorrect; there is no evidence to support this. Answer (B) is incorrect; in fact, the neutron star is often the by-product of the supernova explosion. Answer (D) is incorrect; this is a false premise. Answer (E) is incorrect; the opposite is true, according to McClintock, when he says it "beggars description."

DEALING WITH NEW INFORMATION

Another type of question requires you to deal with new information presented after the selection in the questions themselves. Dealing with new information demands a different skill; you must assess the new data and apply this new material to what you have gathered from the reading passage. Read this selection and keep in mind that you are reading to prepare yourself to *deal with new information.*

Line   Lead poisoning may be observed in the acute or chronic form. Most cases of acute salt poisoning are accidental and seldom homicidal. Acute cases result from the ingestion of large amounts of soluble salt (acetate or nitrate) or many small doses
5   at intervals. Retention of lead is cumulative, so that a sudden attack may occur after a long period of administration.

    The continued intake of small doses when released suddenly by the body stores may give rise abruptly to a type of poisoning similar to that following the ingestion of a large
10   amount. Removal of old paint by workers in a closed environment or with minimal ventilation may be responsible for on-the-job lead poisoning. Ingestion of lead-containing paint and plaster by children still accounts for many cases of poisoning.

    Although the symptoms of acute poisoning are varied, the
15   patient may complain of a metallic taste, a dry burning sensation in the throat, cramps, retching, and persistent vomiting. Hematemesis (vomiting of blood) may occur. In children, absorbed lead is often deposited near the epiphyseal ends of the bones and can often be seen on X rays as a dark band near the cartilage.

20   Lead, after absorption, is carried by the blood to different organs, where it produces a multiform symptomatology. Symptoms can include weakness, anorexia, loss of weight, abdominal colic, constipation, backache, headache, hypertension, and a variety of neurological signs. The three organ areas where lead
25   has the greatest effect are the hematopoietic system (blood and blood-producing organs), the central nervous system, and the kidneys.

Question:

1. Based on the passage above, one can see that laws prohibiting the use of lead paint and lead in gasoline:

    (A) are useless in preventing the serious effects of the poisoning.
    (B) are only sporadically enforced around the country.
    (C) can help to reduce the incidence of this preventable disease.
    (D) can cost construction and oil companies millions of dollars.
    (E) can do nothing to control the fumes of the poison.

    The correct answer is (C). Legislation can begin to prevent the disease. Answer (A) is incorrect; there is no mention of lead poisoning as uncontrollable. Answer (B) is incorrect. There is nothing in the passage that refers to the enforcement of laws. Answer (D) is incorrect. Although control of lead poisoning can be expensive, there is nothing in the passage that reveals that the cost to private companies is in the millions of dollars. Answer (E) is incorrect; nothing in the passage indicates that lead poisoning cannot be controlled.

Question:

1. Based on the information provided about the organ areas most affected by lead, one can conclude:

    (A) the most serious damage would be to the nervous system.
    (B) the poison can be transported throughout the body by the blood system.
    (C) a patient suffering from severe poisoning will eventually experience kidney failure.
    (D) one of the most obvious effects is nausea.
    (E) all of the above.

    The correct answer is (E). All of the statements in answers (A), (B), (C), and (D) are logical outcomes of the details provided about lead poisoning.

SYNTHESIS

A synthesis question requires you to combine or blend information to reach a conclusion. Frequently, your task will require you to arrive at a composite based on details in the passage and the question. This kind of question involves the ability to blend new details with other data. Read this brief passage and keep in mind that you are reading to prepare yourself *to synthesize information.*

Line   No step in life is more important than the choice of a vocation. The wise selection of the business, profession, trade, or occupation to which one's life is to be devoted and the development of full efficiency in the chosen field are matters of the deepest

5   moment to young men, young women, and the public. These vital problems should be solved in a careful, scientific way, with due regard to each person's aptitudes, abilities, ambitions, resources, and limitations, and the relations of these elements to the conditions of success in different industries. If a man takes

10   up a line of work to which he is adapted, he will achieve far greater success than if he drifts into an industry for which he is not fitted. An occupation out of harmony with the worker's aptitudes and capacities means inefficiency, unenthusiastic and perhaps distasteful labor, and low pay, while an occupation in

15   harmony with the nature of the man means enthusiasm, love of work, and high economic values—superior product, efficient service, and good pay. If a young woman chooses her vocation so that her best abilities and enthusiasms will be united with her daily work, she has laid the foundations of success and happi-

20   ness. But, if her best abilities and enthusiasms are separated from this daily work or do not find in it fair scope and opportunity for exercise and development; if this occupation is merely a means of making a living and the work she loves to do is sidetracked into the evening hours or pushed out of her life

25   altogether, she will be only a fraction of the person she ought to be. Efficiency and success are largely dependent on adaptation.

Question:

1. A thought that is contrary to the feeling of the author is that:

    (A) one cannot simply relegate one's real interest in life to "spare time."

    (B) a happy worker is an efficient one.

    (C) if one wants to, he can work at his really important interests after he has completed his day's work.

    (D) tying one's interests and enthusiasms to one's job can lead to a happy work experience.

    (E) choosing one's career is something that calls for great care and thoughtfulness.

    Be sure to read the question carefully. This question calls for the "contrary." The correct answer is (C). Everything in the selection points in just the opposite direction of that statement. The author warns that a person who relegates his really important interests to after-hours "will be only a fraction of the man he ought to be." Answers (A), (B), (D), and (E) are incorrect. Each of these statements is part of the author's thinking as reflected in the selection.

DERIVING IMPLICATIONS

One type of question often asked depends on your ability to figure out or derive what the author implies in the selection. As you read, keep in mind such verbs as *convey, denote, hint, insinuate, signify,* and *suggest.* Although the writer is unlikely to use these words, they can guide you to recognition of what the author is suggesting. Read this brief passage and keep in mind that you are reading to *derive the implications* of the selection.

Line   One by one, it seems, American values are being restored. First, there was Liberty in New York, then Freedom in Washington— statues, that is, both stalwart women worn by a century or more of exposure to the elements. Liberty received her facelift right
5   on her pedestal in New York Harbor in the mid-1980s, but before Freedom could be cleaned and repaired in 1993, the 19.5-foot, 7.5-ton bronze figure had to be removed from the top of the U.S. Capitol.

One morning in May 1993, a Sikorsky S-64F rose quickly
10   from the Capitol grounds and hovered above the dome. With the aid of a gyro-coupled flight control system, the pilot held that spot in the sky while a rigging crew on the dome attached four dangling cables to a framework of bars and nylon straps that supported the statue. With the connections secure, the helicop-
15   ter's hoist began lifting, threading the statue through the scaffolding that had been erected around it. The statue swayed slightly but did not twist on the short trip down. The helicopter has a suspension system that ensures that the load turns only with the helicopter.
20   A cheer rose from hundreds of onlookers as the helicopter lowered the statue to the ground and workers bolted it to a temporary base constructed on the Capitol's East Plaza, the statue's temporary home. This was the first time Freedom had been moved since 1863, when pieces of the statue were first
25   hoisted atop the dome by steam engine and bolted together. It took less than 10 minutes to lift the statue off the dome. Freedom was returned to its original position after the restoration.

Question:

1. The author implies that:

    (A) statues should be refurbished often.
    (B) using a helicopter for such a delicate operation is inefficient.
    (C) today's technology allows major tasks to be performed in an efficient manner when viewed in a historical perspective.
    (D) helicopters are made for a variety of tasks.
    (E) our nation's historical statues must receive care that will allow them to extend into the next century.

This question requires you to derive the author's implication. Ask yourself, "What is the writer trying to convey? What does he suggest?" The correct answer is (C); the comparison between the steam engine that placed the statue on the dome and the fact that it took less than 10 minutes to hoist it by helicopter implies that modern technology, when viewed in a historical perspective, is far more efficient than technology in the past. Answer (A) is incorrect; there is no indicator that statues should be refurbished often. Answer (B) is incorrect; indeed, the use of the efficient helicopter is applauded. Answer (D) is incorrect; while this is a true statement, it is not the author's inference. Answer (E) is not correct; although probably true, it is not what the author implies.

Now read this passage, again looking for implications suggested by the author.

Line | There were many reasons why the whole character of the twentieth century should be very different from that of the nineteenth. The great wave of vitality and national expansion, which, during the Victorian period, swept both England and
5 | America to a high-water mark of national prosperity, left in its ebb a highly developed industrial civilization and a clear path for all the currents of scientific and mechanistic thought that were to flood the new century. However, literature, which had been nourished by the general vigor of the time but not at all by the
10 | practical interests of the period, declined as the spirit itself dispersed. Before the end of the century, that positive, homogeneous, energetic social culture that collaborated with the great Victorian writers had disintegrated. The literary coterie of the nineties already marked the arrival of an entirely new idea. Art
15 | had begun to be created for Art's sake. The great age of groups and "movements" began. The eighteenth-century poets did not

call themselves classicists, nor did the nineteenth-century poets call themselves romanticists; their poetic coloring was simply the quality of their whole response to the whole of life. But the
20 literary history of the late nineteenth and early twentieth centuries is full of theories and "isms"

Symbolism, Futurism, Imagism, Vorticism, Expressionism, Dadaism, and Surrealism provided artistic creeds for various groups and set the individual artist apart from the community in
25 the popular opinion.

Question:

1. The statement "Art had begun to be created for Art's sake" implies that:

    (A) art is basically untrue and unreal for most people.
    (B) there were malicious forces at work among the artists.
    (C) art is basically to be created for society.
    (D) the author is critical of art and artists in general.
    (E) there had been a steady movement of art toward Art.

    The correct answer is (C). The sense of the entire selection and certainly the implication of the statement that "Art had begun to be created for Art's sake" (especially with the capital "A") indicate the author's feeling that art must be related to people—hence, to society. Answer (A) is incorrect; actually, the opposite of this is indicated, especially in the discussion of the richness of the Victorian period in its art as well as its industry. Answer (B) is incorrect; there is no indication of such "plotlike" activity either among the artists or in society among the artists or in society in general. Answer (D) is incorrect; this is a matter of semantics: the term "critical" usually implies some condemnation or disapproval. Actually, the author is discussing art and culture in a historical context. Answer (E) is incorrect; again, the use of the difference between the small "a" and the capital "A" implies a critical comment that is not warranted here.

Part VI

PRACTICE READING COMPREHENSION TESTS

PRACTICE TEST 1

Directions: Each passage in this group is followed by questions based on its content. After reading a passage, choose the best answer to each question. Answer all questions following a passage on the basis of what is stated or implied in that passage.

Passage 1

Line We are profoundly ignorant about the origins of language and have to content ourselves with more or less plausible speculations. We do not even know for
5 certain when language arose, but it seems likely that it goes back to the earliest history of man, perhaps half a million years. We have no direct evidence, but it seems probable that
10 speech arose at the same time as tool making and the earliest forms of specifically human cooperation. In the great Ice Ages of the Pleistocene period, our earliest human ancestors
15 established the Old Stone Age culture; they made flint tools and, later, tools of bone, ivory, and antler; they made fire and cooked their food; they hunted big game, often by methods that called for
20 considerable cooperation and coordination. As their material culture gradually improved, they became artists and made carvings and engravings on bones and pebbles as well as wonderful
25 paintings of animals on the walls of caves. It is difficult to believe that the makers of these Paleolithic cultures lacked the power of speech. It is a long step, admittedly, from other earliest
30 flint weapons to the splendid art of the late Stone Age: the first crude flints date back perhaps to 500,000 B.C., while the finest achievements of Old Stone Age man are later than 100,000
35 B.C.; and in this period we can envisage a corresponding development of language, from the most primitive and limited language of the earliest human groups to a fully developed language in
40 the flowering time of Old Stone Age culture.

How did language arise in the first place? There are many theories about this, based on various types of indirect
45 evidence, such as the language of children, the language of primitive societies, the kinds of changes that have taken place in language in the course of recorded history, the behav-
50 ior of higher animals like chimpanzees, and the behavior of people suffering from speech defects. These types of evidence may provide us with useful pointers, but they all suffer from
55 limitations and must be treated with caution.

When we consider the language of children, we have to remember that

their situations are quite different from
60 those of our earliest human ancestors
because the child, growing up in an
environment where there is already a
fully developed language, is surrounded
by adults who use that language and
65 are teaching it to him. For example, it
has been shown that the earliest words
used by children are mainly the names
of things and people ("doll," "spoon,"
"Mummy"), but this fact does not prove
70 that the earliest words of primitive man
were also the names of things and
people. When the child learns the
name of an object, he may then use it
to express his wishes or demands:
75 "Doll!" often means, "Give me my doll!"
or "I've dropped my doll. Pick it up for
me!" The child is using language to get
things done, and it is almost an
accident of adult teaching that the
80 words used to formulate the child's
demands are mainly nouns instead of
words like "Bring!" "Pick up!" and so
on.

Questions 1–6

1. The main idea of this excerpt is:

   (A) to provide evidence of the origin
   of language.
   (B) to present the need for language.
   (C) to discuss how early man commu-
   nicated.
   (D) to present the culture of early
   man.
   (E) to narrate the story of English.

2. Theories of the origin of language
   include all of the following EXCEPT:

   (A) changes occurring throughout the
   years.
   (B) the need to communicate.
   (C) language of children.
   (D) the first man's extensive vocabu-
   lary.
   (E) communication among primitive
   men.

3. The purpose of the discussion of the
   word "doll" is to:

   (A) trace the evolution of a noun.
   (B) support the fact that naming
   things is most important.
   (C) indicate how adults teach
   language to children.
   (D) show the evolution of many
   meanings for one word.
   (E) evince man's multiple uses of
   single words.

4. The implication of the author regarding
   the early elements of language is that:

   (A) there were specific real steps
   followed to develop our language.
   (B) care must be taken when exhum-
   ing what we consider the roots of
   language.
   (C) we owe a debt of gratitude to the
   chimpanzee contribution.
   (D) adults created language in order
   to instruct their children.
   (E) language was fully developed by
   primitive man.

5. If we accept that primitive man existed for a very long period of time without language, then we may assume that:

   (A) language is not necessary to man's existence.

   (B) language developed with the developing culture of primitives.

   (C) primitives existed in total isolation from one another.

   (D) children created a need for language.

   (E) mankind was not intended to communicate.

6. After a reading of this article, one might infer that:

   (A) society creates problems with language.

   (B) language is for adults to instruct children.

   (C) society uses language to improve itself.

   (D) with the evolution of language came wisdom.

   (E) language brings power.

Passage 2

Line We live in an era that has ostensibly become concerned with the natural environment, conservation, and pollution. Every day there is something
5 new to be worried about in the resources we use, including the air we breathe, the food we eat, and the water we drink. If we destroy what we have, use it up, or pollute it, we will inevita-
10 bly lose these valuable natural resources. Among the many possible victims of environmental exploitation are lakes, streams, soils, monuments, statues, and ancient ruins. All of these
15 static, vulnerable treasures are in

danger of being eaten away by a recently recognized phenomenon called acid precipitation.

   Although acid precipitation
20 includes snow, hail, sleet, water vapor, mist, and even dew, it is often termed simply "acid rain." Describing the "acid" portion of the phrase is more complicated. A general chemistry
25 textbook defines an acid as a substance dissolved in water that produces a solution of pH less than seven. So what does pH mean? The pH scale is one that describes the concentration of
30 hydrogen ions in a substance. The more the ions, the more "acid;" the less the ions, the more "basic." A lower pH value indicates high acidity, while a higher pH indicates high alkalinity
35 (basicity). The pH goes from 1 to 14. One is highly acidic, 14 is highly basic, and 7 is normal (neither acidic nor basic)—the ions are in balance.

   Normal precipitation has an aver-
40 age pH of 5.6, already on the acidic side of the scale but not dangerously so. The various "rained-on" substrates can handle this slight acidity, mainly because they possess a "buffering capacity." That
45 is, they contain enough of certain materials that can, in effect, combine with the acids to produce harmless substances and thus decrease the acidity. They "buffer" the medium (lake, soil, even a
50 statue) against the acid by neutralizing the effects it can have.

   What are these effects? What do acids do to lakes, streams, and other substances? Acids have different effects
55 on different materials. In the cases of statues, monuments, and some buildings, acids simply break down the composition of minerals—slowly, for certain, but there is a definite break-

60 down. If you pour soda onto a hard
crust of bread, the crust will hold up
for a while, but soon it will start to
melt away and will eventually fall apart.
Of course, the presence of buffers
65 combats the destruction, but if somehow the acids become stronger (or the
buffers weaker), the defense will be
less powerful. More immediately
noticeable effects can be seen in
70 aquatic and terrestrial environments.
Acids can leach essential nutrients from
lakes, streams, and soils. They can also
increase the ability of toxic metals (lead
and mercury, for example) to dissolve
75 into a medium. When these metals are
released into water, for example, they
can cause pipes to corrode faster, fish
to become contaminated and die, and
plants to be destroyed. Whole habitats
80 can be wiped out; some actually have
been. There are lakes in the Adiron-
dacks that have become completely
barren of all life because of the
devastation of acid rain.

85 　　How, then, do acids get into the
atmospheric precipitation? Now we
come to the core of the problem—the
source of the acids. There are certain
substances that, when added to rain,
90 dew, and mist, can decrease the pH to
4.5 through 4 and lower, increasing
acidity. This precipitation falls from the
sky into lakes and onto soil and pelts
monuments such as the Lincoln
95 Memorial, wreaking its havoc.

Questions 7–12

7. The author's purpose in this passage is to:

　(A) narrate.
　(B) inform.
　(C) instruct.
　(D) persuade.
　(E) describe.

8. According to the writer, in the day and age in which we live, there is:

　(A) no hope of having clean water.
　(B) cause for each person to be concerned.
　(C) only a slight chance of problems.
　(D) no danger to our environment.
　(E) no soil pollution.

9. The pH value is important to the environment because it measures:

　(A) the amount of pollutants in the air.
　(B) pollution in water to deter developing bacteria.
　(C) the oxygen level in the air.
　(D) soil sterility.
　(E) the concentration of hydrogen ions.

10. The reader can infer that the author's attitude is one of:

　(A) detachment.
　(B) concern.
　(C) disinterest.
　(D) amusement.
　(E) fear.

11. Noticeable effects of acid rain include all of the following EXCEPT:

(A) leaching of nutrients.
(B) dissolution of metals.
(C) eventual demise of Earth's crust.
(D) a hole in the ozone.
(E) contamination of aquatic life.

12. According to the article, the source of the acids that get into the atmospheric precipitation is:

(A) a diminishing ozone layer.
(B) municipal waste disposal.
(C) not explained.
(D) pollution from fuel from airplanes and jets.
(E) a deliberate disregard for natural resources.

Passage 3

Line The essential feature of Post-traumatic Stress Disorder is the development of characteristic symptoms following exposure to an extremely traumatic
5 stress involving direct personal experience of an event that encompasses actual or threatened death or serious injury or other threat to one's physical integrity or another person; or learning
10 about unexpected or violent death, serious harm, or threat of death or injury experienced by a family member or other close associate. The person's response to the event must entail
15 intense fear, helplessness, or horror (or, in children, the response must involve disorganized or agitated behavior). The characteristic symptoms resulting from the exposure to the extreme trauma
20 include persistent reexperiencing of the traumatic event, persistent avoidance of stimuli associated with the trauma,

numbing of general responsiveness, and persistent symptoms of increased
25 arousal. The full symptom picture must be present for more than one month, and the disturbance must cause clinically significant distress or impairment in social, occupational, or other
30 important areas of functioning.

Traumatic events that are experienced directly include, but are not limited to, military combat, violent personal assault (sexual assault, physical
35 attack, robbery, mugging, being kidnapped, being taken hostage, terrorist attack, torture, incarceration as a prisoner of war or in a concentration camp), natural or man-made disasters,
40 severe automobile accidents, or being diagnosed with a life-threatening illness. For children, sexual traumatic events may include developmentally inappropriate sexual experiences without
45 threatened or actual violence or injury. Witnessed events include, but are not limited to, observing the serious injury or unnatural death of another person because of violent assault, war or
50 disasters, or unexpectedly witnessing a dead body or body parts. Even events experienced by others that are learned about include, but are not limited to, violent personal assault, serious
55 accident, or serious injury experienced by a family member or close friend; learning about the sudden, unexpected death of a family member or close friend; or learning that one's child has a
60 life-threatening disease. The disorder can be especially severe or long lasting when the stressor is of human design (e.g., torturous rape). The likelihood of developing this disorder may increase
65 as the intensity of physical proximity to the stressor increases.

The traumatic event can be reexperienced in various ways. Commonly, the person has recurrent and
70 intrusive recollections of the event or recurrent distressing dreams during which the event is replayed. In rare instances, the person experiences dissociative states that last from a few
75 seconds to several hours or even days, during which components of the event are relived and the person behaves as though they are experiencing the event at that moment. Intense psychological
80 distress or physiological reactivity often occurs when a person is exposed to triggering events that resemble or symbolize an aspect of the traumatic event (e.g., anniversaries of the
85 traumatic event; cold, snowy weather; uniformed guards for survivors of death camps in cold climates; hot, humid weather for combat veterans of the South Pacific; entering any elevator for
90 a woman who was raped in an elevator).

Questions 13–17

13. The author's purpose is to:

(A) narrate.
(B) instruct.
(C) explain.
(D) define.
(E) persuade.

14. Post-traumatic Stress Disorder is:

(A) developed from genetic disorders.
(B) characterized by direct personal experiences.
(C) induced by climatic changes.
(D) the result of biological changes.
(E) all of the above.

15. The biological conclusion one might reach after reading this selection is that:

(A) Post-traumatic Stress Disorder recurs unexpectedly.
(B) all of us are vulnerable to Post-traumatic Stress Disorder.
(C) victims of this disorder are mostly veterans.
(D) this disorder is life-threatening.
(E) only adults are victims.

16. The time requirement to qualify for Post-traumatic Stress Disorder is:

(A) interminable.
(B) brief.
(C) one week.
(D) one month.
(E) one year.

17. According to this selection, one may infer that the name Post-traumatic Stress Disorder implies:

(A) a recurring chronic pain.
(B) the presence of memory-inducing stressors.
(C) the recurring stressors of childhood experiences.
(D) stressors that evoke biological reactions.
(E) genetic conditions that recur without warning.

Passage 4

Line There were two traditional conceptions
of matter, both of which have had
advocates ever since scientific specula-
tion began. There were the atomists,
5 who thought that matter consisted of
tiny lumps that could never be divided;
the atoms were supposed to hit each
other and then bounce off in various
ways within the matter. After Newton,
10 atoms were no longer supposed to
actually come into contact with each
other but rather to attract and repel
each other and move in orbits around
each other. Then there were those who
15 thought that there is matter of some
kind everywhere and that a true
vacuum is impossible. Descartes held
this view and attributed the motions of
the planets to vortices in the aether.
20 The Newtonian theory of gravitation
caused the view that there is matter
everywhere to fall into discredit,
moreso as light was thought by Newton
and his disciples to be due to actual
25 particles traveling from the source of
the light. But when this view of light
was disproved and it was shown that
light consisted of waves, the aether was
revived so that there should be
30 something to undulate. The aether
became still more respectable when it
was found to play the same part in
electromagnetic phenomena as in the
propagation of light. It was even hoped
35 that atoms might turn out to be a mode
of motion in the aether. At this state,
the atomic view of matter was, on the
whole, getting the worst of it.
Leaving relativity aside for the
40 moment, modern physics has provided
proof of the atomic structure of
ordinary matter while not disproving

the arguments in favor of the aether, to
which no such structure is attributed.
45 The result was a sort of compromise
between the two views, the one
applying to what was called "gross"
matter, the other to the aether. There
can be no doubt about electrons and
50 protons, though, as we shall see
shortly, they need not be conceived of
as atoms were conceived of traditionally. The truth is that relativity demands
abandonment of the old conception of
55 "matter," which is infected by the
metaphysics associated with "substance" and represents a point of view
not really necessary in dealing with
phenomena. This is what must now be
60 investigated.
In the old view, a piece of matter
was something that survived all through
time while never being at more than
one place at a given time. This way of
65 looking at things is obviously connected with the complete separation of
space and time in which people
formerly believed. When we substitute
space-time for space and time, we shall
70 naturally expect to derive the physical
world from constituents that are as
limited in time as in space. Such
constituents are what we call "events."
An event does not persist and move
75 like the traditional piece of matter; it
merely exists for its little moment and
ceases. A piece of matter will thus be
resolved in a series of events. Just as, in
the old view, an extended body was
80 composed of a number of particles, so
now each particle, being extended in
time, must be regarded as composed of
what we may call "event-particles." The
whole series of these events makes up

85 the whole history of the particle, and the particle is regarded as being its history, not some metaphysical entity to which the events happen. This view is rendered necessary by the fact that

90 relativity compels us to place time and space more on a level than they were in the older physics.

Questions 18–22

18. The purpose of this article is to:

(A) persuade.
(B) discuss.
(C) narrate.
(D) inform.
(E) instruct.

19. The author disassociates matter from substance by:

(A) introducing new concepts.
(B) embracing traditional concepts.
(C) asking for better definitions.
(D) dismissing both as irrelevant.
(E) demonstrating their invalidity.

20. The traditional concepts of "matter" should be abandoned, according to the author, because of all of the following EXCEPT:

(A) the infection of metaphysics
(B) an association with "substance"
(C) the terminology is archaic
(D) the representation of an outmoded point of view
(E) not needed to deal with phenomena

21. Newton's theory of gravitation fell into discredit when:

(A) Einstein introduced his theory of relativity.
(B) light was shown to consist of waves.
(C) light was found to contain actual particles.
(D) matter was found to exist everywhere.
(E) electromagnets were found to propagate light.

22. The importance of "events" to matter is demonstrated by which of the following?

   I. An event does not persist and move like traditional matter.
  II. A piece of matter is resolved into a series of events.
  III. An event exists for its little moment and ceases.

(A) I.
(B) II.
(C) III.
(D) Both I and II.
(E) I, II, and III.

PRACTICE TEST 2

Directions: Each passage in this group is followed by questions based on its content. After reading a passage, choose the best answer to each question. Answer all questions following a passage on the basis of what is stated or implied in that passage.

Passage 1

Line One of the most difficult parts of education for many students is learning to write effectively. All career paths require one stepping stone that
5 involves effective written communication, whether the writing calls for completion of a job application blank or the creation of a resumé, interoffice memo, business letter, or product
10 presentation. One of the most effective ways to write effectively is the use of freewriting, an activity in which all individuals can participate.

Freewriting involves writing for 10
15 minutes without guidelines, restrictions, or inhibitions. The activity means totally "free" writing, without stopping to correct punctuation, spelling, capitalization, or structure. Of course,
20 the easiest way to accomplish this goal is to write whatever one thinks. For the writer who finds this task difficult, writing the same word over and over can accomplish freewriting. The main
25 stipulation is to *never* stop writing.

Because there is no requirement in freewriting, it is a teacherless activity that provides maximum student involvement. Such writing is not
30 evaluated or graded. The writer simply writes for 10 minutes and later 20

minutes or more. As a student's proficiency grows, the student may choose to write longer. The problem
35 with most writing instruction is that the student writes for the *teacher* and not for self. Because of this perspective, many students bog down in editing and reediting to adhere to perceived rules.
40 This procedure often takes the life out of the writing, which should be spontaneous and fresh.

Freewriting, on the other hand, is not usually an end itself. Reading for
45 pleasure is comparable to freewriting. The goal is to help the student become more comfortable with language and confident about expressing ideas. As in most other endeavors, the more a
50 student practices, the greater his prowess. The opportunity will eventually come, however, when a writer will need to focus some attention on proper form and grammatical rules. Fortu-
55 nately, in today's world of computers with word processing programs, a student can check spelling and grammar in his writing without bogging down in editing and revising. Early
60 experience with freewriting can engender greater facility with language.

Questions 1–8

1. According to this selection, one may refer to good writing as:

    (A) a necessity for a good grade.
    (B) effective communication.
    (C) the result of effective editing.
    (D) an outcome of classroom instruction.
    (E) a teacher's legacy.

2. Freewriting involves:

   (A) spontaneity.
   (B) correct spelling.
   (C) accurate punctuation.
   (D) flawless sentence structure.
   (E) selection of an appropriate subject.

3. After reading this selection, one may assume that the time period for freewriting activities:

   (A) is 10 minutes.
   (B) is a class period.
   (C) changes as the writer becomes more proficient.
   (D) is closely controlled.
   (E) requires overseeing.

4. Writing instruction teaches that one must consider the audience; the audience for freewriting is:

   (A) the teacher.
   (B) an editor.
   (C) one's peers.
   (D) the reader.
   (E) self.

5. The purpose of this article is to:

   (A) persuade.
   (B) narrate.
   (C) explain.
   (D) instruct.
   (E) compare.

6. Based upon this writing, the reader sees the author as:

   (A) disjointed.
   (B) unattached.
   (C) concerned.
   (D) dispassionate.
   (E) malfunctioning.

7. The main idea in this article is to:

   (A) pass on an idea to facilitate easy writing.
   (B) instruct in good composition technique.
   (C) create passive communication.
   (D) convince the reader that one can become a good communicator.
   (E) make writing more stringent for students.

8. After reading this article, one can infer that freewriting can:

   (A) eliminate "writer's block."
   (B) reduce a student writer's anxiety about writing.
   (C) help a student writer avoid having to learn rules of punctuation.
   (D) be intimidating to reluctant writers.
   (E) always result in better writing skills.

Passage 2

Line   Istanbul's Grand Bazaar is one place most tourists want to visit when they travel to the largest city in Turkey. Istanbul, formerly known as Byzantium
5   and Constantinople, is the only major city in the world that lies in both Asia and Europe, and this colorful city reflects the influences of both continents. The covered bazaar, known as
10   Kapa Çar, has been the center of trade in Istanbul for many years.

    The bazaar has been repaired a number of times because of earthquakes and fires; it was enlarged each
15   time until after the earthquake in 1894. After this great quake, the bazaar took the shape it has today. This shopping center, a forerunner to today's subur-

ban malls, has withstood 12 strong
20 earthquakes and 9 big fires. Reconstruc-
tion after a major fire in 1954 resulted
in the most comprehensive restoration.
This huge bazaar can be entered
through one of its 18 gates; however, it
25 is best approached by the Nuruos-
maniye Gate, which faces Nuruos-
maniye Mosque, one of more than
2,000 mosques in Istanbul today.
    During the Ottoman Empire, the
30 bazaar was not only a shopping and
trade center but also a financial district.
This combination served as a model for
markets in other Eastern countries. At
that time, the streets of the bazaar were
35 lined with stalls selling spices, cloth, or
wood. In addition, until the 1850s, it
served as a slave market. Currently
containing more than 4,000 shops, the
bazaar continues to be a virtual
40 labyrinth with something for just about
everyone: carpets, glassware, brass,
ceramics, clothing, jewelry, and leather
goods, just to name a few popular
items.
45   Wandering some of the 80 streets
and roads is an adventure a visitor will
never forget. In this arcade, an incred-
ible array of goods offered by aggres-
sive salesmen makes it difficult to walk
50 through without buying something. The
tradesmen are congenial and eager to
show their wares to prospective
buyers. These salesmen can easily spot
tourists, especially Americans, who
55 always seem to be ready to purchase
something. If a shopper stops strolling
to look at some item in a shop window
or on display, a salesman immediately
offers his services. Sometimes, sellers
60 actually accost shoppers in the street,
enticing them to enter their shop.
Often, merchants even serve tea as they

demonstrate their goods and negotiate
prices. Since haggling over prices is a
65 time-honored tradition, Western
travelers seeking bargains can expect to
be approached by experienced salesmen who know how to sell. The
process of negotiation is a key ingredi-
70 ent in the sale. Along with their
purchases, visitors bring home vivid
memories of bargaining for their
treasures in Kapa Çar.

Questions 9–12

9. The purpose of this article is to:

(A) explain.
(B) narrate.
(C) compare.
(D) persuade.
(E) describe.

10. From this article, the reader can infer that "bazaar" means:

(A) unusual.
(B) a carnival.
(C) foreign.
(D) marketplace.
(E) visitor center.

11. Because of its unusual characteristics, the Grand Bazaar is compared to a:

(A) maze.
(B) palace.
(C) flea market.
(D) the catacombs in Rome.
(E) the Ottoman Empire.

12. The city of Istanbul has had several names:

(A) because it was the property of warring kingdoms.

(B) because it was settled by several different groups of people.

(C) but the article offers no explanation.

(D) but the current name was given by the Turks in the 1400s.

(E) because the Romans, then the Byzantine, and finally the Turks controlled it.

Passage 3

Line   Not long ago, the region between the extreme northern section of California and southern British Columbia was considered an unlikely setting for an
5   earthquake of great magnitude; however, such earthquakes have occurred in the past and will in all probability occur in the future.

To determine the chronology of
10   earthquakes in the Pacific Northwest area of Cascadia, researchers have sought traces of past earthquakes in the geologic record. Excavation of coastal salt marshes indicated that distinct
15   layers below the present marshes (spaced at successive depths of about a meter) contain peat formed from remains of vegetation identical to flora currently extant in the intertidal zone.
20   Many of the buried peat layers are covered by sand washed in by huge tsunamis that rushed into the subsided coast. Theoretical modeling, as well as preserved geologic effects on the
25   shoreline, indicates that these attained heights of 10 meters on the open coast.

After the tsunami dissipated, mud filled the subsided region, and marsh vegetation returned. Repeated se-
30   quences of peat, sand, and mud make the geologic point but do not provide sufficient evidence to date the events with certainty. However, coastal fir trees have been found that were
35   drowned by the ocean after the land abruptly subsided. Examining growth rings and measuring radiocarbon in these trees, researchers have estimated that they died in the last great earth-
40   quake to hit the area, about 300 years ago.

The existence of the last great quake and of similar events that apparently struck at irregular intervals
45   of about 500 years is suggested by unusual deposits found on the ocean floor at quite a distance from land. When scientists studied these sea-floor sediments, they found fine-grained mud
50   alternating with sandier layers. Mud, accumulating from continuous precipitation of sediment from the ocean above, is common. High-energy earthquakes might have initiated huge
55   submarine landslides that carried coastal sediments out into the deep ocean floor.

The sediments themselves do not ordinarily provide precise chronology.
60   A particular sample, however, contains volcanic ash from the cataclysmic eruption 7,700 years ago of the former Mt. Mazama, whose legacy is Crater Lake, in Oregon. Assuming a steady
65   precipitation of mud onto the sea floor, the calendar in the seabed coincides with that of the coastal peat deposits and places the most recent event at 300 years ago, with the 12 previous

70   landslides separated by 300- to 900-year
periods.

     Reports of a disaster are preserved
in the oral history of the natives of
British Columbia. According to native

75   tradition records, an earthquake
devastated Pachena Bay on the west
coast of Vancouver Island one winter
night, obliterating the village at the
head of the bay. A similar account, to

80   which no precise date can be attributed, has been found in the unwritten
lore of northernmost California.

     Japanese written records indicate
that a 20-meter-high tsunami washed

85   onto the coast of Honshu nearly 300
years ago. The earthquake that generated the tsunami occurred along the
American coast on January 26, 1700, at
about 9 p.m., which was determined by

90   adjusting for time zone changes and for
the time required for the wave to reach
Japan.

Questions 13–19

13. The occurrence of identical flora in the intertidal zone and in layers of peat probably indicates that:

(A) the sea has risen over the eons.
(B) a former salt marsh sank and was inundated by ocean water.
(C) the flora in question thrive in an ocean environment as well as on land.
(D) the flora grow only in an environment of sand.
(E) theoretical modeling can be inaccurate.

14. Which of the following statements is most directly supported by the text?

(A) It is difficult to date peat accurately.
(B) All peat contains marine plant life.
(C) Peat is located only on ocean floors.
(D) Peat bogs cause instability that gives rise to earthquakes.
(E) Where sand covers peat, an unstable suspension occurs.

15. The most appropriate title for the article would be:

(A) Cascadia's Story
(B) Secrets of the Geologic Record
(C) In Search of Cascadia's Quake History
(D) Scientists Find Answers in Cascadia
(E) Giant Earthquakes of the Pacific Northwest

16. Which evidence is LEAST conclusive as proof that earthquakes have occurred in Cascadia?

(A) Existence of identical layers of peat beneath present peat marshes.
(B) Geologic evidence on the shoreline.
(C) Repeated sequences of peat, sand, and mud.
(D) Fine-grained mud alternating with sandier layers.
(E) Documentation of the date of the Honshu tsunami.

17. The author mentions the "drowned" coastal fir trees in paragraph 5:

    (A) to document the devastation of earthquakes.
    (B) as a contrast to dates obtained in peat.
    (C) to explain the presence of radiocarbon.
    (D) as evidence used to date the last quake.
    (E) for comparison with the Honshu quake.

18. Which of the following kinds of evidence were used by the author in reaching the conclusion that large earthquakes do occur in Cascadia?

    I. native stories
    II. sedimentary deposits
    III. Japanese writing
    IV. geologic effects on the shoreline

    (A) I and III
    (B) II, III, and IV
    (C) I, III, and IV
    (D) I, II, and III
    (E) All of the above

19. The author provides information related to the Honshu tsunami primarily to:

    (A) compare the geologic past of Honshu with that of the Pacific Northwest.
    (B) prove that even early written records contain references to earthquakes.
    (C) present evidence that coincides historically with previously presented evidence.
    (D) add validity to the unwritten native stories of the Pacific Northwest.
    (E) provide the reader with a diversion from the previous, more technical discussions.

Passage 4

Line   In an era when the value of a good education is as important as it has ever been, controversy still exists about the merits of coed vs. single-sex education.
5   Advocates of both sides contend their views are superior, although most agree that having a choice of the two types is ideal. Many people, however, do not have the luxury of that option. Parents
10   who lack financial resources and those who do not live in metropolitan areas are two groups for whom this choice usually does not exist.

        Those who do have the privilege of selection typically face the choice
15   when their child enters high school, usually in the ninth grade. Primary education in grades 1–8 is largely coeducational in both public and
20   private schools. However, some choice is offered in both high school years and college. Parents can choose the setting they think is best for their child. Making this choice is an important
25   responsibility; therefore, it must be based on a sound examination of key factors.

        Proponents of single-sex education point to a number of benefits. Students
30   of the same sex are less likely to be distracted during class. They are instead more likely to join class discussions and offer comments and questions during class—even the shiest of students.
35   Attire is not as important in a single-sex classroom because there is no need to impress the opposite sex. Clothing then becomes less important. Often, as a matter of fact, single-sex schools have a
40   dress code or require students to wear uniforms. Consequently, both girls and boys can concentrate on academics,

devoting more attention to learning. This lack of distraction is probably the

45   most important characteristic influencing parents who choose single-sex education for their children. Other advantages appeal as well.

Some studies have shown that girls

50   particularly benefit from being in a single-sex classroom because, in traditional class settings, they may be overshadowed by their male counterparts, who are more likely to control

55   class discussion. Furthermore, studies have shown that teachers are more likely to call on male students. Unless a girl is unusually confident, she is likely to be overlooked. In addition, girls

60   sometimes suffer from "math phobia," which may limit their achievement. They may be afraid to ask for help in class or to request further explanation for fear of embarrassment.

65   Likewise, boys can also profit from single-sex instruction. Some studies have reported that boys feel restrained in a class discussion dominated by girls. This feeling mirrors the girls' response

70   and contradicts studies that have shown how boys control the class. The discrepancy may hinge on the personality and perhaps the gender of the teacher, who may be completely

75   unaware of any biases.

Those opposed to single-sex education contend that the worst result of this approach is that both sexes will not have the opportunity to acquire

80   and polish important social skills for interaction with the opposite sex. Likewise, although attire is correctly downplayed, sometimes a concomitant lack of concern about personal hygiene

85   or appearance is another negative side effect. When girls and boys are to-

gether, they may lack the social skills necessary for successful relationships. To offset these factors, single-sex

90   schools often have a "brother" or a "sister" school; students of the two schools can work together on community projects and social occasions such as dances. Working in groups, further-

95   more, offers students a less threatening way to socialize.

Parents who have the opportunity to choose either a coed or a single-sex school for their child should consider

100   the advantages and disadvantages of each.

Questions 20–24

20. The purpose of this article is to:

(A) narrate.
(B) describe.
(C) persuade.
(D) inform.
(E) instruct.

21. Typically, parents select a single-sex school for their child because:

(A) single-sex schools are less expensive.
(B) single-sex schools prepare students better for college.
(C) single-sex schools ideally provide fewer distractions in the classroom.
(D) students can achieve greater athletic prowess in single-sex schools.
(E) single-sex schools are usually boarding schools.

22. "Math phobia" sometimes affects girls:

    (A) who are uncertain of their skills in mathematics.
    (B) who are actually afraid of mathematics.
    (C) who excel in English and social sciences.
    (D) who transfer from public to private schools.
    (E) who have only brothers rather than sisters as siblings.

23. The article supports all of the following inferences EXCEPT:

    (A) Coed classrooms are likely to include distracting elements for students.
    (B) Coed classes may be intimidating to especially shy students of both sexes.
    (C) Coed classrooms usually have more students per class.
    (D) Coed classes help students learn how to interact with classmates of both sexes.
    (E) Coed classes usually do not have rules about attire.

24. Among the following suggestions, the best title for this article is:

    (A) Coed Is the Way to Learn
    (B) Coeds Prefer Single-Sex Schools
    (C) Easy Choices in Education
    (D) Socialization vs. Academics
    (E) Choosing a School

PRACTICE TEST 3

Directions: Each passage in this group is followed by questions based on its content. After reading a passage, choose the best answer to each question. Answer all questions following a passage on the basis of what is stated or in that passage.

Passage 1

Line   Today, the Great Smoky Mountains constitute the largest and highest range in the eastern United States. The foundation for what became the Great
5   Smoky Mountains National Park began millions of years ago when sediments were deposited on a sea floor along an ancient coastline. The source of the sediment was a decaying mountain
10   range being worn away by flowing water. Slowly, the sediment collected in masses of black mud that settled in several layers. Eventually, this mud was fertile enough to support a variety of
15   flora, but since this life lacked hard parts, this part of the sediment contained no fossils. As the old mountain range was eroded by the flow of water, a new range was forming. Subse-
20   quently, these processes developed various layers of shale and sandstone as a result of fossilized remains of some living creatures in the ocean.
         Another important factor in the
25   development of the Smokies occurred when movements of oceanic crust brought North America and Africa closer, with land extending from Scandinavia to Alabama, thus creating a
30   magnificent mountain range as broad as the Andes. Friction and then heat generated by these shifts of oceanic

rock in turn helped to form layers of metamorphic rock. As time passed,

35 about 180 million years ago, the process of creating the mountains was completed with a spectacular range, or chain, of mountains. The processes of erosion and decay continue to be

40 forces that shape the Smokies.

The Smokies were home to Cherokee Indians for years before the arrival of the European pioneers. In words and illustrations that vividly

45 conveyed his interest, the botanist William Bartram first described this area as a result of his travels in the Southeast. His encounters with the Cherokees were friendly; later treatment of

50 the Cherokees would be a shameful chapter in American history. The first white settlers arrived in the Smokies in the late 1790s and early 1800s. As arable land was exhausted, most of

55 these pioneers moved to better farmland, but those who remained behind were virtually forgotten, cut off from the rest of the world almost entirely. Loggers arrived in the early

60 1900s to cut the abundant timber, logging about 65 percent of the timber and devastating forests.

About the same time that timber companies focused their attention on

65 the Smokies, the national park movement was building interest. Then, no national park existed east of the Mississippi River. After considerable study and investigation of sites,

70 Congress gave the secretary of the interior the power to determine the boundaries of two areas: a Shenandoah park in Virginia and the Great Smoky Mountain park in North Carolina and

75 Tennessee. Negotiations with a variety of timber companies as well as fund-

raising on a national scale ensued to make the park a reality. Schoolchildren saved nickels and dimes to contribute

80 to this movement. By 1935, with sufficient funds raised thanks in part to a large gift from John D. Rockefeller, full national park status was granted. Today, more than 150 types of trees

85 exist in the Smokies, as do miles and miles of hiking trails, including the famous Appalachian Trail. Several pioneer cabins and homesteads are maintained within the park today. It is

90 possible, therefore, for visitors, millions of whom go to the Smokies yearly, to get a feel for life in the 1790s in this mountain area.

Questions 1–5

1. The main idea of this passage can best be expressed as follows:

   (A) The Cherokees were not given fair treatment.
   (B) The national park was established over a long period of time.
   (C) The history of the Great Smoky Mountain National Park.
   (D) A geological examination of the Smokies.
   (E) The effects of erosion and decay in the Smokies.

2. The primary geological force creating the mountain chain was:

   (A) flowing water.
   (B) sediment of mud.
   (C) shifts in oceanic crust.
   (D) friction of oceanic rocks.
   (E) all of the above.

3. Timber companies were attracted to the Smokies because:

   (A) of the varieties of hardwood indigenous to the area.
   (B) of the amount of virgin hardwood available.
   (C) of the accessibility of the trees.
   (D) of the fine quality of the trees.
   (E) of the ease with which timber could be transported by river.

4. Which of the following may be inferred from the passage?

   (A) The Great Smoky Mountain National Park is one of the largest in the country.
   (B) The Smokies are named for the haze or mist that often covers the mountains.
   (C) The land formation responsible for creating the mountains was a singular event.
   (D) The white settlers drove the Cherokees out of the Smokies in the 1790s.
   (E) The Great Smoky Mountain National Park charges no admission for visitors.

5. The information provided in the passage implies that:

   (A) the Great Smoky Mountain National Park is the largest national park.
   (B) establishing the park involved a national effort.
   (C) few people actually live in the park today.
   (D) the plant life in the park is endangered.
   (E) the Cherokees were forced to move when the park was opened.

Passage 2

Line The first gold nugget discovered in what became the state of California appeared in January 1848. When the discovery was confirmed by President
5 James K. Polk in his State of the Union speech in December 1848, the California gold rush officially began. As gold fever spread across the country, the population of California grew from
10 15,000 to more than a quarter of a million within three years—a phenomenal growth. This rapid increase put great strain on the rough communities that sprang up, largely populated by
15 men who had left their families back in the East.
    The original "mother lode" was an area that ran more than 100 miles between Mariposa in the south and
20 Auburn in the north, ranging from a width of two miles to only a few yards. By 1865, the lode had yielded more than $750 million. Ironically, neither John Sutter, who owned the property
25 on which the gold was first discovered, nor James Marshall, who made the original discovery of gold, ever got rich from the discovery.
    Such a rapid population growth,
30 called a boom, lasted about 20 years, but it brought remarkable changes to the area. More than 500 mining towns sprang up. Businesses that flourished included gambling and brothels as well
35 as the arts and opera houses. The state capital, Sacramento, was the key center of commerce during the period of prosperity because of businesses such as the Pony Express and the transconti-
40 nental railroad. A fair share of crime followed the gold strike, too.

A number of America's most favorite writers began their careers writing about life during the gold rush.
45 Bret Harte wrote about mining camps in *The Outcasts of Poker Flat*, and Mark Twain offered humor in *The Celebrated Jumping Frog of Calaveras County*.

Questions 6–10

6. This passage about life in the California gold rush days could be titled:

(A) Early Crime in California
(B) Bustling Business in Boom Times
(C) Effects of the Gold Strike in California
(D) California's Capital
(E) Going for the Gold

7. It can be inferred that the gold strike at Sutter's Mill:

(A) took place in the year before California became a state.
(B) occurred in a very limited area.
(C) happened by accident.
(D) occurred before Sacramento became the capital.
(E) was the only site in California where gold was discovered.

8. The article includes no mention of the scars caused by gold mining because:

(A) the purpose of the article is to provide positive information.
(B) there was no lasting damage caused by gold mining.
(C) scars have healed long ago.
(D) the wealth sparked by the gold rush more than offset any damage.
(E) cities like Sacramento were built over the damaged areas.

9. The person who first discovered gold in California:

(A) owned the land on which the gold was discovered.
(B) never became rich because of his discovery.
(C) founded the Pony Express.
(D) became a storekeeper in Sacramento.
(E) was John Sutter himself finding gold on his own property.

10. The population of early mining camps:

(A) was composed entirely of gold miners.
(B) included representatives from all kinds of professions.
(C) fluctuated with strikes.
(D) had to develop their own systems of justice.
(E) was primarily composed of men, many of whom had left families in the East.

Passage 3

Line The development of new food crops is one of the most important ways that scientists benefit society. With his work on the peanut, American scientist
5 George Washington Carver made an enormous contribution to American agriculture. During the 1800s and into the 1900s, cotton was the chief crop grown in the southern part of the
10 United States. However, cotton robs the soil of nutrients when it is planted in the same field year after year; thus, the yield dwindles yearly. Southern farmers, therefore, especially those who farmed
15 small plots, made little money growing this crop, and their future was precarious.

Their rescue came from a fellow Southerner, George Washington Carver,
20 who wanted to help the Southern farmer. After receiving his master's degree in agriculture in 1896, Carver became head of the newly formed Agriculture Department at the Tuskegee
25 Institute in Tuskegee, Alabama. Carver set up a laboratory and experimental plots for agricultural research. Employing students to help carry out experiments on different crops and on
30 products that could be made from those crops, he sought ways to help these farmers. Carver was especially interested in the peanut and the sweet potato, two crops that harbor bacteria
35 that add nutrients to the soil on their roots. Carver discovered about 300 products that could be made from peanuts and more than 100 products that could be made from sweet
40 potatoes. These products included flour, cheese, milk, cosmetics, dyes, rubber, and peanut butter.

Carver's impressive list of products established the importance of the
45 peanut and the sweet potato. Southern farmers began to grow these crops, which were especially suited to the warm weather and the sandy soil of that region. In 1921, Carver went to
50 Washington, D.C., to testify before Congress about the importance of the peanut. Because of Carver's testimony, Congress acted to promote the growth of peanuts in the United States. In time,
55 the soil-enriching peanut became the second-largest crop in the South. By 1950, it had become the sixth-leading crop in the nation.

The peanut is a legume, a plant
60 that bears fruit in the form of pods containing one or more seeds. In fact,

this legume is more closely related to peas than to nuts. Peanut seeds consist of almost 50 percent oil, which is
65 commonly used to fry foods because it smokes only at high temperatures and does not absorb odors easily. Low grades of peanuts are used as an ingredient in soaps, cosmetics, shaving
70 creams, shampoos, paints, and even nitroglycerin. Even the shells of peanuts have used, because they can be ground into powder to be used in plastics, cork substitutes, wallboard, and abrasives.
75 Carver continued his research. He published articles on practical matters such as improved farm techniques and food preservation. His work was especially appreciated during the Great
80 Depression of the 1930s, when many people were out of work and had little money to buy food. Carver was also an influential teacher, inspiring young people to find ways to make science
85 work for the betterment of all.

Questions 11–20

11. The main idea of this passage can be expressed as follows:

   (A) Carver wanted to become wealthy because of his agricultural research.
   (B) Ordinary plants can have a multitude of uses besides food.
   (C) The peanut can be used in more ways than any other nut or vegetable.
   (D) Carver helped the South recover from the Civil War.
   (E) Scientific research can quickly solve agricultural problems.

12. The main purpose of this article is to:

(A) praise the peanut.

(B) delineate Carver's contribution to farming.

(C) compare and contrast peanuts and sweet potatoes.

(D) promote the growing of peanuts and sweet potatoes.

(E) illustrate the effect of the Great Depression.

13. One may infer from this article that:

(A) the South would have failed agriculturally without Carver's peanut research.

(B) Carver's research and experimentation were applied all over the world.

(C) sweet potatoes are just as useful as peanuts.

(D) the most popular use of the peanut is peanut butter.

(E) peanut oil is the most common oil in salad dressings.

14. The author's attitude toward Carver can best be described as:

(A) ambiguous because he offers both positive and negative qualities.

(B) nebulous because there is not sufficient evidence to determine his attitude.

(C) positive because he relates the outstanding contributions Carver made through science.

(D) negative because Carver focused his research on the South only.

(E) biased because the author is probably a peanut farmer.

15. The peanut is similar to a pea in which of the following ways?

(A) It bears fruit in a shell or pod.

(B) It usually has one or two peanut seeds in a pod.

(C) It can be used for food.

(D) It is shaped like a pea.

(E) All of the above.

16. Peanuts were an especially appropriate choice to replace cotton in the South because:

(A) the sandy soil and warm climate were conducive to growing peanuts.

(B) peanuts are low-growing plants that look just like cotton growing in fields.

(C) peanuts can be harvested with cotton gins.

(D) the growing season is identical to cotton's.

(E) it provided much-needed food instead of fiber.

17. In the passage, the writer implies that:

(A) careful, dedicated research can solve virtually all agricultural problems.

(B) careful, dedicated research can result in remarkably beneficial conclusions.

(C) Carver focused his attention on Southern agricultural problems because he lived in the South.

(D) sweet potatoes are more valuable than peanuts.

(E) farmers in the South should grow peanuts and sweet potatoes exclusively.

18. Suppose you learn that the sweet potato is a member of the morning glory family (a type of trumpet-shaped flower that grows on vines). You conclude:

   (A) that sweet potatoes also grow on vines.
   (B) that morning glories also must have many uses.
   (C) that the two plants share some characteristics, but you don't know which.
   (D) that morning glories must also be edible.
   (E) that the seeds of both plants must look similar.

19. The purpose of this passage is to:

   (A) describe.
   (B) narrate.
   (C) compare and contrast.
   (D) explain.
   (E) defend.

20. According to this passage, perhaps Carver's most significant contribution to American history is:

   (A) his creation of peanut butter, second only to hamburgers as America's favorite food.
   (B) his promotion of the lowly peanut as a source of roughage for maintaining road surfaces.
   (C) his research involving peanuts and sweet potatoes.
   (D) his speech before Congress in 1921.
   (E) his role as head of the Tuskegee Institute.

Passage 4

Line Because carpets, especially floor coverings, are destroyed through use, very few rugs from before the sixteenth century have survived. There are two

5 basic types of carpet: flat-weaves and pile, or knotted. Both can be made on either vertical or horizontal frames. The best known flat-weaves today are Turkish kilims, which are typically

10 woven in wool with bold, geometric patterns and sometimes embroidered details. Kilim weaving is done in the tapestry technique, which allows free placement of each area of color.

15   Knotted carpets are an ancient invention. The oldest known example, excavated in Siberia and dating to the fourth or fifth century B.C., has designs evocative of Archaemenid Persian art,

20 suggesting that the technique may have originated in ancient Persia. In knotted rugs, the pile—the plush, thickly tufted surface—is made by tying colored strands, usually wool but occasionally

25 silk for deluxe carpets, onto the vertical elements (*warp*) or a yarn grid. These knotted loops are later sheared, cut, and trimmed to form the plush surface of the carpet. Rows of knots alternate

30 with flat-woven rows (*weft*) that hold the carpet together. The weft is usually in undyed yarn and is eventually hidden by the colored knots. Two common tying techniques are the symmetrical

35 "Turkish" knot, which works well for straight-line designs, and the asymmetrical "Persian" knot, used for rendering curvilinear patterns. The greater the number of knots, the denser and more

40 durable the pile. The finest carpets have 100 knots per square inch, each one tied separately by hand. Because

these rugs are not mass-produced, the size and shape may not be exact and
45 colors may vary slightly; however, these "flaws" are proof of authenticity.

Although royal workshops produced the most luxurious carpets, most knotted rugs have traditionally
50 been made in tents and homes. Carpets were woven by either women or men, depending on the local custom. Today, an older woman generally works with a young girl, who learns the art of carpet
55 weaving at the loom and eventually passes it on to the next generation. Working between September and May, these women may weave five carpets, tying up to 5,000 knots a day. Oriental
60 rugs are considered valuable because they have complex designs and take a long time to produce. Knotted rugs from Persia and Turkey were so highly prized among Westerners that they
65 were often displayed on tables rather than on floors. Persian taste favored intricate, elegant designs that evoked the gardens of paradise. Written accounts indicate that such designs
70 appeared on Persian carpets as early as the seventh century. In one fabled royal carpet, garden paths were rendered in real gold, leaves were modeled with emeralds, and highlights on flowers,
75 fruits, and birds were created with pearls and other jewels. Carpets such as this one were definitely as much status symbols within the Islamic world as they were beyond it.

Questions 21–30

21. The purpose of this passage is:
    (A) narration.
    (B) persuasion.
    (C) description.
    (D) comparison and contrast.
    (E) analysis.

22. Since the weavers work from September to May, their work time implies:
    (A) they have to shear animals and spin yarn in the interim.
    (B) working during the hot summer months is unbearable.
    (C) they weave during the months their children are in school.
    (D) they need the summer to clean the looms.
    (E) the summer months are used to clean and size the completed rugs.

23. The finest carpets today are characterized by:
    (A) 5,000 knots per carpet.
    (B) 100 knots per square inch.
    (C) asymmetrical designs.
    (D) flat weaves.
    (E) Islamic designs exclusively.

24. Elegant Persian carpets, often preferred by collectors,
    (A) feature ornate, exquisite designs with garden patterns.
    (B) are usually room-size because of the amount of work required to produce them.
    (C) contain aniline dyes that provide brilliant colors.
    (D) are actually made in China today, not Persia.
    (E) are created with complicated looms.

25. The terms *warp* and *weft* refer to:

    (A) two typical kinds of knots used in Turkish rugs.
    (B) decorative details on elaborate Oriental rugs.
    (C) two kinds of Persian rugs produced in Iran today.
    (D) the grid or foundation for the rug on which the knots are tied.
    (E) two kinds of looms on which to create the rug.

26. The art of making rugs continues because:

    (A) it is passed on from one generation to the next.
    (B) the demand for high-quality rugs is high.
    (C) few rugs survive from prior to the sixteenth century.
    (D) it represents an important type of Oriental art.
    (E) the consumer is willing to pay high prices for good rugs.

27. A flat-weave carpet such as a Turkish kilim:

    (A) is seldom characterized by bright colors.
    (B) is woven with free placement of colored areas.
    (C) typically has asymmetrical designs of two colors.
    (D) almost always has an off-white background with a geometric design.
    (E) is typically produced in huge workshops.

28. Oriental rugs are sometimes characterized by variations or "flaws" in shape and color because:

    (A) they are made by hand, not by machine.
    (B) little quality control exists to ensure consistency.
    (C) the complicated designs are difficult to create, especially in large rugs.
    (D) the materials used respond to dyes in different ways.
    (E) so many different artisans are likely to contribute to the making of a single rug.

29. An exotic rug with an elaborate design, complete with jewels and gold thread, would most likely:

    (A) be used in a sultan's palace, probably in public areas where he received guests.
    (B) be created and used in secret because of its great value.
    (C) hang on a wall instead of being placed on the floor.
    (D) be a wondrous wedding gift.
    (E) take almost a lifetime for an artisan to complete.

30. The main idea of this passage is to:

    (A) provide some general information about Oriental rugs.
    (B) offer a history of Oriental rugs.
    (C) explain some little-known aspects about Oriental rugs.
    (D) supply detailed commentary about the rug-making process.
    (E) present a comparison-contrast between woven and knotted rugs.

PRACTICE TEST 4

Directions: Each passage in this group is followed by questions based on its content. After reading a passage, choose the best answer to each question. Answer all questions following a passage on the basis of what is stated or implied in that passage.

Passage 1

Line Censorship was hardly a concern of educators, although it was an obvious concern for librarians, until recently. Before World War II, censorship rarely
5 surfaced in schools, although some works—such as John Steinbeck's *Of Mice and Men* and *The Grapes of Wrath*—did cause some discussion in the newspapers of the time. When
10 students began to read the books, the furor spread into the schools. Following World War II, Norman Mailer published *The Naked and the Dead*, and J.D. Salinger wrote *Catcher in the Rye*,
15 which described the society of that day as overly permissive, lax, and even immoral. Youth and young adults were caught up in that description. Most of the objections were aimed at the
20 writers and publishers, and certainly some were aimed at the bookstores stocking the books. Few high school teachers taught the controversial books for many years; even fewer librarians
25 would stock them. But both teachers and librarians became aware anew that they needed to be more careful about books they allowed students to read for extra credit and for book reports.
30 Paperback books offered little of intellectual or pedagogical value to

teachers before World War II. After the war, many teachers blithely assumed that paperbacks had not changed, and,
35 given the lurid covers, teachers seemed to have a point, though it was more superficial than real. Teachers and parents continued to object to student use of paperbacks even after the
40 publication of *The Bible*, Plato's *Dialogues*, and *Four Tragedies of Shakespeare* proved that paperbacks had merit. Students discovered even earlier that paperbacks were handy to
45 stick into a purse or pocket, and the titles were appealing, not stodgy, as on textbooks. Paperbacks came to schools, censors notwithstanding, and these posed problems galore for teachers.
50 Perhaps as important, until about 1967, young-adult books were generally safe, pure, and simplistic, devoid of the reality that young people faced daily— violence, pregnancy, premarital sex,
55 profanity, alcohol, drugs, tobacco, abortion, runaways, alienation, the generation gap, suicide, death, preju- dice, poverty, class distinction, and divorce, among other social problems.
60 The looming topics were sports, going to the prom, getting a car for the Friday-night date, and the first kiss. Young people read them for fun, knowing that they were nothing more
65 than escape reading and had little relationship to reality or to anything of real significance.
Then, in 1967, Ann Head's *Mr. and Mrs. Bo Jo Jones* and S.E. Hinton's
70 *The Outsiders* appeared and the face of young-adult literature changed, never going back to the good old pure days.
The books that followed were not always great or honest, but a surprising
75 number were. English teachers and

librarians who had accepted the possibility of censorship with adult authors popular with their students—Steinbeck, Fitzgerald, and Hemingway,
80 for example—now learned that the once-safe young-adult novel was no longer "safe." Censorship attacks soon began. Many of the works were denounced.

85 Since 1963, the enactment of censorship in communities and schools has increased. Teachers and librarians eager to promote reading as a means of learning about life found themselves
90 expected to sit quietly while the censors trod all over them. In 1982, a survey of high school librarians found that 34 percent of them reported a challenge to at least one book, com-
95 pared to 30 percent in 1977. A 1986 Canadian survey was no better.

So it was that schools found themselves embroiled in an emotional and pedagogical dilemma that was the
100 stuff of which novels were made, but it was also very real to the people represented in the daily newspapers' accounts of challenges and students in the middle. Censorship became a real
105 part of the American education system, affecting the youth and young adults not only of the 1980s but stretching into the 1990s as well.

Questions 1–10

1. Based on the material presented in this selection, the reader should conclude that:

   (A) too much attention has been given to subjects that are real in the lives of students today.
   (B) focusing on the problems students face is not what students want.
   (C) school personnel are diligent in selecting only books that present material about life today.
   (D) local reaction to the subject material of books in schools has grown radically during the past 30 years.

2. The author's mention of Steinbeck's works is intended to:

   (A) remind the reader to avoid these works as questionable.
   (B) portray Steinbeck as an innovative writer whose works are generally appealing.
   (C) illustrate what "bad" books really are and warn students to shun them.
   (D) present works that are familiar as an example of what censorship really is.

3. The fact that some censors insist that all young-adult books just be examined by parents, teachers, and librarians, with the ultimate decision made by those not in education, would most directly challenge the assumption:

(A) of freedom of the press.
(B) that young people can choose for themselves.
(C) that subject matter is changing and must be closely watched.
(D) that parents should not be involved in education.

4. On the basis of statements made in the passage, one is justified in concluding that the:

(A) teachers and librarians have given over the choice of reading material to students.
(B) school administrators have refused to allow parents and community leaders to have a say in library holdings.
(C) authors of today fear writing about matters of concern to youth.
(D) censorship of books for school libraries will continue to grow even though new authors are writing about new subjects.

5. The author's presentation of the rise in the publication of paperbacks is intended to:

(A) show that students prefer informal presentation.
(B) indicate the questionable topics for which paperbacks were first known.
(C) illustrate why censorship became important as the popularity of paperbacks grew.
(D) show the increased availability of books because of the decrease in price.

6. Based upon the passage, which of the following would likely characterize the young-adult novel?

   I. Plots about teen issues of pregnancy, abortion, and adoption.
   II. Plots about drug and alcohol abuse.
   III. Issues of divorce, suicide, and prejudice.

(A) II only
(B) III only
(C) I and II only
(D) II and III only

7. According to this article, information contained in the modern young-adult novel is considered:

(A) old-fashioned, good, and pure.
(B) absolutely honest and forthright.
(C) surprisingly great and honest.
(D) more superficial than real.

8. The fact that some teachers and librarians choose to include the paperback young-adult novels on reading lists would most directly challenge the assumption that:

   (A) educators more than parents and community leaders know the needs and preferences of students.
   (B) taking a chance with censorship is a popular trend in education today.
   (C) censorship should be a priority concern before books are purchased and/or recommended to students.
   (D) students will read the books that are available to them in the school setting.

9. The word *pedagogical* is used to illustrate to the reader the:

   (A) appeal to the intellectual offered by the paperback.
   (B) dearth of appropriate subject matter chosen for the books.
   (C) emotional appeal to young people of the literature presented.
   (D) lack of teaching value in the paperbacks available before World War II.

10. To illustrate a difference between the paperbacks available immediately after World War II and those available today, the author describes:

    (A) unattractive titles.
    (B) questionable authors.
    (C) cheap conversation.
    (D) subject matter.

Passage 2

Line During the normal development of self, a child is affected by certain influential factors. One of the most important involves his relationship with his
5 mother. Infants form an attachment with the mother that must undergo a process of separation and individuation. Object relations psychology examines this relationship, which depends on the
10 ability of the child to separate himself from his object, the mother, and realize that he is a separate individual. By the age of six months, an infant will usually protest if separated from this mother;
15 eventually, he grows to realize that not only when she leaves, she usually will return, but also that he is separate from his mother. A safe, loving environment is another necessary component for the
20 development of a healthy self-concept. Certainly, affectionate, caring parents are essential as well. As the child begins to develop his sense of self, he must master certain developmental
25 tasks that are part of growing up, such as acquisition of language and toilet training. Anything that interrupts the development of these important skills may interfere with developing a healthy
30 self-concept. Obviously, there are other aspects of early childhood development that also influence this crucial facet of childhood.
   What, then, effect does adoption
35 have on the development of a healthy sense of self? Since an infant's relationship with his mother is so important, according to many psychologists, what effect does being separated from the
40 biological mother have on the adopted child? For infants adopted at birth, the effect may be minimal, for the infant

has often had no opportunity to bond with the biological mother. But what
45 about a child who is older when he is adopted? What effect does adoption have on a toddler?

Even if a toddler has been in one foster home since birth and has
50 therefore attached himself to his foster mother, he will likely experience a series of reactions when separated from this caregiver—protest, despair, and detachment—unless his experience is
55 monitored to help him handle the change. Consider a toddler adopted at the age of 18 months who has lived in the same foster home since birth. When he is placed with an adoptive
60 family, he is likely to experience separation anxiety from his foster mother, who can be regarded as symbolically abandoning him as his own biological mother did. His behav-
65 ior may demonstrate his distress; he may cry inconsolably or act out in other ways.

His transition to living in an adoptive home may be difficult as he
70 adjusts to new surroundings and caregivers because, by the age of 18 months, he has already begun to develop a sense of self in relation to others. On the other hand, he is past
75 the crucial age of 7 to 12 months, when an infant may sustain the most severe damage to his mental and physical development if deprived of mothering by one significant individual.
80 Now it seems as though he has to start over; his protesting may give way to despair as he yearns for people who used to be in his life. The adoptive family should offer as much affection
85 and security as possible to reassure the child that he is safe, that they are

reliable sources of loving care, and that they will help him through this difficult stage.
90 Despite these actions, sometimes a child may continue to suffer from separation anxiety. Although he may not mind the actual separation from his mother when he goes to playschool or
95 day care, he may become obsessed about the time when his mother is supposed to pick him up at day care or kindergarten; tardiness may provoke fears about car accidents or death. His
100 anxieties may burgeon with unusual fears of ghosts, robbers, and loud noises such as sirens and thunder. Psychological counseling and/or medication may help reduce the child's
105 anxiety.

On the other hand, some psychologists believe that a child who is given more affection is sometimes more strongly attached and therefore more
110 prone to separation anxiety than are some of those who are treated more roughly. Since such "dependence" in the well-loved child is outgrown and later provides the basis for a stable
115 independence, it would be a mistake to suppose it to be pathological. On the contrary, the capacity to experience separation anxiety can be regarded as a sign of the healthy personality. An
120 adopted child, then, has at least an average chance of successful individuation, assuming he is adopted by loving parents.

Questions 11–15

11. According to the article, adopted children:

    (A) are less likely to develop separation anxiety than those who are not adopted.
    (B) who develop separation anxiety never recover.
    (C) struggle to develop a healthy sense of self.
    (D) always experience feelings of protest, despair, and detachment.

12. A child's relationship with his mother:

    (A) is a crucial factor in his personality development.
    (B) is the most important influence in his personality development.
    (C) teaches him how to interact with others.
    (D) is more important than his relationship with his father.

13. From the article, one can infer that children who are adopted as toddlers may present special problems, such as:

    (A) delayed motor skills development.
    (B) delayed toilet training.
    (C) difficulty in interacting with peers.
    (D) inability to express affection.

14. The effect of adoption on the development of a healthy self-concept:

    (A) varies with the age of the child.
    (B) depends on the adoptive family.
    (C) can be influenced by a foster mother.
    (D) all of the above.

15. A child suffering from separation anxiety may:

    (A) fear his parents have been injured in a car wreck.
    (B) be unable to play with his peers.
    (C) not develop motor skills at appropriate ages.
    (D) have an irrational fear of spiders.

Passage 3

Line Petroglyphs are figures scratched or carved into rocks. These artistic designs are found in the ruins of numerous ancient Indian dwellings in the Ameri-
5 can Southwest. Although many of the designs are difficult to distinguish, in many instances we can decipher figures of various animals, such as deer, lizards, and wolves. Although the multitude of
10 scratchings on cave walls and crude drawings depict animals, only one from the pre-Columbian people is anthropomorphic: Kokopelli. Because this figure occurs in so many places and on so
15 many relics from that era, anthropologists today have concluded that Kokopelli must have played a strong role in Native American culture.

   This easily recognized figure is
20 characterized by having a hunchback and playing a flute. This male symbol appears throughout the Southwest, dating as early as 200 A.D. and as late as the sixteenth century, when it
25 appears with men on horseback. The arrival of Spanish conquistadors, unfortunately, brought disaster to the Indians who scratched the figures of Kokopelli. The Spaniards brought with
30 them disease, starvation, and slavery, virtually wiping out life in the Southwest for the Indians living there.

Finding petroglyphs, however, offers a window into the past. Trying to
35 date drawings done before the arrival of these explorers is difficult. Because the process of dating the scratching or etching of a petroglyph takes time and because time eventually will cause the
40 design to become invisible, scientists are trying to find information as quickly as possible. Newspaper Rock in Utah and another smaller version in Arizona offer fascinating glimpses into the lives
45 of Indians with no written language. Visits to these sites as well as other sites, such as Canyon de Chelly and Chaco Canyon, will yield remarkable experiences of seeing these petro-
50 glyphs. Like Kokopelli, some other designs depict kachinas, which are important figures to the Hopi tribe.
Not only is Kokopelli always depicted playing a flute, but also he is
55 frequently a vivid phallic figure. It is reasonable to conclude that Kokopelli played an important role in fertility rites. Perhaps his shape is based on a superstition that all hunchbacked
60 people are fertility symbols. Perhaps he may also be a kind of traveling sales-man who plays his flute as a signal to all that he comes in peace.

Questions 16–20

16. The purpose of the selection is:

(A) to narrate.
(B) to persuade.
(C) to describe.
(D) to convince.

17. According to the passage, the figure of a hunchbacked man:

(A) appears in sculpture also.
(B) only appears as drawings or etchings on walls or rocks.
(C) sometimes is depicted with a wife.
(D) can also be seen playing a drum.

18. Since Kokopelli appears in a number of places in the American Southwest, one can infer that:

(A) Kokopelli was part of a voodoo ritual.
(B) Kokopelli was supposed to scare off enemies.
(C) Kokopelli was a powerful deity for many Native Americans.
(D) Traveling tribes marked their journeys with drawings of him.

19. Because Kokopelli is associated with fertility, one can conclude that:

(A) he is connected with harvesting crops.
(B) he was sometimes depicted with a wife of his own.
(C) he was sometimes surrounded by magic herbs.
(D) he may appear with six toes.

20. Petroglyphs are most commonly found on:

(A) cave walls and rocks in the Pacific Northwest, particularly in Montana, where the climate preserves them.
(B) rocks on Hopi Indian reservations as part of religious rituals.
(C) centrally located rocks such as News-paper Rock for communication.
(D) ruins of Native American dwell-ings in the Southwest.

ANSWERS AND EXPLANATIONS

PRACTICE TEST 1

Answers to Passage 1

1. The correct answer is (A). This is a main idea question. The first line of paragraph 2 states, "How did language arise in the first place?" Answer (B) is incorrect, for there is no evidence presented concerning the "need" for language. Answer (C) is incorrect; the communication of early man is presented to introduce the origin of language. Answer (D) is incorrect; the culture of early man is not the main idea but an example. Answer (E) is incorrect; the language "English" is not mentioned. "Language" is the focus.

2. The correct answer is (D). This question is based on details or evidence from the passage. There is no indication that primitive men had an extensive vocabulary. The reverse is actually indicated. Paragraph 2 lists the theories as (A) changes occurring through the years, (C) the language of children, and (E) communication among primitive men. Answer (B) is found in the last part of paragraph 2.

3. The correct answer is (C). This is an implication question. The reader must determine what the author implies by the information supplied. Paragraph 3 indicates that the use of words like "doll" is an accident of adult teaching. Answer (A) is incorrect; there is no evidence to trace evolution of a noun. Answer (B) is incorrect; the fact that most of the early language was nouns is a supporting fact to the origin of language but not an indicator of the most important part of the beginning. Answer (D) is incorrect; the evolution of the word "doll" is not developed. Answer (E) is incorrect because there is no mention of multiple uses.

4. The correct answer is (B). This is an implication question. The last sentence of paragraph 2 states, "The types of evidence . . . must be treated with caution." Answer (A) is incorrect; there was NO specific route to developing language. Answer (C) is incorrect; chimpanzee behavior is observed as a precursor to language but not a part of it. Answer (D) is incorrect; the statement is made that adults *teach* language to their children, but that is not a reason for its development. Answer (E) is incorrect; paragraph 1 makes the point that primitive man had no language.

5. The correct answer is (B). This is an inference question. The reader must draw a conclusion based on the information supplied. Paragraph 1 indicates the lack of early language but asserts that as cultures grew, so did language. Answer (A) is incorrect; the opposite of this is true: The indication from this selection is that man does want and need to communicate. Answer (C) is incorrect; the evidence presented in paragraph 1 indicates that primitives were social. Answer (D) is incorrect; the point is made that adults do instruct children, but there is no indication that the children created the need for language. Answer (E) is incorrect; there is no evidence that mankind was not intended to communicate.

6. The correct answer is (E). This is an inference question. Paragraph 1 states, "It is difficult to believe . . . Palaeolithic cultures lacked the power of speech." The implication is that without speech they would have been unable to make tools, fire, or cooperate with each other in order to hunt big game. Answer (A) is incorrect; there is no evidence of this in the passage. Answer (B) is incorrect; the PURPOSE of language is NOT merely for adults to instruct children. Answers (C) and (D) are incorrect; while these may be true statements, neither is the logical assumption from this selection.

Answers to Passage 2

7. The correct answer is (B). This is a primary purpose question. The author seeks to inform the reader of the definition of acid rain. Answer (A) is incorrect; the author does not tell a story. Answer (C) is incorrect; there is no attempt to instruct. Answer (D) is incorrect; the author does not seek to convince the reader but merely states facts. Answer (E) is incorrect; the author does not describe as much as define.

8. The correct answer is (B). This question is based on details or evidence from the passage. The first paragraph indicates the universal concern for the problems of acid rain. Answer (A) is incorrect; this point is made in the second sentence of the first paragraph. Answer (C) is incorrect; the second paragraph states the universal danger. Answer (D) is incorrect; the dangers to the environment are spelled out in the fourth sentence in paragraph 1 concerning environmental exploitation. Answer (E) is incorrect; the same sentence points out the environmental exploitation of the soil.

9. The correct answer is (E). This question is based on details or evidence from the passage. Paragraph 2 defines pH as "the concentration of hydrogen ions in substance. Answer (A) and Answer (B) are incorrect; sentence 5 of paragraph 2 offers a correct definition. Answer (C) is incorrect; the pH does not measure the oxygen level in the air. Answer (D) is incorrect; the pH does not measure soil sterility.

10. The correct answer is (B). This is an inference question. The author's informational approach indicates research born of concern exemplified by the continued references to lakes, soil, and statuary. Answer (A) is incorrect; there is no indication of detachment. Answer (C) is incorrect; the author's interest is apparent in the beginning. Answer (D) is incorrect; there is no indication of amusement on the part of the author. Answer (E) is incorrect. While the author may have fear, it is not expressed in the passage.

11. The correct answer is (D). This is an evidence question. There is no mention of ozone in this article. Answers (A), (B), (C), and (E) are indicated in paragraph 4.

12. The correct answer is (C). This is an evidence question. The passage is concerned with the effects of acid rain, not the causes. Answer (A) is incorrect; although the statement is true, it is not relevant to this article. Answer (B) is incorrect; while it may be an accurate statement, it is not pertinent to this article. Answer (D) is incorrect; there is no mention of airplanes or jets. Answer (E) is incorrect, for there is no evidence of a *deliberate* disregard of natural resources. Even though this comment may be true, there is no evidence in the article to support it.

Answers to Passage 3

13. The correct answer is (C). This is a primary purpose question. The passage offers a description of general symptoms of the disorder, causes for these behavior, and ways the traumatic or causative event can be re-experienced. Answer (A) is incorrect because the author does not tell a story. Answer (B) is incorrect; there is no evidence of this goal. Answer (D) is incorrect; the passage goes beyond a definition of the disorder. Answer (E) is incorrect; there is no evidence that the author is attempting to persuade the reader to accept an argument.

Peterson's Logic & Reading Review

14. The correct answer is (B). This is an evidence question. The opening sentence of the passage notes this characteristic. Answer (A) is incorrect, for there is no evidence that genetics has any role in the disorder. Answer (C) is incorrect; the disorder can be re-experienced—not *induced*—by climatic changes according to paragraph 3. Answer (D) is incorrect; biological changes are not relevant. Answer (E) is incorrect because only one of the choices is correct.

15. The correct answer is (B). This is an inference question. According to the information presented, anyone can experience the disorder. Answer (A) is incorrect; sentence 2 in the final paragraph notes that apparently recurrences are common. Answer (C) is incorrect; victims can include veterans, but there is no evidence that victims are mostly veterans. Answer (D) is incorrect; the event that triggered the disorder may be life-threatening, but there is no evidence that the disorder itself is life-threatening. Answer (E) is incorrect; children are mentioned in paragraphs 1 and 2.

16. The correct answer is (D). This is an evidence question. The time requirement is cited in the final sentence of the first paragraph. Answer (A) is incorrect; "interminable" suggests the time is unending. Answers (B), (C), and (E) are incorrect because the specific time appears in the first paragraph.

17. The correct answer is (B). This is an inference question. The definitions of the varying disorders all imply a previous event, which, when recalled, induces stress. Answer (A) is incorrect; there is no pain indicated. Answer (C) is incorrect; the experiences recalled are not necessarily from childhood. Answer (D) is incorrect; there are no biological indicators. Answer (E) is incorrect; there is no mention of genetic conditions.

Answers to Passage 4

18. The correct answer is (D). This is a primary purpose question. This article informs the reader about the definition of matter. Answer (A) is incorrect; there is no effort made to convince or persuade. Answer (B) is incorrect; there is no discussion of varying ideas but rather a presentation of facts. Answer (C) is incorrect because the author does not tell a story. Answer (E) is incorrect; the reader is not instructed in how to use matter but informed of definitions.

19. The correct answer is (A). This is an evidence question. In paragraph 3, the writer introduces new concepts including "space-time" and "event-particles." Answer (B) is incorrect; traditional concepts are challenged throughout paragraph 1, not embraced. Answer (C) is incorrect; there are no definitions requested. Answer (D) is incorrect; this selection dismisses neither as irrelevant. Answer (E) is incorrect; neither is demonstrated as invalid.

20. The correct answer is (C). This is an evidence question. There is no evidence in this article of archaic terminology. The ending of paragraph 2 states that "relativity demands the abandonment of the old conception of 'matter,' which is . . . (A) infected by metaphysics, (B) associated with "substance," (D) "represents a point of view" (E) "not needed to deal with phenomena." Therefore, all answers EXCEPT (C) are covered.

21. The correct answer is (B). This is an evidence question. Paragraph 1 states that "when this view of light was disproved and it was shown that light consisted of waves," Newton's theory of gravitation fell into discredit. Answer (A) is incorrect; there is no mention of Einstein in this selection. Answer (C) is incorrect; Newton's theory, according to paragraph 1, held that light contained particles. Answer (D) is incorrect; that matter existed everywhere was the beginning of Newton's thesis. Answer (E) is incorrect; electromagnets play no part in Newton's theory.

22. The correct answer is (E). This is an evidence question. Paragraph 3 states that (I) An event does not persist and move, like traditional matter, (II) A piece of matter is resolved into a series of events, and (III) An event exists for its little moment and ceases. Therefore, all three statements are correct.

PRACTICE TEST 2

Answers to Passage 1

1. The correct answer is (B). This is an implications question. Paragraph 1 makes the statement that good writing is good communication. Answer (A) is incorrect; the implication is that one should not write only for a good grade. Answer (C) is incorrect; paragraph 3 makes the statement that over-editing makes writing lifeless. Answer (D) is incorrect; the statement is made that free-writing is "teacherless." Answer (E) is incorrect; there is no mention of the teacher's legacy as a part of good writing.

2. The correct answer is (A). This is an inference question. Because free-writing is immediate, the result is spontaneous and does not require (B) correct spelling, (C) accurate punctuation, (D) flawless sentence structure, or (E) selection of an appropriate subject.

3. The correct answer is (C). This is an inference question. The statement is made that one begins with a 10-minute period and can expand to 20 minutes. Answer (A) is incorrect because of the foregoing. Answer (B) is incorrect; this task is deemed a teacherless activity and does not involve the class period time. Answer (D) is incorrect; free-writing is not closely controlled. Answer (E) is incorrect; free-writing is personal and not overseen.

4. The correct answer is (E). This question calls for knowledge of evidence in the passage. This selection states that free-writing is read by one's self. Answer (A) is incorrect; free-writing is teacherless. Answer (B) is incorrect; there is no editor in free-writing. Answer (C) is incorrect; one's peers are not a factor in free-writing. Answer (D) is incorrect; there is no reader involved.

5. The correct answer is (D). This is a primary purpose question. The author is instructing the reader on effective writing. Answer (A) is incorrect; there is no effort to persuade. Answer (B) is incorrect; this is not a narrative because it tells no story. Answer (C) is incorrect; there is no attempt to explain with reasoning. Answer (E) is incorrect; there is no effort to compare free-writing to other writing.

6. The correct answer is (C). This is an author's attitude question. The author's instructions reveal a concern for good writing. Answer (A) is incorrect; there is no evidence that the writer is disjointed or confused. Answer (B) is incorrect; the author is obviously attached to and cares about the subject. Answer (D) is incorrect; there is evidence of the writer's passion throughout the selection. Answer (E) is incorrect; the writer succeeds in functioning to reveal methods for good communication.

7. The correct answer is (A). This is a main idea question. The author is passing on an idea to make writing easier. Answer (B) is incorrect; there is no mention of free-writing as a composition technique. Answer (C) is incorrect; passive communication is the least of the writer's intents as stated in the last two sentences of paragraph 3. Answer (D) is incorrect; while this may be an underlying intent, there is no effort to convince. Answer (E) is incorrect; making writing more stringent is not the writer's intent.

8. The correct answer is (B). This is an inference question. This inference can be based on details in the passage that explain how free-writing is essentially a nonthreatening activity because only the writer sees his writing. Answer (A) is incorrect; there is no reference to "writer's block" nor any mention of dispelling obstacles to successful writing. Answer (C) is incorrect; although free-writing does not depend on a knowledge of punctuation rules, the activity does not preclude a knowledge of these rules. Answer (D) is incorrect; there is no mention of intimidation; in fact, the free-writing is designed to encourage reluctant writers. Answer (E) is incorrect; the article does not state that better writing skills are always the result of free-writing.

Answers to Passage 2

9. The correct answer is (E). This is a primary purpose question. The selection describes the Grand Bazaar in Istanbul. Answer (A) is incorrect; no analysis of details leading to explanation is present. Answer (B) is incorrect; the author is not telling a story. Answer (C) is incorrect, for the main idea is not to compare the bazaar to anything. Answer (D) is incorrect; the author does not attempt to persuade.

10. The correct answer is (D). This is an inference question. The Grand Bazaar is a marketplace. Answer (A) is not correct; "bizarre," which is pronounced like "bazaar," means "unusual." Answer (B) is incorrect; although "bazaar" can mean "carnival," it does not in this article. Answer (C) is incorrect; "foreign" is not relevant to the question. Answer (E) is incorrect; although many travelers visit the Grand Bazaar, there was no mention of a visitor center.

11. The correct answer is (A). This is a synthesis question. The first sentence of paragraph 4 compares the bazaar to a "labyrinth," which is a maze. Answer (B) is incorrect; there is no mention of a palace in the article. Answer (C) is incorrect; while the term "flea market" may come to mind when the reader considers the Grand Bazaar, the article does not include any reference to a flea market. Answer (D) is incorrect; the Roman catacombs are not mentioned in the article. Answer (E) is incorrect; although the Ottoman Empire was an important period in Turkish history, it bears no relevance to the article.

12. The correct answer is (C). This question depends on evidence from the passage. Remember that you must answer each question on the basis of what is presented in the article. Answer (A) is incorrect because there is no mention of warring kingdoms. Answer (B) is incorrect; the article includes no mention of how the city was settled. The details in answer (E) are also true, but once again, the article does not specifically include these points. There is only a brief reference in sentence 2 of paragraph 1 to the city's different names without any explanation of their source.

Answers to Passage 3

13. The correct answer is (B). This is an inference question. Since peat layers below the current salt marshes contain the same kinds of plants, and since those peat layers were covered by sand washed in by huge waves, it can be assumed that a previous marsh sank and was covered by ocean water and sand. Answer (A) is an unlikely choice since the passage makes no reference to the rise or fall of ocean levels. Answer (C) is incorrect since the "identical flora" are not growing in the ocean. Although the plants obviously grow in sandy environments, this passage does not discuss or imply other locations; answer (D) is beyond the data of this passage. Answer (E) uses a technical term from the passage ("theoretical modeling") pulled from a sentence discussing wave heights, not flora.

14. The correct answer is (A). This question depends on evidence from the passage. The passage (in paragraph 3) states that sequences of peat, sand, and mud do not provide evidence to date the events with certainty. The passage tells the reader that peat contains plant life (flora), but not that all peat contains marine plant life; thus, answer (B) is not correct. Answer (C) can be eliminated because the passage does not indicate that *any* peat is on ocean floors. The cause-effect relationship stated in answer (D) is nearly a converse of the correct relationship: earthquakes can give rise to peat bogs. Answer (E) is not acceptable because the reader has no basis upon which to make a decision regarding unstable suspensions.

15. The correct answer is (C). This is a main idea question. This title is the most specific available that blankets the content of the passage as a whole. Answer (A) is more vague (what story?), as are answers (B) (what secrets?) and (D) (what answers?). Answer (E) is too broad; this passage does not discuss the earthquakes themselves but focuses upon evidence indicating that they did occur.

16. The correct answer is (D). This is an evidence question. The passage states in paragraph 4 that huge earthquakes *might* have caused mudslides. All other answers are presented as definite cause-effect situations.

17. The correct answer is (D). This is an author's purpose question. Growth rings and radiocarbon dating establish that the trees died 300 years ago when a large earthquake produced an ocean wave that drowned their roots, killing the trees. The age of dead trees does not document the seriousness of an earthquake, so answer (A) can be eliminated. Peat layers do not provide sufficient evidence to date the layers with accuracy, and peat data does not contrast with tree data; thus, answer (B) is incorrect. Answer (C) is incorrect, since drowned trees do not explain the presence of radiocarbon, which occurs in all living things. As for answer (E), there was no Honshu quake, only a Honshu tsunami.

18. The correct answer is (E). This is an evidence question. All answers are correct. Native stories from different locations told of quakes. Sedimentary deposits on the ocean floor enabled researchers to date such a quake. Japanese writing also enabled a date to be established. Geologic evidence on shorelines is cited in paragraph 2.

19. The correct answer is (C). This is a primary purpose question. The author has presented information that enables the conclusion that (1) earthquakes have occurred in this region; and (2) the last one occurred about 300 years ago. The documentation of the date of the Honshu tsunami coincides with the period of time the drowned pine trees have been dead and with the date indicated by the ocean floor layer that contained volcanic ash. Answer (A) is incorrect because it gives no purpose for the comparison. Answer (B) is not specific in regard to time or location. Answer (D) is the second-best choice, but answer (C) is better because it relates to the passage as a whole. Answer (E) suggests that the author included loosely related material, which is not correct.

Answers to Passage 4

20. The correct answer is (D). This is a primary purpose question, to inform the reader about the qualities of both types of education. Answer (A) is not correct, because the author is not telling a story. Answers (B) and (C) are incorrect; the author is not trying to persuade or convince the reader that one answer is superior to the other. Answer (E) is incorrect; the author is not trying to teach or instruct the reader.

21. The correct answer is (C). This is an evidence question. Paragraph 3 offers supporting evidence for this answer. Answer (A) is incorrect; there is no evidence of cost being less expensive in single-sex schools. Answer (B) is incorrect; there is no specific evidence in the article that supports this view. Answer (D) is incorrect; the article makes no mention of athletics. Answer (E) is incorrect; boarding schools are not mentioned in the article.

22. The correct answer is (A). This is another evidence question. Evidence appears in paragraph 4. Answer (B) is incorrect; the expression "math phobia" does not necessarily describe a genuine fear of mathematics. Answer (C) is incorrect; there is no mention of performance in English or social sciences. Answer (D) is not correct; the article does not include information about transferring from one school to another. Answer (E) is incorrect; family relationships are not mentioned in the article.

23. The correct answer is (C). This is an evidence question. The article does not offer information about class size. Answer (A) is incorrect; evidence appears in paragraph 3. Answer (B) is incorrect; supporting evidence for this statement also appears in paragraph 3. Answer (D) is incorrect; this inference is valid based on information presented in paragraph 6. Answer (E) is incorrect; this inference is based on information presented in paragraph 3.

24. The correct answer is (E). This is a main idea question. The author offers information to inform the reader of pros and cons of both choices. Answer (A) is incorrect; there is no evidence to support this view. Answer (B) is incorrect; the author offers no evidence of coeds' preferences. Answer (C) is incorrect; the decision is more than likely the opposite. Answer (D) is incorrect; the article deals with more than these areas.

PRACTICE TEST 3

Answers to Passage 1

1. The correct answer is (C). This is a main idea question. All four paragraphs deal with this topic. Answer (A) is incorrect; although the statement is true, this topic is not the main focus of the passage. Answer (B) is incorrect; this information is only partially true. The land formation took many years, but the creation of the national park was not as long. Answer (D) is incorrect; only the opening paragraph deals with this topic. Answer (E) is incorrect because it is also too limited.

2. The correct answer is (E). This is an evidence question. All of the choices are cited in the passage.

3. The correct answer is (B). This is an evidence question. See the final sentence of paragraph 3: "abundant timber" supports this claim. Answer (A) is incorrect; while this statement is true, no evidence in the passage supports this claim. Answer (C) is incorrect; there is no evidence in the passage to support this claim. Answer (D) is incorrect because there is no mention of this point. Answer (E) is incorrect; there is no evidence to support this point.

4. The correct answer is (A). This is an inference question. The opening sentence of the passage notes that the mountain range is the largest in the eastern United States. Answer (B) is incorrect; although this statement is true, there is no evidence in the passage to support this inference. Answer (C) is incorrect; the passage points out several geological forces responsible for forming the mountain range. Answer (D) is incorrect; the Cherokees were forced to leave but not in the 1790s. Answer (E) is incorrect; this is also true, but there is no evidence in the passage to support this statement.

5. The correct answer is (B). This is an implications question. Note that American schoolchildren even contributed nickels. Answer (A) is incorrect; there is no evidence that this is the nation's largest park. Answer (C) is incorrect; even though this information is probably true, there is no evidence in the passage to support this choice. Answer (D) is incorrect; there is no reference to endangering the plant life. Answer (E) is incorrect; evidence in the passage notes that the Cherokees were forced out long before the park was established.

Answers to Passage 2

6. The correct answer is (C). This is a main idea question. Answer (A) is incorrect because it is too limited. Answer (B) is incorrect; although the gold strike leads to boom times, the passage discusses more than business. Answer (D) is incorrect; information offered covers more than the capital. Answer (E) is incorrect; the passage does not focus solely on hunting for gold.

7. The correct answer is (D). This is an inference question. Answer (A) is incorrect because the passage does not offer specific information about when California achieved statehood. Answer (B) is incorrect; the vein of gold extended over 100 miles. Answer (C) is incorrect; there is no explanation of how the discovery was made. Answer (E) is incorrect; there is no evidence that this was the only site of a gold strike.

8. The correct answer is (A). This is a primary purpose question. Because of the lack of negative information, the reader can infer that the author sought only to offer positive details. Answer (B) is incorrect; there is no mention of damage. Answer (C) is incorrect; there is no mention of scars. Answer (D) is incorrect; no evidence indicates that wealth accrued offset damage. Answer (E) is incorrect; there is no mention of cities' being built on mine sites.

9. The correct answer is (B). This is an evidence question. The article notes that neither James Marshall, who found the gold, nor John Sutter, on whose property the discovery was made, ever became rich. Answer (A) is incorrect. Sutter owned the land. Answer (C) is incorrect; there is no mention of who founded the Pony Express. Answer (D) is incorrect; there is no evidence to support this idea. Answer (E) is incorrect; Sutter owned the land but did not make the discovery.

10. The correct answer is (E). This is an evidence question. The relevant information appears at the end of paragraph 1. Answer (A) is incorrect; there is no evidence to support this idea. Answer (B) is incorrect; while this point is probably true, there is no supporting evidence in the passage. Answer (C) is incorrect; there is no mention of changing populations. Answer (D) is incorrect; while the point may be true, there is no mention of justice systems in the passage.

Answers to Passage 3

11. The correct answer is (B). This is a main idea question. After careful reading you should recognize that the main idea in this passage is (B). Carver's research proved that peanuts and sweet potatoes could be used in a variety of ways in addition to being edible. Answer (A) is incorrect; there is no mention of Carver's desire to be wealthy or of any financial success he achieved. Answer (C) is incorrect; although the passage notes that the peanut has a wide variety of uses, there is no evidence that the peanut can be used in more ways that any other nut or vegetable. Answer (D) is incorrect; there is no evidence that Carver's work contributed to the era immediately following the Civil War; he began his research around the turn of the century. Answer (E) is incorrect; there is no evidence that speed was a factor in Carver's research.

12. The correct answer is (B). This question requires you to determine the primary purpose of the passage. The passage discusses the ways in which Carver's research helped farming. Answer (A) is incorrect because the passage does more than merely praise the peanut. Answer (C) is incorrect; no comparison or contrast between these two plants is included. Answer (D) is incorrect; although the passage does point out the benefits of growing peanuts and sweet potatoes, the writer does not necessarily encourage the reader to cultivate these plants. Answer (E) is incorrect; although the Great Depression is mentioned in the passage, it is not the main focus.

13. The correct answer is (A). This is an inference question. The reader draws conclusions based on the evidence presented. His research offered a substitute crop for cotton, which was rapidly depleting the soil in the South. Answer (B) is incorrect; there is no mention of Carver's work being applied internationally. Answer (C) is incorrect because there is no basis for this assertion. Answer (D) is incorrect; while it may be true, nothing in the passage supports this conclusion. Answer (E) is incorrect; while this statement is a true one, nothing in the passage supports this inference.

14. The correct answer is (C). This question requires you to determine the author's attitude. The author's description of Carver's accomplishments is presented in a positive manner. Answer (A) is incorrect; there are no negative qualities offered. Answer (B) is incorrect; the author's positive tone is clear. Answer (D) is incorrect; even though Carver's research was focused on the South, the results were applied elsewhere as well. Answer (E) is incorrect; there is no evidence of the author's occupation.

15. The correct answer is (E). This question depends on specific evidence from the passage. All of the statements are correct. Paragraph 4 includes details to support all of these assertions.

16. The correct answer is (A). This is another evidence question. Supporting details can be seen in paragraph 3. Answer (B) is incorrect; there is no mention of the appearance of plants growing in the fields. Answer (C) is incorrect; there is no mention of how peanuts are harvested. Answer (D) is incorrect; there is no evidence of the length of the growing season of either plant. Answer (E) is incorrect; there is no mention of food vs. fiber as an important issue.

17. The correct answer is (B). This is an implications question. It is the only one with sufficient evidence to support it in the passage. Answer (A) is incorrect; there is no mention of solving "virtually all" agricultural problems. Answer (C) is incorrect; there is no mention of Carver's home as a significant factor in his research. Answer (D) is incorrect; there is no evidence to prove this assertion. Answer (E) is incorrect; nothing in the passage supports this idea.

18. The correct answer is (C). This question requires you to use new information. You are given new information and asked to combine it with details from the passage before you answer the question. Of the possible answers, this is the only one that can be defended. Answer (A) is incorrect; there is no evidence to indicate how sweet potatoes grow. Answer (B) is incorrect; there is no evidence of any uses of morning glories. Answer (D) is incorrect; there is no evidence that these flowers can be eaten. Answer (E) is incorrect; no evidence supports this assertion.

19. The correct answer is (D). This question asks you to determine the purpose of the passage. Answer (A) is incorrect; description is not evident in the passage. Answer (B) is incorrect; the writer is not telling a story. Answer (C) is incorrect; the writer is not comparing or contrasting anything. Answer (E) is incorrect; the writer is not defending a position or point of view.

20. The correct answer is (C). This is another inference question. Answer (A) is incorrect; he is not credited with creating peanut butter. Answer (B) is incorrect; there is no mention of roads. Answer (D) is incorrect; the speech is mentioned but not emphasized as important. Answer (E) is incorrect; Carver was head of Tuskegee Institute, but the passage deals with more than this aspect of his career.

Answers to Passage 4

21. The correct answer is (C). This question asks you to determine the purpose of the passage. Answer (A) is incorrect; the passage does not tell a story. Answer (B) is incorrect; the writer makes no attempt to persuade the reader. Answer (D) is incorrect. The process of comparison or contrasting is not used in the passage. Answer (E) is incorrect; analysis requires an examination of causes and results.

22. The correct answer is (B). This is an implications question. You consider information from the passage and decide what the writer is implying by his remarks. Answer (A) is incorrect; there is no mention of shearing animals or spinning yarn. Answer (C) is incorrect; there is no reference to children or school. Answer (D) is incorrect; there is no mention of cleaning the looms. Answer (E) is incorrect; there is no mention of clean and sizing the rugs.

23. The correct answer is (B). This is a question that is based on evidence from the passage, which is pointed out in the last sentence of the second paragraph. Answer (A) is incorrect; sometimes a weaver may tie 5,000 knots in a day, according to the fourth sentence of paragraph three. Answer (C) is incorrect; asymmetrical designs are mentioned but not specified as a characteristic of the finest rugs. Answer (D) is incorrect. Kilim rugs are characterized as flat weaves, but there is no mention of them as "finest carpets today." Answer (E) is incorrect; there is no mention of Islamic designs.

24. The correct answer is (A). This question depends on evidence from the passage. Answer (B) is incorrect; there is no mention of the size of any rugs. Answer (C) is incorrect; there is no mention of a special kind of dye. Answer (D) is incorrect; while some Oriental rugs are indeed made in China, the passage does not include any information about them. Answer (E) is incorrect; the rugs are hand-knotted, but the backing or foundation is woven.

25. The correct answer is (D). This question also deals with specific evidence from the passage. Sentences 3 and 4 in the second paragraph present these details. Answer (A) is incorrect; there are actually two types of knots, but they are not named in this passage. Answer (B) is incorrect; the terms refer to more basic elements of the rug, not decorations. Answer (C) is incorrect; the two terms refer to the backing or foundation of the rug. Answer (E) is incorrect; there is no mention of different kinds of looms.

26. The correct answer is (A). This question is an inference question. You read the passage and draw conclusions. Answer (B) is incorrect; there is no mention of the demand for rugs. Answer (C) is incorrect; this answer is not relevant to the question. Answer (D) is incorrect; while the statement is true, it is not a logical inference. Answer (E) is incorrect. Again, the statement may be true, but it is not relevant to the question.

27. The correct answer is (B). This question is one that calls for specific details from the passage. Evidence appears at the end of the first paragraph. Answer (A) is incorrect; there is no evidence to support this response. Answer (C) is incorrect; there is no evidence to support this response. Answer (D) is incorrect; the color of the background is never discussed. Answer (E) is incorrect; there is no mention of large workshops.

28. The correct answer is (E). This is an inference question. Answer (A) is incorrect; there is no indication that more than two people make a rug. Answer (B) is incorrect; there is no mention of quality control or the need for it. Answer (C) is incorrect; difficult designs do not necessarily mean the rugs are likely to be flawed. Answer (D) is incorrect; there is no reference to dyes.

29. The correct answer is (C). This question is another inference question. Answer (A) is incorrect; although the statement may be true, there is no evidence in the passage to support this choice. Answer (B) is incorrect; there is no evidence to support this choice. Answer (D) is incorrect; there is no mention of rugs as gifts. Answer (E) is incorrect; there is no evidence in the passage to support this choice.

30. The correct answer is (D). This is a question that requires you to determine the main idea of the passage. The passage offers information without focusing too much attention on specific details. Answer (A) is incorrect; the rug-making process is not carefully examined. Answer (B) is incorrect; only some general historical information is offered. Answer (C) is incorrect; the passage does not depend on unusual facets. Answer (E) is incorrect; there is no comparison-contrast provided.

PRACTICE TEST 4

Answers to Passage 1

1. The correct answer is (D). This is an inference question. You make a decision based solely on what is available in the passage. Answer (A) is incorrect; although young-adult literature strives to deal with honest subjects, censorship of books still continues into the 1990s. Answer (B) is incorrect; the opposite is true. Answer (C) is incorrect; while there may be some communities that are doing this, there is no evidence to prove it as a real factor.

2. The correct answer is (D). This is an author's purpose question. Answers (A) and (C) are incorrect; there is no evidence of the author's attempts to urge the avoidance of any works. Answer (B) is incorrect; although this may be a true statement, it is not part of the selection.

3. The correct answer is (B). This is an implication question. Answer (A) is incorrect; although there may be some truth here, there is nothing in the article to support this argument. Answer (C) is incorrect; while on the surface, this seems to be true, the reader must realize that there is no indicator of the need to watch the subject matter. Answer (D) is incorrect; the point is made that parents DO have a voice in these choices.

4. The correct answer is (D). You must draw an inference to answer this question. Answer (A) is incorrect; there is no evidence of this. In fact, the choice is given to the censors. Answer (B) is incorrect; there is evidence that parents and community leaders do have a choice. Answer (C) is incorrect; again, evidence shows the opposite of this choice.

5. The correct answer is (A). This question asks you to determine the author's purpose. Answer (B) is incorrect; while the dubious beginning is implied, it is not the author's purpose. Answer (C) is incorrect; again, while there is some evidence, the premise is not supported. Answer (D) is incorrect; there is no evidence that this is true.

6. The correct answer is (D). This question requires you to recall specific evidence from the passage. Answer (A) is incorrect; there is no mention of adoption. Answers (B) and (C) are incorrect because each is only partly correct.

7. The correct answer is (C). This question calls for an inference. The author states that while all the novels were "hardly great or honest, a surprising number were." Answer (A) is incorrect; the point is made that today's young-adult novels are not the "good-old-pure" ones of yesterday. Answer (B) is incorrect; there is no mention of the works as "forthright." Answer (D) is incorrect; the word "superficial" is used to describe the paperback books that predate the young-adult novel.

8. The correct answer is (C). This is an inference question. To have the books made available would challenge the priority of censorship. Answer (A) is incorrect; if the books were available, this would agree with the statement of answer (C). Answer (B) is incorrect; there is no mention of censorship as a popular trend in education. Answer (D) is incorrect; while this point may be true, the article does not state this as a certainty.

9. The correct answer is (D). This is a kind of purpose question, focusing on the use of a specific term. "Pedagogy" means the art of teaching; therefore the books were lacking in material that was teachable. Answer (A) is incorrect; the point is made that there was a lack of intellectual appeal. Answer (B) is incorrect; the lack of appropriate subject matter was not relevant to the question. Answer (C) is incorrect; while there may be truth in the statement, it is not borne out in this article.

10. The correct answer is (D). This is a question that requires you to use evidence or details from the passage. The author lists the subjects with which today's paperback young-adult novels deal and relates them to life. Answer (A) is incorrect; there is no mention of unattractive titles. Answer (B) is incorrect; the author does not describe any authors as questionable. Answer (C) is incorrect; the cheap price of the book is referred to as a positive factor but not in relation to the construction of the book.

Answers to Passage 2

11. The correct answer is (A). This is a question that depends on evidence in the passage. Paragraph 3 supports this response. Answer (B) is incorrect; there is no evidence that children *never* recover. Answer (C) is incorrect; while the statement may be correct, there is no clear-cut evidence in the article to support this choice. Answer (D) is incorrect; the use of *always* is a clue. There is no evidence that children *always* experience these feelings.

12. The correct answer is (C). This is a question that depends on specific evidence. The article emphasizes the role of this relationship. Answer (A) is incorrect; there is no mention of interaction with peers. Answer (B) is incorrect; the article does not indicate that the relationship is the "most important." Answer (D) is incorrect; the child's relationship with his father is not discussed.

13. The correct answer is (B). This is an inference question. This response is supported by paragraph 1. Answer (A) is incorrect; development of motor skills is not mentioned. Answer (C) is incorrect because interaction with peers is not mentioned. Answer (D) is incorrect; the child's ability to express affection is not examined in the article.

14. The correct answer is (D). This is a question that depends on your knowledge of details or evidence from the passage. All of the choices are supported by the article.

15. The correct answer is (A). This question calls for a knowledge of evidence in the passage. Paragraph 5 supports this choice. Answer (B) is incorrect; the article makes no mention of peers. Answer (C) is incorrect; there is no mention of inability to develop appropriate motor skills. Answer (D) is incorrect; although this fear is common in children, the article makes no mention of it.

Answers to Passage 3

16. The correct answer is (C). This is a primary purpose question. The passage describes the physical details of Kokopelli as well as some of the places where he is found. Answer (A) is incorrect; there is no story being told here. Answer (B) is incorrect; the author is not attempting to persuade the reader about anything. Answer (D) is incorrect; the author is not trying to convince the reader either.

17. The correct answer is (B). The question depends on evidence from the passage. These sites are the only ones mentioned. Answer (A) is incorrect because no sculpture is mentioned. Answer (C), though true, is incorrect because the passage does not include any reference to Kokopelli's wife. Answer (D) is incorrect because there is no mention of a drum.

18. The correct answer is (C). This is an inference question. Because Kokopelli was a fertility figure, it is safe to assume he was an important figure. Answer (A) is incorrect because there was no mention of voodooism, which is not indigenous to the American Southwest. Answer (B) is incorrect; Kokopelli is not described as fearsome or as being used to scare away anybody. Answer (D) is incorrect; there is no reference to traveling tribes.

19. The correct answer is (B). This is another inference question. Based on the information provided in the passage, one can conclude that he was sometimes depicted with a wife of his own. It is also the best choice of the four possible answers. Answer (A) is incorrect because it is illogical. Being associated with fertility and the planting of crops makes more sense. Answer (C) is incorrect; there is no mention of magic herbs. While Kokopelli may indeed be depicted with six toes, that fact is not included in the passage, and it has no relevance to fertility.

20. The correct answer is (D). This is an evidence question. Answer (A) is incorrect; there is no mention of the Pacific Northwest. Answer (B) is incorrect; there is no mention of specific Indian reservations. Answer (C) is incorrect; the petroglyphs appear in other locations as well.

QUICK-SCORE ANSWERS

ANSWERS TO PRACTICE TESTS 1–4

Practice Test 1	Practice Test 2	Practice Test 3	Practice Test 4
1. A	1. B	1. C	1. D
2. D	2. A	2. E	2. D
3. C	3. C	3. B	3. B
4. B	4. E	4. A	4. D
5. B	5. D	5. B	5. A
6. E	6. C	6. C	6. D
7. B	7. A	7. D	7. C
8. B	8. B	8. A	8. C
9. E	9. E	9. B	9. D
10. B	10. D	10. E	10. D
11. D	11. A	11. B	11. A
12. C	12. C	12. B	12. C
13. C	13. B	13. A	13. B
14. B	14. A	14. C	14. D
15. B	15. C	15. E	15. A
16. D	16. D	16. A	16. C
17. B	17. D	17. B	17. B
18. D	18. E	18. C	18. C
19. A	19. C	19. D	19. B
20. C	20. D	20. C	20. D
21. B	21. C	21. C	
22. E	22. A	22. B	
	23. C	23. B	
	24. E	24. A	
		25. D	
		26. A	
		27. B	
		28. E	
		29. C	
		30. D	

Peterson's Logic & Reading Review

FINANCING YOUR GRADUATE AND PROFESSIONAL EDUCATION

If you're considering attending graduate school but fear you don't have enough money, don't despair. Financial support for graduate study does exist, although, admittedly, the information about support sources can be difficult to find.

Support for graduate study can take many forms, depending upon the field of study and program you pursue. For example, some 60 percent of doctoral students receive support in the form of either grants/fellowships or assistantships, whereas most students in master's programs rely on loans to pay for their graduate study. In addition, doctoral candidates are more likely to receive grants/fellowships and assistantships than master's degree students, and students in the sciences are more likely to receive aid than those in the arts and humanities.

For those of you who have experience with financial aid as an undergraduate, there are some differences for graduate students you'll notice right away. For one, aid to undergraduates is based primarily on need (although the number of colleges that now offer undergraduate merit-based aid is increasing). But graduate aid is often based on academic merit, especially in the arts and sciences. Second, as a graduate student, you are automatically "independent" for federal financial aid purposes, meaning your parents' income and assest information is not required in assessing your need for federal aid. And third, at some graduate schools, the awarding of aid may be administered by the academic departments or the graduate school itself, not the financial aid office. This means that at some schools, you may be involved with as many as three offices: a central financial aid office, the graduate school, *and* your academic department.

FINANCIAL AID MYTHS

- Financial aid is just for poor people.
- Financial aid is just for smart people.
- Financial aid is mainly for minority students.
- I have a job, so I must not be eligible for aid.
- If I apply for aid, it will affect whether or not I'm admitted.
- Loans are not financial aid.

Be Prepared

Being prepared for graduate school means you should put together a financial plan. So, before you enter graduate school, you should have answers to these questions:

- What should I be doing now to prepare for the cost of my graduate education?
- What can I do to minimize my costs once I arrive on campus?
- What financial aid programs are available at each of the schools to which I am applying?
- What financial aid programs are available outside the university, at the federal, state, or private level?
- What financing options do I have if I cannot pay the full cost from my own resources and those of my family?
- What should I know about the loans I am being offered?
- What impact will these loans have on me when I complete my program?

You'll find your answers in three guiding principles: think ahead, live within your means, and keep your head above water.

Think Ahead

The first step to putting together your financial plan comes from thinking about the future: the loss of your income while you're attending school, your projected income after you graduate, the annual rate of inflation, additional expenses you will incur as a student and after you graduate, and any loss of income you may experience later on from unintentional periods of unemployment, pregnancy, or disability. The cornerstone of thinking ahead is following a step-by-step process.

1. **Set your goals.** Decide what and where you want to study, whether you will attend full- or part-time, whether you'll work while attending, and what an appropriate level of debt would be. Consider whether you would attend full-time if you had enough financial aid or whether keeping your full-time job is an important priority in your life. Keep in mind that some employers have tuition reimbursement plans for full-time employees.

2. **Take inventory.** Collect your financial information and add up your assets—bank accounts, stocks, bonds, real estate, business and personal property. Then subtract your liabilities—money owed on your assets including credit card debt and car loans—to yield your net worth.

3. **Calculate your need.** Compare your net worth with the costs at the schools you are considering to get a rough estimate of how much of your assets you can use for your schooling.

4. **Create an action plan.** Determine how much you'll earn while in school, how much you think you will receive in grants and scholarships, and how much you plan to borrow. Don't forget to consider inflation and possible life changes that could affect your overall financial plan.

5. **Review your plan regularly.** Measure the progress of your plan every year and make adjustments for such things as increases in salary or other changes in your goals or circumstances.

Live Within Your Means

The second step in being prepared is knowing how much you spend now so you can determine how much you'll spend when you're in school. Use the standard cost of attendance budget published by your school as a guide. But don't be surprised if your estimated budget is higher than the one the school provides, especially if you've been out of school for a while. Once you've figured out your budget, see if you can pare down your current costs and financial obligations so the lean years of graduate school don't come as too large a shock.

Keep Your Head Above Water

Finally, the third step is managing the debt you'll accrue as a graduate student. Debt is manageable only when considered in terms of five things:

1. Your future income

2. The amount of time it takes to repay the loan

3. The interest rate you are being charged

4. Your personal lifestyle and expenses after graduation

5. Unexpected circumstances that change your income or your ability to repay what you owe

To make sure your educational debt is manageable, you should borrow an amount that requires payments of between 8 and 15 percent of your starting salary.

The approximate monthly installments for repaying borrowed principal at 5, 8–10, and 12 percent are indicated in the table below.

Estimated Loan Repayment Schedule
Monthly Payments for Every $1000 Borrowed

Rate	5 years	10 years	15 years	20 years	25 years
5%	$18.87	$10.61	$ 7.91	$ 6.60	$ 5.85
8%	20.28	12.13	9.56	8.36	7.72
9%	20.76	12.67	10.14	9.00	8.39
10%	21.74	13.77	10.75	9.65	9.09
12%	22.24	14.35	12.00	11.01	10.53

You can use this table to estimate your monthly payments on a loan for any of the five repayment periods (5, 10, 15, 20, and 25 years). The amounts listed are the monthly payments for a $1000 loan for each of the interest rates. To estimate your monthly payment, choose the closest interest rate and multiply the amount of the payment listed by the total amount of your loan and then divide by 1,000. For example, for a total loan of $15,000 at 9 percent to be paid back over ten years, multiply $12.67 times 15,000 (190,050) divided by 1,000. This yields $190.05 per month.

If you're wondering just how much of a loan payment you can afford monthly without running into payment problems, consult the chart below.

HOW MUCH CAN YOU AFFORD TO REPAY?

Of course, the best way to manage your debt is to borrow less. While cutting your personal budget may be one option, there are a few others you may want to consider:

- *Ask Your Family for Help:* Although the federal government considers you "independent," your parents and family may still be willing and able to help pay for your graduate education. If your family is not open to just giving you money, they may be open to making a low-interest (or deferred-interest) loan. Family loans usually have more attractive interest rates and repayment terms than commercial loans. They may also have tax consequences, so you may want to check with a tax adviser.

- *Push to Graduate Early:* It's possible to reduce your total indebtedness by completing your program ahead of schedule. You can either take more courses per semester or during the summer. Keep in mind, though, that these options reduce the time you have available to work.

- *Work More, Attend Less:* Another alternative is to enroll part-time, leaving more time to work. Remember, though, to qualify for aid, you must be enrolled at least half time, which is usually considered six credits per term. And if you're enrolled less than half time, you'll have to start repaying your loans once the grace period has expired.

ROLL YOUR LOANS INTO ONE

There's a good chance that as a graduate student you will have two or more loans included in your aid package, plus any money you borrowed as an undergraduate. That means when you start repaying, you could be making loan payments to several different lenders. Not only can the recordkeeping be a nightmare, but with each loan having a minimum payment, your total monthly payments may be more than you can handle. If that is the case, you may want to consider consolidating your federal loans.

There is no minimum or maximum on the amount of loans you must have in order to consolidate. Also, there is no consolidation fee. The interest rate varies annually, is adjusted every July 1, and is capped at 8.25 percent. Your repayment can also be extended to up to thirty years, depending on the total amount you borrow, which will make your monthly payments lower (of course, you'll also be paying more total interest). With a consolidated loan, some lenders offer graduated or income-sensitive repayment options. Consult with your lender or the U.S. Department of Education about the types of consolidation provisions offered.

PLASTIC MANIA

Any section on managing debt would be incomplete if it didn't mention the responsible use of credit cards. Most graduate students hold one or more credit cards, and many students find themselves in financial difficulties because of them. Here are two suggestions: use credit cards only for convenience, never for extended credit; and, if you have more than one credit card, keep only the one that has the lowest finance charge and the lowest limit.

Credit: Don't Let Your Past Haunt You

Many schools will check your credit history before they process any private educational loans for you. To make sure your credit rating is accurate, you may want to request a copy of your credit report before you start graduate school. You can get a copy of your report by sending a signed, written request to one of the four national credit reporting agencies at the address listed below. Include your full name, social security number, current address, any previous addresses for the past five years, date of birth, and daytime phone number. Call the agency before you request your report so you know whether there is a fee for this report. Note that you are entitled to a free copy of your credit report if you have been denied credit within the last sixty days. In addition, Experian currently provides complimentary credit reports once every twelve months.

Credit criteria used to review and approve student loans can include the following:

- Absence of negative credit
- No bankruptcies, foreclosures, repossessions, charge-offs, or open judgments
- No prior educational loan defaults, unless paid in full or making satisfactory repayments
- Absence of excessive past due accounts; that is, no 30-, 60-, or 90-day delinquencies on consumer loans or revolving charge accounts within the past two years

Types of Aid Available

There are three types of aid: money given to you (grants, scholarships, and fellowships), money you earn through work, and loans.

Grants, Scholarships, and Fellowships

Most grants, scholarships, and fellowships are outright awards that require no service in return. Often they provide the cost of tuition and fees plus a stipend to cover living expenses. Some are based exclusively on financial need, some exclusively on academic merit, and some on a combination of need and merit. As a rule, grants are awarded to those with financial need, although they may require the recipient to have expertise in a certain field. Fellowships and scholarships often connote selectivity based on ability— financial need is usually not a factor.

Federal Support

Several federal agencies fund fellowship and trainee programs for graduate and professional students. The amounts and types of assistance offered vary considerably by field of study.

CREDIT REPORTING AGENCIES

Experian
P.O. Box 9530
Allen, Texas 75013
888-397-3742

Equifax
P.O. Box 105873
Atlanta, Georgia 30348
800-685-1111

CSC Credit Services
Consumer Assistance Center
P.O. Box 674402
Houston, Texas 77267-4402
800-759-5979

Trans Union Corporation
P.O. Box 390
Springfield, Pennsylvania 19064-0390
800-888-4213

Jacob Javits Fellowship. This is a grant program for students in the arts, humanities, and social sciences to use at the school of their choice. Graduate students apply directly to the U.S. Department of Education. The application deadline is in February. The school the Javits Fellow attends receives up to $10,222 toward the cost of tuition. If the tuition exceeds $10,222, the school is obliged to cover the additional cost in the form of a grant. Javits Fellows receive as much as $15,000 in stipend, depending on financial need and available funding. No funding is guaranteed beyond the 1998 fiscal year. For more information, call 202-708-8596.

National Institutes of Health (NIH). NIH sponsors many different fellowship opportunities. For example, it offers training grants administered through schools' research departments. Training grants provide tuition plus a twelve-month stipend of $11,496. For more information, call 301-435-0714.

National Science Foundation. Graduate Research Program Fellowships include tuition and fees plus a $15,000 stipend for three years of graduate study in engineering, mathematics, the natural sciences, the social sciences, and the history and philosophy of science. The application deadline is in early November. For more information, write to the National Science Foundation at Oak Ridge Associated Universities, P.O. Box 3010, Oak Ridge, Tennessee 37831-3010, or call 423-241-4300.

Graduate Assistantships in Areas of National Need. This program was designed to offer fellowships to oustanding doctoral candidates of superior ability. It is designed to offer financial assistance to students enrolled in specific programs for which there is both a national need and lack of qualified personnel. The definition of national need is determined by the Secretary of Education. Current areas include chemistry, engineering, mathematics, physics, and area studies. Funds are awarded to schools who then select their recipients, based on academic merit. Awardees must also demonstrate financial need. Awards include tuition plus a living expense stipend of up to $14,000. Awards are not to exceed four years. Contact the graduate dean's office or academic department to see whether it participates in this program.

Foreign Language and Area Studies Fellowships (FLAS). FLAS fellowships are designed to finance graduate training in foreign languages and related area studies. Administered by the U.S. Department of Education, this program was developed to promote a wider knowledge and understanding of certain cultures and countries. Universities apply directly to the Department of Education for these funds and schools themselves select the recipients based on academic merit. Few fellowships are awarded to first-year students. Application deadlines vary by school.

Veterans' Benefits. Veterans may use their educational benefits for training at the graduate and professional levels. Contact your regional office of the Veterans Administration for more details.

State Support

Some states offer grants for graduate study, with California, Michigan, New York, North Carolina, Texas, and Virginia offering the largest programs. States grant approximately $2.9 million per year to graduate students. Due to fiscal constraints, however, some states have had to reduce or eliminate their financial aid programs for graduate study. To qualify for a particular state's aid you must be a resident of that state. Residency is established in most states after you have lived there for at least twelve consecutive months prior to enrolling in school. Many states provide funds for in-state students only; that is, funds are not transferable out of state. Contact your state scholarship office to determine what aid it offers.

Institutional Aid

Educational institutions using their own funds provide more than $3 billion in graduate assistance in the form of fellowships, tuition waivers, and assistantships. Consult each school's catalog for information about aid programs. More information about institutional aid programs can be found in Books 2 through 6 of this series.

Corporate Aid

Some corporations provide graduate student support as part of the employee benefits package. Most employees who receive aid study at the master's level or take courses without enrolling in a particular degree program.

Aid from Foundations

Most foundations provide support in areas of interest to them. For example, for those studying for the Ph.D., the Howard Hughes Institute funds students in the biomedical sciences, while the Spencer Foundation funds dissertation research in the field of education.

The Foundation Center of New York City publishes several reference books on foundation support for graduate study. For more information, call 212-620-4230 or access their Web site at http://fdncenter.org.

Mellon Fellowships in the Humanities. Eighty entry-level, one-year, portable merit fellowships are awarded each year. Fellowships are for one year only and you should plan to seek support elsewhere for subsequent years. The stipend for Mellon fellows entering graduate school in 1998 is $14,000 plus tuition and mandated fees. Awards are highly competitive. Any college senior or graduate of the last five years who is a citizen or permanent resident of the United States and is applying to a Ph.D. program in a humanities field is encouraged to compete. The application deadline is in December. Contact Woodrow Wilson Fellowship Foundation, Mellon Fellowships CN5329, Princeton, New Jersey 08543-5329, 609-452-7007, e-mail: mellon@woodrow.org, Web site: http://www.woodrow.org.

Financial Aid for Minorities and Women

Patricia Roberts Harris Fellowships. This federal award provides support for minorities and women. Awards are made to schools, and the schools decide who receives these funds. Fellows receive a stipend of $14,400 for up to four years, and their institutions receive up to $9493 per year. No funding is guaranteed beyond the 1998 fiscal year. Consult the graduate school for more information.

Bureau of Indian Affairs. The Bureau of Indian Affairs (BIA) offers aid to students who are at least one quarter American Indian or native Alaskan and from a federally recognized tribe. Contact your tribal education officer, BIA area office, or call the Bureau of Indian Affairs at 202-208-3710.

The Ford Foundation Doctoral Fellowship for Minorities. Provides three-year doctoral fellowships and one-year dissertation fellowships. Predoctoral fellowships include an annual stipend of $14,000 to the fellow and an annual institutional grant of $7500 to the fellowship institution in lieu of tuition and fees. Dissertation fellows receive a stipend of $18,000 for a twelve-month period. Applications are due in early November. For more information, contact the Fellowship Office, National Research Council at 202-334-2872.

National Consortium for Graduate Degrees in Engineering and Science (GEM). GEM was founded in 1976 to help minority men and women pursue graduate study in engineering by helping them obtain practical experience through summer internships at consortium work-sites and finance graduate study toward a master's or Ph.D. degree. GEM administers the following programs:

Engineering Fellowship Program. Each fellow receives a GEM-sponsored summer internship and a portable fellowship tenable at one of seventy-seven GEM universities. The fellowship consists of tuition, fees, and a $6000 stipend per academic year.

Ph.D. Fellowship Program. The Ph.D. Science Fellowship and the Engineering Fellowship programs provide opportunities for minority students to obtain a Ph.D. in the natural sciences or in engineering through a program of paid summer research internships and financial support. Open to U.S. citizens who belong to one of the ethnic groups underrepresented in the natural sciences and engineering, GEM fellowships are awarded for a twelve-month period. Fellowships are tenable at universities participating in the GEM science or engineering Ph.D. programs. Awards include tuition, fees, and a $12,000 stipend. After the first year of study fellows are supported completely by their respective universities and support may include teaching or research assistantships. Forty fellowships are awarded annually in each program. The application deadline is December. For more information, contact GEM, Box 537, Notre Dame, Indiana 46556, call 219-631-7771, or visit their Web site at http://www.nd.edu/⎪P5gem/.

National Physical Sciences Consortium. Graduate fellowships are available in astronomy, chemistry, computer science, geology, materials science, mathematics, and physics for women and Black, Hispanic, and Native American students. These fellowships are available only at member universities. Awards may vary by year in school and the application deadline is November 5. Fellows receive tuition plus a stipend of between $10,000 and $15,000. For more information, contact National Physical Sciences Consortium, Department 3NPS, c/o New Mexico State University, P.O. Box 30001, Las Cruces, New Mexico 88033-8003, call 505-646-6037, or visit their Web site at http://www.npsc. org.

In addition, below are some books available that describe financial aid opportunities for women and minorities.

The Directory of Financial Aids for Women by Gail Ann Schlachter (Reference Service Press, 1997) lists sources of support and identifies foundations and other organizations interested in helping women secure funding for graduate study.

The Association for Women in Science publishes *Grants-at-a-Glance,* a booklet highlighting fellowships for women in science. It can be ordered by calling 202-326-8940 or by visiting their Web site at http://www.awis.org.

Books such as *Financial Aid for Minorities* (Garrett Park, MD: Garrett Park Press, 1998) describe financial aid opportunities for minority students. For more information, call 301-946-2553.

Reference Service Press also publishes four directories specifically for minorities: *Financial Aid for African Americans, Financial Aid for Asian Americans, Financial Aid for Hispanic Americans,* and *Financial Aid for Native Americans.*

For more information on financial aid for minorities, see the Minority On-Line Information Service (MOLIS) Web site at http://web.fie.com/web/mol/.

Disabled students are eligible to receive aid from a number of organizations. *Financial Aid for the Disabled and Their Families, 1996–98* by Gail Ann Schlachter and David R. Weber (Reference Service Press) lists aid opportunities for disabled students. The Vocational Rehabilitation Services in your home state can also provide information.

Researching Grants and Fellowships

The books listed below are good sources of information on grant and fellowship support for graduate education and should be consulted before you resort to borrowing. Keep in mind that grant support varies dramatically from field to field.

Annual Register of Grant Support: A Directory of Funding Sources, Wilmette, Illinois: National Register Publishing Co. This is a comprehensive guide to grants and awards from government agencies, foundations, and business and professional organizations.

Corporate Foundation Profiles, 10th ed. New York: Foundation Center, 1998. This is an in-depth, analytical profile of 250 of the largest company-sponsored foundations in the United States. Brief descriptions of all 700 company-sponsored foundations are also included. There is an index of subjects, types of support, and geographical locations.

The Foundation Directory, edited by Stan Olsen. New York: Foundation Center, 1998. This directory, with a supplement, gives detailed information on U.S. foundations, with brief descriptions of the purpose and activities of each.

The Grants Register 1998, 16th ed. Edited by Lisa Williams. New York: St. Martin's, 1998. This lists grant agencies alphabetically and gives information on awards available to graduate students, young professionals, and scholars for study and research.

Peterson's Grants for Graduate & Postdoctoral Study, 5th ed. Princeton: Peterson's, 1998. This book includes information on 1,400 grants, scholarships, awards, fellowships, and prizes. Originally compiled by the Office of Research Affairs at the Graduate School of the University of Massachusetts at Amherst, this guide is updated periodically by Peterson's.

Graduate schools sometimes publish listings of support sources in their catalogs, and some provide separate publications, such as the *Graduate Guide to Grants,* compiled by the Harvard Graduate School of Arts and Sciences. For more information, call 617-495-1814.

The Internet as a Source of Funding Information

If you have not explored the financial resources on the World Wide Web (the Web, for short), your research is not complete. Now available on the Web is a wealth of information ranging from loan and entrance applications to minority grants and scholarships.

University-Specific Information on the Web

Many universities have Web financial aid directories. Florida, Virginia Tech, Massachusetts, Emory, and Georgetown are just a few. Applications of admission can now be downloaded from the Web to start the graduate process. After that, detailed information can be obtained on financial aid processes, forms, and deadlines. University-specific grant and scholarship information can also be found, and more may be learned about financing information by using the Web than by an actual visit. Questions can be answered on line.

Scholarships on the Web

Many benefactors and other scholarship donors have pages on the Web listing pertinent information with regard to their specific scholarship. You can reach this information through a variety of methods. For example, you can find a directory listing minority scholarships, quickly look at the information on line, decide if it applies to you, and then move on. New scholarship pages are being added to the Web daily. Library and Web resources are productive—and free.

The Web also lists many services that will look for scholarships for you. Some of these services cost money and advertise more scholarships per dollar than any other service. While some of these might be helpful, beware. Check references to make sure a bona fide service is being offered. Your best bet initially is to surf the Web and use the traditional library resources on available scholarships.

Bank and Loan Information on the Web

Banks and loan servicing centers have pages on the Web, making it easier to access loan information. Having the information on screen in front of you instantaneously is more convenient than being put on hold on the phone. Any loan information such as interest rate variations, descriptions of loans, loan consolidation programs, and repayment charts can all be found on the Web.

Work Programs

Certain types of support, such as teaching, research, and administrative assistantships, require recipients to provide service to the university in exchange for a salary or stipend; sometimes tuition is also provided or waived.

Teaching Assistantships

Because science and engineering classes are taught at the undergraduate level, you stand a good chance of securing a teaching assistantship. These positions usually involve conducting small classes, delivering lectures, correcting class work, grading papers, counseling students, and supervising laboratory groups. Usually about 20 hours of work is required each week.

Teaching assistantships provide excellent educational experience as well as financial support. TAs generally receive a salary (now considered taxable income). Sometimes tuition is provided or waived as well. In addition, at some schools, TAs can be declared state residents, qualifying them for the in-state tuition rates. Appointments are based on academic qualifications and are subject to the availability of funds within a department. If you are interested in a teaching assistantship, contact the academic department. Ordinarily you are not considered for such positions until you have been admitted to the graduate school.

Research Assistantships

Research Assistantships usually require that you assist in the research activities of a faculty member. Appointments are ordinarily made for the academic year. They are rarely offered to first-year students. Contact the academic department, describing your particular research interests. As is the case with teaching assistantships, research assistantships provide excellent academic training as well as practical experience and financial support.

Administrative Assistantships

These positions usually require 10 to 20 hours of work each week in an administrative office of the university. For example, those seeking a graduate degree in education may work in the admissions, financial aid, student affairs, or placement office of the school they are attending. Some administrative assistantships provide a tuition waiver, others a salary. Details concerning these positions can be found in the school catalog or by contacting the academic department directly.

Federal Work-Study Program (FWS)

This federally funded program provides eligible students with employment opportunities, usually in public and private nonprofit organizations. Federal funds pay up to 75 percent of the wages, with the remainder paid by the employing agency. FWS is available to graduate students who demonstrate financial need. Not all schools have these funds, and some only award undergraduates. Each school sets its application deadline and work-study earnings limits. Wages vary and are related to the type of work done.

Additional Employment Opportunities

Many schools provide on-campus employment opportunities that do not require demonstrated financial need. The student employment office on most campuses assists students in securing jobs both on and off the campus.

LOANS

Most needy graduate students, except those pursuing Ph.D.'s in certain fields, borrow to finance their graduate programs. There are basically two sources of student loans—the federal government and private loan programs. You should read and understand the terms of these loan programs before submitting your loan application.

FEDERAL LOANS

Federal Stafford Loans

The Federal Stafford Loan Program offers government-sponsored, low-interest loans to students through a private lender such as a bank, credit union, or savings and loan association.

There are two components of the Federal Stafford Loan program. Under the *subsidized* component of the program, the federal government pays the interest accruing on the loan while you are enrolled in graduate school on at least a half-time basis. Under the *unsubsidized* component of the program, you pay the interest on the loan from the day proceeds are issued. Eligibility for the federal subsidy is based on demonstrated financial need as determined by the financial aid office from the information you provide on the Free Application for Federal Student Aid (FAFSA). A cosigner is not required, since the loan is not based on creditworthiness.

Although Unsubsidized Federal Stafford Loans may not be as desirable as Subsidized Federal Stafford Loans from the consumer's perspective, they are a useful source of support for those who may not qualify for the subsidized loans or who need additional financial assistance.

Graduate students may borrow up to $18,500 per year through the Stafford Loan Program, up to a maximum of $138,500, including undergraduate borrowing. This may include up to $8,500 in Subsidized Stafford Loans, depending on eligibility, up to a maximum of $65,000, including undergraduate borrowing. The amount of the loan borrowed through the Unsubsidized Stafford Program equals the total amount of the loan (as much $18,500) minus your eligibility for a Subsidized Stafford Loan (as much as $8500). You may borrow up to the cost of the school in which you are enrolled or will attend, minus estimated financial assistance from other federal, state, and private sources, up to a maximum of $18,500.

The interest rate for the Federal Stafford Loans varies annually and is set every July. The rate during in-school, grace, and deferment periods is based on the 91-Day U.S. Treasury Bill rate plus 2.5 percent, capped at 8.25 percent. The rate in repayment is based on the 91-Day U.S. Treasury Bill rate plus 3.1 percent, capped at 8.25 percent. However, the interest rate may soon be based on the ten-year Treasury Bill, pending current legislation.

Two fees are deducted from the loan proceeds upon disbursement: a guarantee fee of up to 1 percent, which is deposited in an insurance pool to ensure repayment to the lender if the borrower defaults, and a federally mandated 3 percent origination fee, which is used to offset the administrative cost of the Federal Stafford Loan Program.

Under the *subsidized* Federal Loan Program, repayment begins six months after your last enrollment on at least a half-time basis. Under the *unsubsidized* program, repayment of interest begins within thirty days from disbursement of the loan proceeds, and repayment of the principal begins six months after your last enrollment on at least a half-time basis. Some lenders may require that some payments may be made even while you are in school, although most lenders will allow you to defer payments and will add the accrued interest to the loan balance. Under both components of the program repayment may extend over a maximum of ten years with no prepayment penalty.

Federal Direct Loans.

Some schools are participating in the Department of Education's Direct Lending Program instead of offering Federal Stafford Loans. The two programs are essentially the same except with the Direct Loans, schools themselves originate the loans with funds provided from the federal government. Terms and interest rates are virtually the same except that there are a few more repayment options with Federal Direct Loans.

Federal Perkins Loans.

The Federal Perkins Loan is a long-term loan available to students demonstrating financial need and is administered directly by the school. Not all schools have these funds, and some may award them to undergraduates only. Eligibility is determined from the information you provide on the FAFSA. The school will notify you of your eligibility.

Eligible graduate students may borrow up to $5000 per year, up to a maximum of $30,000, including undergraduate borrowing (even if your previous Perkins Loans have been repaid.) The interest rate for Federal Perkins Loans is 5 percent, and no interest accrues while you remain in school at least half-time. There are no guarantee, loan, or disbursement fees. Repayment begins nine months after your last enrollment on at least a half-time basis and may extend over a maximum of ten years with no prepayment penalty.

Deferring Your Federal Loan Repayments.

If you borrowed under the Federal Stafford Loan Program or the Federal Perkins Loan Program for previous undergraduate or graduate study, some of your repayments may be deferred (i.e., suspended) when you return to graduate school, depending on when you borrowed and under which program.

There are other deferment options available if you are temporarily unable to repay your loan. Information about these deferments is provided at your entrance and exit interviews. If you believe you are eligible for a deferment of your loan repayments, you must contact your lender to complete a deferment form. The deferment must be filed prior to the time your repayment is due, and it must be refiled when it expires if you remain eligible for deferment at that time.

Supplemental Loans

Many lending institutions offer supplemental loan programs and other financing plans, such as the ones described below, to students seeking assistance in meeting their expected contribution toward educational expenses.

If you are considering borrowing through a supplemental loan program, you should carefully consider the terms of the program and be sure to "read the fine print." Check with the program sponsor for the most current terms that will be applicable to the amounts you intend to borrow for graduate study. Most supplemental loan programs for graduate study offer unsubsidized, credit-based loans. In general, a credit-ready borrower is one who has a satisfactory credit history or no credit history at all. A creditworthy borrower generally must pass a credit test to be eligible to borrow or act as a cosigner for the loan funds.

Many supplemental loan programs have a minimum annual loan limit and a maximum annual loan limit. Some offer amounts equal to the cost of attendance minus any other aid you will receive for graduate study. If you are planning to borrow for several years of graduate study, consider whether there is a cumulative or aggregate limit on the amount you may borrow. Often this cumulative or aggregate limit will include any amounts you borrowed and have not repaid for undergraduate or previous graduate study.

The combination of the annual interest rate, loan fees, and the repayment terms you choose will determine how much the amount is that you will repay over time. Compare these features in combination before you decide which loan program to use. Some loans offer interest rates that are adjusted monthly, some quarterly, some annually. Some offer interest rates that are lower during the in-school, grace, and deferment periods, and then increase when you begin repayment. Most programs include a loan "origination" fee, which is usually deducted from the principal amount you receive when the loan is disbursed, and must be repaid along with the interest and other principal when you graduate, withdraw from school, or drop below half-time study. Sometimes the loan fees are reduced if you borrow with a qualified cosigner. Some programs allow you to defer interest and/or principal payments while you are enrolled in graduate school. Many programs allow you to capitalize your interest payments; the interest due on your loan is added to the outstanding balance of your loan, so you don't have to repay immediately, but this increases the amount you owe. Other programs allow you to pay the interest as you go, which will reduce the amount you later have to repay.

For more information about supplemental loan programs or to obtain applications, call the customer service phone numbers of the organizations listed below, access the sponsor's site on the World Wide Web, or visit your school's financial aid office.

American Express Alternative Loan.

An unsubsidized, credit-based loan for credit-ready graduate students enrolled at least half-time, sponsored by American Express/California Higher Education Loan Authority (800-255-8374).

CitiAssist Graduate Loan.

An unsubsidized, credit-based loan for graduate students in all disciplines, sponsored by Citibank (800-745-5473 or 800-946-4019; World Wide Web: http://www.citibank.com/student).

CollegeReserve Loan.

An unsubsidized, credit-based loan for credit-worthy graduate students enrolled at least half-time, sponsored by USA Group (800-538-8492; World Wide Web: http://www.usagroup.com).

EXCEL Loan.

An unsubsidized, credit-based loan for borrowers who are not credit-ready or who would prefer to borrow with a creditworthy cosigner to obtain a more attractive interest rate, sponsored by Nellie Mae (888-2TUITION).

GradAchiever Loan.

An unsubsidized, credit-based loan for graduate students enrolled at least half-time, sponsored by Key Education Resources (800-KEY-LEND; World Wide Web: http://www.key.com/education/grad.html).

GradEXCEL Loan.

An unsubsidized, credit-based loan for credit-ready graduate students enrolled at least half-time, sponsored by Nellie Mae (888-2TUITION).

Graduate Access Loan.

An unsubsidized, credit-based loan for creditworthy graduate students enrolled at least half-time, sponsored by the Access Group (800-282-1550; World Wide Web: http://www.accessgroup.org).

Signature Student Loan.

An unsubsidized, credit-based loan for graduate students enrolled at least half-time, sponsored by Sallie Mae (888-272-5543; World Wide Web: http://www.salliemae.com).

INTERNATIONAL EDUCATION AND STUDY ABROAD

A variety of funding sources are offered for study abroad and for foreign nationals studying in the United States. The Institute of International Education in New York assists students in locating such aid. It publishes *Funding for U.S. Study—A Guide for International Students and Professionals* and *Financial Resources for International Study,* a guide to organizations offering awards for overseas study. To learn more, visit the institute's Web site at http://www.iiebooks.org.

The Council on International Educational Exchange in New York publishes the *Student Travel Catalogue,* which lists fellowship sources and explains the council's services both for United States students traveling abroad and for foreign students coming to the United States. For more information, see the council's Web site at http://www.ciee.org.

The U.S. Department of Education administers programs that support fellowships related to international education. Foreign Language and Area Studies Fellowships and Fulbright-Hays Doctoral Dissertation Awards were established to promote knowledge and understanding of other countries and cultures. They offer support to graduate students interested in foreign languages and international relations. Discuss these and other foreign study opportunities with the financial aid officer or someone in the graduate school dean's office at the school you will attend.

HOW TO APPLY

All applicants for federal aid must complete the Free Application for Federal Student Aid (FAFSA). This application must be submitted *after* January 1 preceding enrollment in the fall. It is a good idea to submit the FAFSA as soon as possible after this date. On this form you report your income and asset information for the preceding calendar year and specify which schools will receive the data. Two to four weeks later you'll receive an acknowledgment, the Student Aid Report (SAR), on which you can make any corrections. The schools you've designated will also receive the information and may begin asking you to send them documents, usually your U.S. income tax return, verifying what you reported.

In addition to the FAFSA, some graduate schools want additional information and will ask you to complete the CSS Financial Aid PROFILE. If your school requires this form, it will be listed in the PROFILE registration form available in college financial aid offices. Other schools use their own supplemental application. Check with your financial aid office to confirm which forms they require.

If you have already filed your federal income tax for the year, it will be much easier for you to complete these forms. If not, use estimates, but be certain to notify the financial aid office if your estimated figures differ from the actual ones once you have calculated them.

APPLICATION DEADLINES

Application deadlines vary. Some schools require you to apply for aid when applying for admission; others require that you be admitted before applying for aid. Aid application instructions and deadlines should be clearly stated in each school's application material. The FAFSA must be filed after January 1 of the year you are applying for aid but the Financial Aid PROFILE should be completed earlier, in October or November.

DETERMINING FINANCIAL NEED

Eligibility for need-based financial aid is based on your income during the calendar year prior to the academic year in which you apply for aid. Prior-year income is used because it is a good predictor of current-year income and is verifiable. If you have a significant reduction in income or assets after your aid application is completed, consult a financial aid counselor. If, for example, you are returning to school after working, you should let the financial aid counselor know your projected income for the year you will be in school. Aid counselors may use their "professional judgment" to revise your financial need, based on the actual income you will earn while you are in graduate school.

Need is determined by examining the difference between the cost of attendance at a given institution and the financial resources you bring to the table. Eligibility for aid is calculated by subtracting your resources from the total cost of attendance budget. These standard student budgets are generally on the low side of the norm. So if your expenses are higher because of medical bills, higher research travel, or more costly books, for example, a financial aid counselor can make an adjustment. Of course, you'll have to document any unusual expenses. Also, keep in mind that with limited grant and scholarship aid, a higher budget will probably mean either more loan or more working hours for you.

TAX ISSUES

Since the passage of the Tax Reform Act of 1986, grants, scholarships, and fellowships may be considered taxable income. That portion of the grant used for payment of tuition and course-required fees, books, supplies, and equipment is excludable from taxable income. Grant support for living expenses is taxable. A good rule of thumb for determining the tax liability for grants and scholarships is to view anything that exceeds the actual cost of tuition, required fees, books, supplies related to courses, and required equipment as taxable.

- If you are employed by an educational institution or other organization that gives tuition reimbursement, you must pay tax on the value that exceeds $5250.

- If your tuition is waived in exchange for working at the institution, the tuition waiver is taxable. This includes waivers that come with teaching or research assistantships.

- Other student support, such as stipends and wages paid to research assistants and teaching assistants, is also taxable income. Student loans, however, are not taxable.

- If you are an international student you may or may not owe taxes depending upon the agreement the U.S. has negotiated with your home country. The United States has tax treaties with more than forty countries. You are responsible for making sure that the school you attend follows the terms of the tax treaty. If your country does not have a tax treaty with the U.S., you may have as much as 30 percent withheld from your paycheck.

A FINAL NOTE

While amounts and eligibility criteria vary from field to field as well as from year to year, with thorough research you can uncover many opportunities for graduate financial assistance. If you are interested in graduate study, discuss your plans with faculty members and advisers. Explore all options. Plan ahead, complete forms on time, and be tenacious in your search for support. No matter what your financial situation, if you are academically qualified and knowledgeable about the different sources of aid, you should be able to attend the graduate school of your choice.

Patricia McWade
Dean of Student Financial Services
Georgetown University